Spiritual Dreaming

A CROSS-CULTURAL AND HISTORICAL JOURNEY

Kelly Bulkeley

PAULIST PRESS
New York/Mahwah, NJ

Cover design by James Brisson

Cover art: Bridgeman/Art Resource, NY
Caspar David Friedrich, "Wanderer in the Mist," Kunsthalle, Hamburg, Germany.

Library of Congress Cataloging-in-Publication Data

Bulkeley, Kelly, 1962-
    Spiritual dreaming : a cross-cultural and historical journey / Kelly
Bulkeley.
        p. cm.
    Includes bibliographical references and index.
    ISBN 0-8091-3592-2 (alk. paper)
    1. Dream—Religious aspects. I. Title.
BL65.D67B84   1995   95-22278
291.4'2—dc20   CIP

Published by Paulist Press
997 Macarthur Boulevard
Mahwah, New Jersey 07430

Printed and bound in the
United States of America

Contents

Acknowledgements v

Introduction 1

1. The Dead 7

2. Snakes 19

3. Gods 30

4. Nightmares 42

5. Sexuality 55

6. Flying 67

7. Lucidity 76

8. Creativity 86

9. Healing 97

10. Prophecy 107

11. Rituals 120

12. Initiation 131

13. Conversion 142

Conclusion 156

Appendix 1: Hermeneutics: The Interpretation
of Spiritual Dreams 161

Appendix 2: Dreams and Conceptions of the Soul, Reality,
and Reason 182

Appendix 3: Methodological Issues 203

Notes 213

Bibliography 240

Index 264

Acknowledgements

I could not have gotten this book launched without the help of Pedro Sanchez, now an anthropology graduate student at Princeton University, whose zeal as a researcher and sophistication as a critic of modern dream studies I admire tremendously. I also relied heavily on the wisdom of Wendy Doniger, of the University of Chicago Divinity School, in both the early and late stages of conceptualizing my work. Many of my friends from the Association for the Study of Dreams, especially Carol Schreier Rupprecht, Jeremy Taylor, Alan Siegel, Johanna King, and Ernest Hartmann, helped me develop particular ideas and themes.

My wife Hilary gave me constant encouragement, reassurance, and support during the long months of writing. I could not ask for a more loving life partner. My son Dylan displayed wonderful patience with his dad's obsessive work habits, and my infant daughter Maya helped me in the best way she could—by sleeping. It was thanks to her two-hour naps every morning and every afternoon that I had the time to write this book. Once I finished a rough manuscript, Harriet Crosby gave me valuable advice about smoothing off the jagged edges. And Lawrence Boadt of Paulist Press has my deep appreciation for his editorial reassurances.

If in my first book I followed the modern west's major pathways into what I metaphorically call the wilderness of dreams, then in *Spiritual Dreaming* I cut away from those pathways and set off to explore the farthest, most inaccessible, most mysterious reaches of that wilderness. This metaphorical exploration has a literal analogue. While writing I found a constant source of renewal and inspiration in the forests along the eastern ridges of the Mount Tamalpais watershed, where I went every Monday afternoon to wander among the hills, creeks, ferns, and redwoods. I've tried to express the spirit of those forests in every word of what I've written here.

For My Parents

*Patrica Molony Bulkley
and
Edward Lawrence Bulkley*

From there to here,
From here to there,
Funny things are everywhere.

> Dr. Seuss,
> *One Fish, Two Fish,*
> *Red Fish, Blue Fish*

Introduction

One of the tales from *The Thousand and One Nights*, the collection of legends, fables, and adventures from medieval Islam, tells the story of a merchant from Baghdad who squandered his fortune and was reduced to a life of misery and destitution. One night the merchant had a dream in which a man appeared and said, "Your fortune lies in Cairo. Go and seek it there." The merchant awoke and, deciding he had nothing to lose, traveled to Cairo. But as the Almighty would have it, when the poor merchant arrived in Cairo he was mistaken for a thief and thrown into prison, where he was mercilessly beaten. Three days later the chief of police questioned the merchant. When asked why he had come to Cairo, the merchant described his dream. The chief of police burst out laughing and said, "You fool, I too have heard a voice in my sleep, not just once but on three occasions. It said: 'Go to Baghdad, and in a cobbled street lined with palm trees you will find such-and-such a house, with a courtyard of grey marble; under the white marble fountain a great sum of money is buried.' But would I go? Of course not. Yet, fool that you are, you have come all the way to Cairo on the strength of one idle dream." The chief of police finally took pity on the gullible merchant and released him. The merchant expressed his humble thanks and hurried back to Baghdad—for the chief's dream had described the merchant's own house, and when he dug under the fountain in his courtyard the merchant uncovered a great treasure.[1]

The basic premise of *Spiritual Dreaming* derives from this lesson which the merchant of Baghdad learned during his journey to Cairo: if we listen carefully to the dreams of *other people* we may be surprised by the valuable treasures we find.

1

Through other people's dreams we gain insights into their experiences and creative expressions, thereby developing a richer understanding of those other people's distinctive identities. At the same time, their dreams help us broaden our appreciation for the hopes, desires, and fears that are shared by humans across differences of culture and history. And finally, learning more about other people's dreams teaches us something new about our own dreams, about the treasures that lie buried in our own backyards.

Dreams have been regarded as a valuable source of spiritual insight, inspiration, and guidance by virtually every cultural and religious tradition in the world. *Spiritual Dreaming* documents the varieties of spiritually significant dreams that people have reported throughout history. The book is not a "how-to" manual; it gives no exercises, no recipes, no tips on how you can meet God when you dream tonight. Instead, it offers a carefully-documented reference guide to the vast but relatively unexplored realm of spiritual dreaming experience. I will be mapping out the major features of this realm, making some observations about striking patterns and themes, and offering comments on the relevance of all this to dreaming experience in modern western culture. In this way I hope to satisfy the research needs of religion scholars, psychologists, anthropologists, historians, literary critics, and other academics. I also hope to offer some useful comments and insights to the many general readers who have personal interests in the subject of dreams and spirituality.

The main body of *Spiritual Dreams* is a comparative survey of thirteen different types of spiritual dreams reported from a variety of times and places. By "spiritual dreams" I mean dreams that reveal an aspect of the sacred, dreams that reveal something of the ultimate powers, truths, and values of reality, however the dreamer conceptualizes them. People experience such dreams with a profound sense of wonder, awe, and even fear. To use Rudolph Otto's term, they are *numinous* dreams, dreams that are experienced as mysterious encounters with "the wholly other," with "that which is quite beyond the sphere of the usual, the intelligible, and the familiar."[2] Such potent dreams address the basic existential questions that lie at the heart of all religious and spiritual traditions—questions about death, about good and evil, about the nature of God or the gods, about suffering and misfortune, about what makes for a happy, fulfilling life. People's beliefs regarding these questions are often deepened and revitalized by their dream experiences. On occasion, a person's entire spiritual world-view may be transformed by a dream encounter with the sacred.

Thus, by the term "spiritual" dreams I refer to those dreams that bring people experientially closer to the powers of the sacred and that speak to their ultimate existential concerns. These dreams do not, however, always have traditionally religious imagery. A person may have a dream that is profoundly spiritual in its symbolism, emotional impact, and existential meaning, even though the dream *appears* on the surface to be quite ordinary and unremarkable. Furthermore, such dreams are experienced by both "religious" people and "secular" people alike. Genuinely spiritual dreams come to avid believers, to die-hard atheists, to skeptical agnostics, and to people who belong to no formal religious institution but who believe in some way or other that human life has a deeper meaning to it.

Attempting to define "spirituality," "religion," or "the sacred" inevitably leads to dry abstractions. These terms will come to life once we begin looking at the dreams themselves.

The first seven chapters of *Spiritual Dreaming* discuss some of the most common contents and experiences that characterize spiritual dreams. Chapter 1 looks at dreams in which the spirit or image of a dead person appears; Chapter 2 presents dreams of snakes, and Chapter 3 discusses dreams of God, the gods, and other supernatural beings. Nightmares are the subject of Chapter 4, flying dreams of Chapter 5, and sexual dreams of Chapter 6. Chapter 7 discusses "lucid" dreams, in which the dreamer becomes aware to some degree of being in a dream state.

From there, the focus turns to the various applications and effects of spiritual dreams. Chapter 8 looks at how people have expressed their spiritual dreams in creative art; Chapter 9 discusses dreams and healing; and Chapter 10 focuses on the power of dreams to prophesize the future. Chapter 11 describes the various rituals that people have used to "incubate," or deliberately evoke, spiritual dreams. Chapter 12 considers the important role dreams have played in spiritual initiations, and Chapter 13 shows how dreams have helped to convert people to new, more fulfilling spiritual world-views. Appendix 1 discusses various systems of classifying and interpreting spiritual dreams, and Appendix 2 reviews the influence dreams have had on religious and philosophical conceptions of the soul, of reality, and of reason.

Living as we do in a post-modern, post-cold war, post-theory world, we know that every typology is an arbitrary, subjective construct. Jorge Luis Borges describes the system used in an ancient Chinese encyclopedia, the *Celestial Emporium of Benevolent Knowledge*, to categorize the members of the animal kingdom:

> On those remote pages it is written that animals are divided into
> a) those that belong to the Emperor,
> b) embalmed ones,
> c) those that are trained,
> d) suckling pigs,
> e) mermaids,
> f) fantastic ones,
> g) stray dogs,
> h) those that are included in this classification,
> i) those that tremble as if they were mad,
> j) innumerable ones,
> k) those drawn with a very fine camel's hair brush,
> l) others,
> m) those that have just broken a flower vase,
> n) those that resemble flies from a distance.[3]

Every typology is ultimately a vain attempt to impose order on a fluid, ever-changing world; every typology is as absurdly idiosyncratic as that devised by Borges' Chinese sages. Typologies are nothing more than maps we draw up to help us explore reality—even the most useful ones are still just maps (see Appendix 3 for a discussion of the various methodological issues raised in the study of spiritual dreams).

This is all a way of saying that the primary subject of *Spiritual Dreaming* is not a thirteen-part typological system, but the spiritual dream experiences that have fascinated, frightened, and inspired people throughout history. The typology that structures this book will, I hope, help readers to appreciate more fully the power of other people's spiritual dreams, and perhaps to recognize the spiritual dimensions of their own dream experiences.

1. The Dead

*P*eople who are mourning the loss of a family member or friend often experience a strong upsurge of dreaming. Many of these dreams take the dreamer back to times when the now-dead person was still alive. Other dreams "rewrite" the death, and show the person as having survived the accident or illness that killed him or her. However, a few of these dreams are *different*. In some dreams the dead person seems to return to the dreamer, and to share or communicate something of strange but deeply valuable meaning. People describe these dreams as incredibly vivid and intense, so unlike "ordinary" dreams that the people wonder if they were even sleeping during the experience. The dead person, they say, was *really there*—even though it was just a dream, it felt as real as anything in waking life.

This type of dream, in which the dreamer has an extraordinarily powerful and vivid encounter with the figure of a dead person, has been widely reported throughout history. Indeed, many of the world's spiritual traditions consider dreams of the dead to be the single most direct means of relating to sacred powers and realities. The following are some accounts of this type of dream, drawn from different cultures and historical eras.

> 1) A medicine man of the Manyika tribe of North America had the following dream experience, as told to anthropologist Wulf Sachs: "I was in a big mountain with my first father. I don't know his face. I was too small when he died. He showed me a hole in a big stone. He told me, I should go inside this stone. I was afraid to go inside this hole although I wanted to very much. Then he went in first and I followed.

I was not afraid then. It was very dark. There was a horn of medicine. There were plenty of horns. There was also a big black snake. He again told me not to be afraid. The snake looks after the horns. I told my father, I know you are dead. How is it you are with me? He answered, 'I am dead, but I walk and you don't see me.' I felt in the dream a bad smell coming from my father, I thought it was his body. Then we came out, father first, and I after him. We went up the mountain. He told me to go on my own. He will look after the medicine. And I went up and up. Then I woke up."[1]

2) Among the Mapuche Indians of Chile, the following dream was reported to anthropologist Lydia Degarrod by a seventy year old woman named Matilde. Matilde said that in her dream "My dead husband came to take me away. He came to the creek nearby our hut. He told me he had everything ready and I should rush because we couldn't waste any time. He told me to dress properly, to wear all my jewelry and my best dress. He would wait for me at the creek. I went to my house and I got ready. When I went to the creek, he was already waiting for me in his carriage. When he saw me, he gave me his hand so I could get hold of him to jump into the carriage. But I lost my balance and I couldn't grab his hand. He told me he was afraid that the carriage wasn't working and he would have to leave the carriage there and take only the horse. He was going to help me to get on the horse, but I woke up."[2]

3) In the *Sefer Hasidim*, a thirteenth-century religious text written by German Jewish pietists, this story is told: "It happened that a saintly sage was buried next to one who was unworthy. The saint came to all the townspeople in a dream and said, 'You did me evil in that you buried me next to a toilet that has a stench. The fumes are hard on me.' They placed stones between the grave of the saint and the grave of the evil-doer as a divider; from that time on he [the saint] did not come to them in a dream."[3]

4) Dream visitations from ancestors play a key role in the religious beliefs of the Xhosa-speaking people of South Africa. One old Xhosa man recounted the following dream of his late father, who had been a minister, coming through a dark wall: "On seeing him I was afraid; he came to me trying to kick me. I was startled and cried, and puzzled

about the reason. He did not say anything at that time."
Although the man's sister told him the dream indicated that
their father was annoyed and wanted him to serve God and
go to church, the man refused to believe it. Then, after
many unhappy years, the man did begin attending church
more regularly, and the dream repeated itself: "While
asleep I dreamt I was praying and singing *Ndiyakholwa* [the
Apostles' Creed] when I saw my father coming from the
wall to me, wearing dark clothes and being angry, wanting
to kick me. When I woke up my face was wet with tears, but
after that nothing troublesome came to me again in
connection with my father, but what now regularly happens
when I am in difficulty is that I see my father in a dream.
He never speaks but just comes, though without being
angry now."[4]

5) Among the Mae Enga, a people who live in the
mountainous regions of New Guinea and who live by
gardening and raising pigs, anthropologist M.J. Meggitt
reports that a man named Anggauwane received an
enormous pig in a village ceremony. He gave the pig to his
father, even though his mother had wanted it. Some years
later, after his parents had died, one of Anggauwane's sows
bore a deformed piglet. Many of his clansmen thought the
deformity was a warning that the ghost of his mother was
angry, and they recommended that Anggauwane sacrifice
the piglet to her. He refused, and gave the pig to a member
of another clan. A few days later, Anggauwane's son
Yakandali became gravely ill. Anggauwane immediately
feared that his mother's ghost had attacked his son. He
sacrificed two fowls and a pig to placate the angry ghost,
but to no avail; his son died, and Anggauwane went into
seclusion to mourn. As Meggitt tells the story, "during the
next few weeks Yakandali's ghost appeared several times in
Anggauwane's dreams and reproached him for his
behavior. Had Anggauwane not sent the deformed pig to
another clan to feed a stranger's ghost, Yakandali said, the
ghost of his mother would not have 'bitten' him.
Anggauwane called in a diviner to discuss the dreams and
ascertain the ghost's intentions. After further divinations,
they sacrificed a pig and offered it to the mother's ghost.
Subsequent omens were favorable, and the diviner declared
the ghost to be satisfied."[5]

6) The nineteenth-century Indian philosopher Debendranath Tagore was a leader of the Brahmo Samaj (Society for Worshiping God), a movement that sought to rationalize and modernize the superstitions of Hinduism. Tagore had a dream that helped him, and his movement, find a balance between modern beliefs and traditional practices: "All these anxieties and troubles would not let me sleep at night, my head felt dazed on the pillow. I would now doze off and again wake up. It was as if I was sleeping on the borderland between waking and sleeping. At such a time some one came to me in the dark and said 'Get up,' and I at once sat up. He said 'Get out of bed,' and I got up; he said 'Follow me' and I followed. He went down the steps leading out of the inner apartments, I did the same and came out into the courtyard with him.... He seemed to be a shadowlike form. I could not see him clearly, but felt myself constrained to do immediately whatever he bade me. From thence he mounted upwards to the sky, I also followed him. Clusters of stars and planets were shedding a bright lustre, right and left and in front of me, and I was passing through them...." The mysterious guide then took Tagore through a spectral city, to a quiet, spacious room of white marble: "I sat silent in that silent room; shortly afterwards the curtain of one of the doors in front of the room was drawn aside and my mother appeared. Her hair was down, just as I had seen it on the day of her death. When she died, I never thought that she was dead. Even when I came back from the burning ground after performing her funeral ceremonies, I could not believe that she was dead. I felt sure that she was still alive. Now I saw that living mother of mine before me. She said 'I wanted to see thee, so I sent for thee. Hast thou really become one who has known Brahma? Sanctified is the family, fulfilled is the mother's desire.' On seeing her, and hearing these sweet words of hers my slumber gave way before a flood of joy. I found myself still tossing on my bed."[6]

7) M.L. Daneel's study of Southern Shona Independent Churches (located in what was Rhodesia) describes the frequent appearance of dead relatives in people's dreams, and the spiritual values attached to these dreams: "The dead communicate with the living through dreams, or by causing illness and misfortune. In the case of dreams the interpretation of the *nganga* [diviner] need not necessarily

be sought because the ancestor's wish may be clear enough.... Should a *sekuru* [paternal grandfather] or *baba* [father] ancestor visit a person in a dream, it is experienced as a real encounter between the dream-soul of the sleeper and the spirit. Guidance about general conduct, medical advice and instructions for a new venture may be given. Complaints about the reluctance of the sleeper to meet the needs of the ancestor for a *jira* (blanket), a *ngombe* (ox), *gono* (bull), or beer, may also be vented. Thus, on the one hand, service is offered by the ancestor while, on the other, demands are made; demands that are legally valid between kinsmen."[7]

8) In Book 23 of Homer's *Iliad*, the Greek warrior Achilleus prepares a funeral pyre for his fallen friend Patroklos. Achilleus then sleeps, and the ghost of Patroklos appears in a dream: "The ghost came and stood over his head and spoke a word to him: 'You sleep, Achilleus; you have forgotten me; but you were not careless of me when I lived, but only in death. Bury me as quickly as may be, let me pass through the gates of Hades." Patroklos says that the other shades of dead men hold him at a distance and refuse to let him cross the river and join them. Still in the dream, Achilleus replies, "I shall do as you tell me. But stand closer to me, and let us, if only for a little, embrace, and take full satisfaction from the dirge of sorrow.' So he spoke, and with his own arms reached for him, but could not take him, but the spirit went underground, like a vapour, with a thin cry, and Achilleus started awake, staring, and drove his hands together, and spoke, and his words were sorrowful: 'Oh, wonder! Even in the house of Hades there is left something, a soul and an image, but there is no real heart of life in it.'"[8]

9) In Bronislaw Malinowski's *The Sexual Life of Savages* he says this of the Trobriand Islanders and their dreams of the dead: "In standardized dreams [i.e. dreams recognized by cultural tradition] a prominent part is played by visions of departed spirits. They appear to people in sleep under appropriate circumstances and at certain seasons. This is in fact one of the chief ways in which they manifest their existence to the living.... Real spirits always come with a purpose and under conditions in which they can be properly

expected. Thus if a recently dead person appears in sleep to a surviving relative, giving him some important message or announcing his death at a distance—such a dream is true."[9]

10) A man from the Ottawa tribe of North America reported the following dream to anthropologist Paul Radin: "I dreamt that I saw my mother coming. I knew that she was dead. I was very glad to see her coming. As she passed she didn't look at me at all, but she spoke and said to me, 'So you are going to leave to-day. Be careful, take good care of yourself and don't be foolish. I don't want you to get hurt or to get into jail.'" In the dream the man then walks through the woods, comes to a camp, and enters a hut. Inside the hut he sees a pile of groceries on a table. A woman there asks him, "Are you looking for work?' 'Yes,' I answered. 'Well, I think you can get a job right here,' she said. I didn't see anybody else and I started to walk away from the camp. I hadn't gone very far when I woke up."[10]

11) The Jewish historian Josephus reports the following dream in his second-century A.D. work *The War of the Jews*. A woman named Glaphyra lost her first husband, Alexander, and later married his brother Archelaus. But after her second marriage "she saw the following dream: She thought she saw Alexander standing by her, at which she rejoiced, and embraced him with great affection; but he complained of her, and said, 'O Glaphyra! thou provest that saying to be true, which assures us that women are not to be trusted. Didst thou not pledge thy faith to me? and wast not thou married to me when thou wast a virgin? and had we not children between us? Yet hast thou forgotten the affection I bear to thee.... However, I will not forget thy former kind affection for me, but will set thee free from every such reproachful action, and cause thee to be mine again, as thou once wast.' When she had related this to her female companions, in a few days' time she departed from this life."[11]

12) Anthropologist Andrew Strathern describes a dream experienced by a young woman of the Melpa people of New Guinea. Her stepmother had recently died, and soon after coming home from the funeral she had this dream: "In the dream she saw her stepmother...at the foot of a large clump of bamboo on a ceremonial ground near her husband's

place.... The dead woman was marketing some peanuts and some fine bananas, and she offered these to her daughter. Then the dead woman said '*nim ukl kae ti in eka*' ('You have done something good'). The daughter asked her, 'How did you know?' and she said, 'I knew a long time ago....' The woman continued, 'My own two daughters did not help him with his school fees but you have done so. This is good, I am happy. Keep on helping him, he will make returns to you, he will not run away.' Still in the dream, the daughter commented to one of her half-sisters who was there on how well the mother was looking, she wasn't like this before (as though the mother had in fact come alive)."[12]

Although these dream accounts come from very diverse cultural settings, they nevertheless share a number of common elements. In all of these examples, the figures who appear in the dreams are *close* to the dreamers. Children, husbands, fathers, mothers, friends, ancestors, spiritual guides—these are people who have been closely, intimately related to the dreamers. In many cases the people have died recently, and their dream appearance relates to the still-painful events surrounding their death. Another common feature of these dream experiences concerns their basic content, in which the dead person speaks to the dreamer, communicating something of value and importance. These dream interactions help to reconnect the interpersonal bonds that were broken by death. That is why so many cultures and spiritual traditions see dreams as a primary way of maintaining contact with the dead.[13]

What the dead most often communicate to the dreamer is a message of guidance, instruction, and counsel. Thus, the mother of Debendranath Tagore reminds him not to forget the traditions of his religious heritage (1.6); Patroklos demands that Achilleus give him a proper burial ceremony (1.8); the Jewish sage commands the townspeople to improve the condition of his grave (1.3). Further such examples can be found in many other parts of the world. The people of China's Shang era (1766–1122 B.C.) believed that dreams were caused by the dead, and most often by the *hsien-kung* and *hsien-pi*, that is, the patriarchal and matriarchal ancestors, whose ghosts demanded sacrificial offerings. Numerous Chinese texts describe dreams in which a dead person appears to ask the dreamer to take better care of the dead person's grave.[14] The Maori of New Zealand believe that in certain dreams "the *wairua* (spirit) of a dead relative, your father maybe, or your child...has come to warn you of impending danger."[15] Contemporary Moroccan Muslims feel that such dreams usually indicate the dead person is unsettled and needs something; if in a dream a deceased relative comes looking bad or badly dressed, the interpretation is that the dreamer has to do something for the relative, such as say special prayers or make a special offering of alms.[16] For the Melpa people of New Guinea, the recently dead appear in dreams in order to make comments on the community's current situation.[17]

As these examples indicate, the guidance given by the dead to the dreamer is not always pleasant or comforting. At times, the message has an angry, reproachful quality that can frighten the dreamer, such as Anggauwane's dream of his dead son (1.5), the Xhosa man's dream of his late father (1.4), and Glaphyra's dream of her dead first husband (1.11). Some cultures fear *all* dreams of the dead, and they go to elaborate lengths to prevent such dreams from occurring. But in most spiritual traditions, the dead are seen as bearing messages meant to help the dreamer in some way or other. Even in the dreams where the dead figure angrily demands a sacrifice or burial ritual, the ultimate *goal* of the dream's message is to promote better relations between the dreamer and the dead person through the performance of an appropriate religious ceremony.

In modern western culture, dreams of the dead have usually been interpreted in psychoanalytic terms. Sigmund Freud's theory of dreams as wish-fulfillments, combined with his theory of the oedipal complex, seems to give a neat, simple explanation for such dreams.[18] In this view, dreams of the dead are so common because they reflect the unconscious turmoil that is always generated by the death of a loved one. The dead appear in our dreams because we wish they were still alive; the vividness of these dreams stems from the powerful nature of the wish. Freud himself gives a moving example of such a dream to open chapter seven of *The Interpretation of Dreams*, in which a child who has just died appears in a dream to his grieving father.[19] Dreams in which the dead person is angry or reproachful reveal another strong unconscious wish, namely the violent, aggressive wish to harm those we love.[20] When a loved one actually *does* die, we feel profoundly guilty because we unconsciously wanted to harm them. This guilt manifests itself in frightening dreams of the vengeful dead.

Freud and other psychoanalytic researchers[21] are certainly right in pointing out the psychological dynamics involved in dreams of the dead. When we examine these dreams we invariably discover deep unconscious emotions and troubling oedipal conflicts. But Freud and his followers remind me of the slow-witted bad guys in an old detective story I read years ago. When the story's hero (a hard-bitten, whiskey-drinking private eye) leaves his cheap motel room, the bad guys sneak in and ransack the place; they rifle through his dresser, and under a folded shirt they find his .38 snub-nosed revolver. Grinning maliciously at this discovery, the bad guys pocket the gun and sneak out again. When the private eye comes back, though, it's his turn to laugh. He knew, of course, that the bad guys would search his room; that's why he hid his *other* .38 directly under the pile of shirts where he had put the first revolver.

We make the same mistake as those easily-duped bad guys if we look at nothing beyond the psychological elements of dreams of the dead. In addition to the psychological level of unconscious emotions and complexes, this type of dream also has a spiritual level of meaning—dreams of the dead provide an especially powerful and uniquely accessible means of opening people to the sacred. No matter what our religious outlook, no matter whether we are from ancient China, the New Guinea highlands, or a modern American metropolis, the death of a loved one forces us to confront one of the great mysteries of human existence. What becomes of people when they die? We see that their physical bodies are dead, and we know that wherever they are they belong now to a realm that is radically different from our own. And yet, despite the infinite gulf that separates us from them, we still feel a strong emotional connection to them. As psychoanalysts rightly point out, our emotional ties to the dead person remain very powerful. Indeed, those ties often become much more powerful after the person has died.

The dead person is gone, and yet not gone. The intensity of this existential paradox creates an opening to the sacred: it is through our living emotional connection to the dead person that we are able to glimpse something of powers and realities that lie beyond our ordinary profane world. In these strangely vivid dreams, the dead person serves as a spiritual guide, leading the dreamer into realms that both frighten and fascinate the living. Who could be a better, more trustworthy guide into these mysterious realms than a person to whom we were close in life and who has just become a member of those realms?

An account of a dream recorded in a Chinese Buddhist text from Yuan times (1279–1368 A.D.) illustrates this process of spiritual guidance.

> 13) A lay believer named Wang Chiu-lien was meditating devotedly, seeking enlightenment in the Pure Land tradition of Buddhism. At night he dreamed of the Buddha, but always in the form of a sculpture, not as the living Buddha. He finally went to a monk and told him about these dreams. "This is easy to deal with," said the monk. "When you think of your late father, can you hold [in your mind] his usual comportment?" "Yes." "Can you see him in your dreams in such a way that he is no different from when he was living?" "There is no difference." "The Buddha in himself has no appearance," said the monk; "the appearance is manifested only in conformity with the way of things. From now on you should think of your late father as Amitabha [the Buddha]. Little by little, imagine that there are white streaks of light in between his brows, that his face is as of real gold, and that he sits on a lotus-flower. You can even imagine that his body grows larger and larger. Then your late father *is* himself the living Buddha." Wang applied this method according to the monk's instructions, so that whenever he dreamed of his father, he told himself, "This is the Buddha." In time, he dreamed that his father led him to sit on the lotus, where he explained to his son the essence of the teachings.[22]

This story makes explicit what lies at the heart of all these dreams: the valuable role of the dead person in guiding the dreamer toward a closer relationship with the sacred—leading the dreamer toward a better understanding of spiritual truths, realities, and powers.

Interestingly, the same basic point is made in a more negative (not to say hysterical) fashion by the sixteenth-century

English writer Thomas Nashe. In his essay *Terrors of the Night*, Nashe insists that *all* dreams are caused by the devil:

> 14) The night is the devil's Black Book, wherein he recordeth all our transgressions.... It will be demanded why in the likeness of one's father or mother or kinsfolks he [the devil] oftentimes presents himself unto us. No other reason can be given of it but this: that in those shapes which he supposeth most familiar unto us, and that we are inclined to with a natural kind of love, we will sooner hearken to him than otherwise. Should he not disguise himself in such subtle forms of affection, we would fly from him as a serpent and eschew him with that hatred he ought to be eschewed.[23]

Nashe is making the same basic argument I am making, namely that the appearance of close relatives in dreams provide a means of connecting with powers that transcend ordinary human life. Nashe, however, regards those powers as demonic, while I refer to them as sacred.

To take seriously the spiritual dimension of this type of dream does not mean we naively ignore their psychological dimension. We should not overlook the unconscious oedipal emotions that often emerge in these dreams. But neither should we reduce all possible spiritual meanings *to* those emotions. It is precisely the deep emotional attachments we feel toward people who have died that open us to the sacred. Our dreams of the dead give us the opportunity to step through that opening. These dreams are a powerful means of encountering the sacred, and they have been cherished by cultures and spiritual traditions all over the world.

Over the years I have heard many people tell me stories about their dreams of people who have recently died. One young woman ("Sheila") had a close friend suddenly commit suicide while they were both freshmen at college; she was shocked by his death, and agonized over the question of what had led him to kill himself. A few weeks after his funeral, Sheila had a dream: her friend comes to her, they sit down at a picnic bench, and he explains to Sheila the reasons for his suicide. He tells her not to worry, and to remember him well. When Sheila woke up, she was trembling; it was just a dream, and yet her dead friend had been so *real*. She didn't know what exactly had happened, whether what had appeared in her dream was a spirit, or a ghost, or an image from her own mind. But whatever it was, Sheila felt that now she did have some understanding of her friend's death. And she finally got the chance to say goodbye to him.

Another story of a strange, uncanny dream following a suicide was told to me by a young man in his mid-twenties ("Harold"). Harold's father had for years suffered from attacks of severe depression, but after a long hospitalization, he seemed to be getting better. Then one day Harold's father went into his study, found a gun, and shot himself in the heart. Harold and his father had just reconciled after a lifetime of bitter struggles, and the suicide stunned Harold. He began having recurrent dreams of his father; in these dreams his father was alive again, either back in the hospital or out doing some activity that he used to enjoy. But one night Harold had a dream that was, he said, "totally different from all the others." In this dream Harold and his father stand in a black, dimensionless void; he knows his father is dead, and his father knows he's dead, and yet there they stand together. When Harold finally asks why his father hasn't gone already, he answers, "They won't let me go," and points to his left. Harold looks, and sees a huge wall stretching infinitely upward. Harold feels confused, and asks if there isn't a light or some kind of tunnel his father should be looking for. He answers no, he doesn't see anything. Harold asks if he's scared; yes, his father says, of course he's scared. What will you do? Harold asks. His father says, in his usual matter-of-fact way, "I guess I'll wait around and see what happens." When Harold told me this dream, he said he couldn't stress enough how "incredibly, incredibly *real*" it was—it felt as though he had really met his father, wherever his father was or whatever he had become. The dream gave Harold a new understanding of death, of that which lies beyond death, and, ultimately, of life.

2. Snakes

Animals of various kinds appear in spiritually meaningful dreams. Birds, dogs, bears, wolves, fish, and even insects have come in people's dreams to deliver important messages from the divine. But the animal that makes perhaps the most powerful spiritual impact in dreams is the snake. People from cultures all over the world report dreams in which they have intensely vivid encounters with snakes. Content analysis studies performed by Robert Van de Castle indicate that even in the dreams of modern Americans, who presumably have little direct contact with snakes, these animals appear with surprising frequency.[1] Many reports of snake dreams emphasize their strange, uncanny quality; the dreamer feels both attracted to and yet repelled by the serpent. As the following examples suggest, many people through history have regarded snake dreams as deeply spiritual experiences—for these dreams reveal the *ambivalent nature* of the sacred, its capacity to be a force of joyful creativity *and* violent destructiveness in human life.

1) A fifty year old woman named Rosie Plummer, of the Paviotso people living on the Walker River reservation in Nevada, told anthropologist Willard Park of her shaman father. Rattlesnakes frequently came to him in his dreams and told him how to cure snake bites and other illnesses. Eighteen years after his death, Rosie started to dream about her father. "She dreamed that he came to her and told her to be a shaman. Then a rattlesnake came to her in dreams and told her to get eagle feathers, white paint, wild tobacco. The snake gave her the songs that she sings when she is curing. The snake appeared three or four times before she believed that she would be a shaman. Now she dreams

19

about the rattlesnake quite frequently and she learns new songs and is told how to cure sick people in this way."[2]

2) Lilias Trotter, a Christian missionary who worked in Algeria in the early part of the twentieth century, had these two dreams reported to her by Muslims who were converting to Christianity. A) Trotter says that an Algerian she knew named Boualem had been involved in an angry conflict with a neighbor. She wanted to help Boualem, but didn't know how; then she says, "Now God has dealt with the matter. Boualem told us that a dream had come. 'I dreamed that a great snake was coiling round my foot and leg, and you [Trotter] were there, and in horror I called to you. You said to the snake: "In the name of Jesus, let go." It uncoiled and fell like a rope, and I woke almost dead with joy.' And the shining of his face told that his soul had got free." B) Trotter says, "Blind Houriya came this morning with 'I want to tell you something that has frightened me very much. I dreamt it Saturday night, but I was too frightened to tell you yesterday. To-day my husband told me, "You must tell them." I dreamed that a great snake was twisting round my throat and strangling me. I called to you [Trotter] but you said: "I cannot save you, for you are not following our road." I went on calling for help, and one came up to me and loosened the snake from off my neck. I said: "And who is it that is saving me, and what is this snake?" A voice said: "I am Jesus and this snake is Ramadan [the Muslim ritual fasting period]."[3]

3) Henry Shipes was the son of an English father and a mother from the Maidu Indians of the Sierra Nevada mountains of California. He grew up at the end of the nineteenth century, during the gold rush era, when the indigenous Maidu culture was coming into conflict with white culture. Henry told anthropologist Arden King of various dreams in which he fought against native shamans who were jealous of his power. In one of these dreams, Henry "had a dream contest with a shaman who was also the headman at Quincy [a Sierra Nevada town]. In this dream Henry and the shaman were contesting with each other to see who had the most power. This was a fight to the death. The shaman acted first. He loosed a snake which pursued Henry Shipes, but was unable to catch him. Henry

then tried his white power. This was stated by him to be specifically white. By ruse he caused the shaman to attempt the lifting of a bucket. The bucket exploded and the dream ended."[4]

4) The Egyptian Pharaoh Tanutamon is reported to have had the following dream experience in the first year of his reign, as presented by philologist A. Leo Oppenheim in his work on dreams in the ancient Near East: "His majesty saw a dream in the night: two serpents, one on his right, the other on his left. His majesty awoke, but he did not find them. His majesty said: 'Why has this happened to me?'" His interpreters told him that the dream means that both Upper Egypt and Lower Egypt now belong to him. Then his majesty said: "True indeed is the dream; it is beneficial to him who places his heart in it but evil for him who does not know it."[5]

5) In Carthage in 203 A.D. Vibia Perpetua, a newly married woman of twenty-two years, and mother to an infant son, was imprisoned and sentenced to death for refusing to renounce her Christian faith. As she waited in prison for the day when she and other Christians would be cast into the arena and killed by wild beasts, her brother came and told her to ask God for a vision to reveal her fate. Perpetua agrees, and says she'll tell him what she learns tomorrow. "And I asked for a vision, and this was shown to me: I saw a bronze ladder, marvellously long, reaching as far as heaven, and narrow too: people could climb it only one at a time. And on the sides of the ladder every kind of iron implement was fixed: there were swords, lances, hooks, cutlasses, javelins, so that if anyone went up carelessly or not looking upwards, he would be torn and his flesh caught on the sharp iron. And beneath the ladder lurked a serpent of wondrous size, who laid ambushes for those mounting, making them terrified of the ascent. But Saturs [a fellow martyr] climbed up first.... And he reached the top of the ladder, and turned and said to me: 'Perpetua, I'm waiting for you—but watch out that the serpent doesn't bite you!' And I said: 'He won't hurt me, in Christ's name!' And under that ladder, almost, it seemed, afraid of me, the serpent slowly thrust out its head— and, as if I were treading on the first rung, I trod on it, and I climbed. And I saw an immense space of garden, and in the

middle of it a white-haired man sitting in shepherd's garb, vast, milking sheep, with many thousands of people dressed in shining white standing all round. And he raised his head, looked at me, and said: 'You are welcome, child.' And he called me, and gave me, it seemed, a mouthful of the cheese he was milking; and I accepted it in both my hands together, and ate it, and all those standing around said: 'Amen.' At the sound of that word I awoke, still chewing something indefinable and sweet." Perpetua tells her dream to her brother, and they both understand that she is to die for her faith.[6]

6) In the 1930s anthropologist Dorothy Eggan collected a number of dreams from a Hopi Indian man she calls "Sam." This is one of Sam's dreams, as recorded by Eggan: He becomes aware of a woman's dance being performed in the plaza. This bothers him, because he believes that performing this dance at this time of year can harm the crops. The people in the plaza ask him to join them, but he refuses and goes to sit under a tree. A crowd gathers around him, whispering curiously, and finally an old man tells Sam that behind him there is something that the people fear. Sam says he isn't afraid of anything, but he gets up and looks: "There I saw a huge snake coiled up. His head must be the size of the mountain lion and around the neck I saw four Pahos (prayer feathers) hanging down. It seems to me that [it] is a sacred snake. "Lay down," said a voice. "Sir, is that you speaking, Snake?" "Yes, I am not going to harm you. You must obey me." I lay down again in the shade and didn't pay any attention to that snake. Well the snake stuck his tongue out and began licking my face and hands. At first I [was] kind of scared, but remembered that the snake would not harm me. Soon the snake put his body over my belly button and was very still. The snake must be around four hundred pounds. Well the snake began to move up to my head and put his nose close to my mouth, but I have to stand it. I remember he is not going to harm me. Well by and by X___ came along, and he must have seen that huge snake over my body. He ran to me and took a stick and tried to chase that snake away, but the snake is too quick for him. He bound X___ round and round and was ready to crush him, but instead of killing X___, he sank down into the

earth. I get up quickly and look down in the hole where the snake sank down into. I can see the movement of the water, a wave, like a boiling water. I notice the ground is shaking and the wind coming up. Everybody who has seen the snake take X___ down into the hole, they get after me. Some are crying. Then the people are running away in order to get away from me. Well I left that hole and went into my house for I wanted to be with my wife and see if the world has come to end. I woke up and find that it is windy.'"[7]

7) In his trilogy of plays known as *The Orestia*, the fifth-century B.C. Greek playwright Aeschylus told the story of Orestes, whose mother Clytemnestra killed his father Agammemnon for having sacrificed their daughter (and Orestes' sister) Iphigenia on the eve of the Trojan war. The following dialogue is from the middle play, *The Libation Bearers*, after Orestes has watched his other sister Electra reluctantly bring offerings from Clytemnestra to the grave of Agammemnon:

Chorus: That godless woman [Clytemnestra] was driven by dreams and by night-wandering terrors to send these offerings.
Orestes: Did you find out about her dream, to be able to tell it rightly?
Chorus: She thought that she gave birth to a snake—that is how she told it.
Orestes: How did her story end? How did it come out?
Chorus: She wrapped the snake in swaddling clothes, like a baby.
Orestes: What food did it need, this newborn monster?
Chorus: She gave it the breast, in her dream.
Orestes: How did the hateful thing not hurt the nipple?
Chorus: It did. It drew clots of blood with the milk.
Orestes: This is not meaningless! It is a vision of man.
Chorus: She started out of her sleep and cried in terror, and many a lamp that was blinded in darkness blazed in the palace walls to pleasure its mistress. And after that, she sent these funeral offerings; she hoped that they would cure all that was wrong.
Orestes: This is *my* prayer, by this land, by my father's grave: may this dream find fulfillment for me! I judge it will, too; all of it fits. For if the snake came from the same place *I* did,

and wore my swaddling clothes, and sucked the breast that
gave me sustenance, mixed the dear milk with clots of
blood, and she was terrified at what happened—then, it
must be so that, as she raised this fearful monster, she must
die violently! For I that became that very snake will kill her,
even as the dream has said.[8]

The snakes in these dreams are *powerful*—in every case the
snake is a figure of strength, energy, and potency. Sometimes
the dreamer struggles *against* the snake, trying to fight its power.
The Algerian Muslims fight to free themselves from the grip
of the snake (2.2), Perpetua confronts a dragon-like creature
blocking her way up a ladder to the heavens (2.5), and Henry
Shipes fends off the snake loosed at him by an antagonistic
shaman (2.3). But sometimes the dreamer becomes an *ally* of
the snake, and is allowed to draw upon the snake's power. Rosie
learns how to become a shaman from a rattlesnake (2.1), Sam is
physically cared for and protected by the sacred snake (2.6), and
Pharaoh Tanutamon extends the range of his kingdom by
"plac[ing] his heart" in his dream of the two snakes lying beside
him (2.4). But even in these latter cases, where the snake's power
has a positive quality, the dreamer feels wary of the snake: it
takes three or four dreams for Rosie to trust the rattlesnake's
message, Sam must continually remind himself in the dream
that the great snake promised not to harm him, and Tanutamon
notes that such a dream would bring evil if it was misunderstood
or ignored.
    Turning to the various interpretations that the world's
cultural and religious traditions have attached to snake dreams,
we find this same complex of reactions:

8) The Temne of West Africa believe that if a person has
sought the aid of a personal river spirit to gain wealth or
children, the spirit may appear in a dream as a snake and
reveal its name.[9]

9) A Muslim treatise on dream interpretation dating from
eighth-century Persia states that "If you see a small snake in
a dream know that you will be in the midst of treasure; and
if you see a big snake, you will be at war with your
enemies."[10]

10) Among the Berti of Africa, snakes in dreams are interpreted as indicating enemies. To dream of killing a snake indicates that the dreamer will defeat an enemy or win a dispute. This dream can also indicate that a village child will die or a pregnant woman will miscarry. To dream of being bitten by a snake means that the dreamer will lose a dispute or fall to an enemy.[11]

11) For the Tzintzuntzan people of Michoacan, Mexico, to dream of "a serpent means one is 'in a state of mortal sin.'"[12]

12) The Lotuko-speaking Lango of Africa believe that "to dream that a snake bites one is a very bad omen. Immediately on waking one bites a piece of charcoal and spits it out and pricks oneself with a thorn. This will avert the omen and even if one meets a snake, as one surely will, it will not bite one."[13]

13) In the *Oneirocritica* of Artemidorus, the second-century Greek text that has so profoundly influenced Western dream studies, it says that "a serpent signifies a king because of its strength. It also signifies time because of its length and because it casts off its old skin and becomes young again.... It also means wealth and possessions, since the serpent guards treasures...." Artemidorus says that if a serpent approaches the dreamer and gives, speaks, or reveals something that is not bad, it means good fortune from the gods. But if the serpent does the opposite, this means bad fortune. Serpents in dreams can portend death, because the snake is a "child of the earth" and thus suggests the burial of the dead. He goes on to say that "A snake signifies sickness and an enemy. The way in which the snake treats the dreamer determines the way in which the sickness or enemy will also treat him." Artemidorus also gives a long list of possible interpretations for a pregnant woman's dream that she gives birth to a serpent.[14]

14) According to the *Oneirocriticon* of Achmet, a Christian from tenth-century Byzantium who patterned much of his work on that of Artemidorus, "The dragon signifies a king, while snakes denote enemies who are very powerful or insignificant in proportion to the snake's size.... If someone dreams that he was fighting with a snake and killed it, he will cut down an enemy whose power is proportionate to

the mightiness of the snake he saw in his dream; if he dreams that he cut or split the snake in two, he will receive from his enemies wealth in proportion to the cut.... If someone dreams that he was eating snake meat, he will find increase of wealth and exult over his enemies."[15]

These different interpretations of snake dreams correspond closely to what we find in the dream experiences themselves. There is, first and foremost, a recognition of the power of the snakes that appear in dreams; there is a tendency to regard such dreams as very negative, as indicating strife, illness, and defeat by one's enemies; there is also a tendency to see snake dreams more positively, as portending wealth, success, and victory; and there is almost always an undercurrent of wariness, fear, and even dread regarding the appearance of snakes in dreams.

So why *snakes*? Why have snakes made such a powerful impact on the human religious imagination, and what exactly is the spiritual significance of their frequent appearances in people's dreams? What is it about this particular animal that has made it so prominent a figure not only in dreams but in myths, folklore, and art from all over the world?[16]

Looking at their "natural" characteristics, snakes are genuine dangers to people, posing a deadly threat either from the quick, poisonous bite of a rattlesnake or the slow, suffocating squeeze of a boa constrictor. At the same time, the capacity of snakes to shed their skins conjures up the image of regeneration, rebirth, and new life.[17] Thus, snakes combine the threat of death with the promise of life. Another "natural" feature of serpents is their lidless eyes; humans find the unblinking gaze of snakes to be both captivating and horrifying, both transcendent and inhuman. This unnerving stare evokes in many people feelings of awe, mystery, and dread.

An obvious explanation refers to the central role that the serpent plays in the book of Genesis. Anyone who is at all familiar with the Bible knows that the serpent is the great tempter, the one whose seductive promises of power persuaded Eve to taste the fruit of the tree of knowledge. The serpent brings evil into the garden of Eden, but also brings the possibility of knowledge: "When you eat [the fruit] your eyes will be opened, and you will be like God, knowing good and evil."[18]

When God discovers what has happened, he ordains that man and serpent shall be eternal enemies.

Another, more "modern" explanation draws on the psychoanalytic theory that snakes symbolize the phallus. Ernest Jones, one of Freud's early followers, says with customary psychoanalytic modesty,

> The idea of a snake, which is never consciously associated with that of the phallus, is regularly so in dreams, being one of the most constant and invariable symbols: in primitive religions the two ideas are quite obviously interchangeable, so that it is often hard to distinguish between phallic from ophitic worship...very rarely can it also symbolize the intestine and its contents, but as far as I know, nothing else.[19]

For Jones, the snake is such a common dream symbol because it enables us to express our strong unconscious feelings about the phallus: the phallus is at once an object of desire and of fear, an object of proud potency and of dreaded impotency, an object that brings great pleasure but that can also bring great pain if it is cut off (as psychoanalysts say men continually fear it will be). The snake's physical shape makes it a uniquely convenient way of representing (and yet *disguising*) the phallus in dreams, myths, and art.

Each of these explanations makes some sense, but none of them adequately answers the question of why snake dreams so often have such a strong *spiritual* impact on people. The "naturalistic" explanation does not account for the vivid dreams of people who have had little direct contact with snakes. The biblical explanation says nothing about the dreams of people who have never had any contact with the Bible. And the psychoanalytic explanation merely sidesteps the question, rightly pointing to the symbolic connection between snakes, penises, and power but failing to relate any of this to people's experiences of the sacred.[20]

We gain a better understanding of snake dreams when we refer to the research of historians of religion like Rudolph Otto and Mircea Eliade. They have found that humans universally feel an *ambivalence* toward the sacred. In virtually all religious and spiritual traditions the divine is portrayed as both enchanting and terrifying; Otto says "the daemonic-divine object may appear to the mind an object of horror and dread, but at the same time it is no less something that allures with a potent charm."[21] The power of the sacred is ambivalent in the true sense of the word— it is both good *and* evil, creative *and* destructive, attractive *and* frightening. If we consider snake dreams in this light, we see that these dreams portray the profoundly ambivalent nature of the sacred. Dream experiences involving snakes have provided people with intensely numinous manifestations of sacred powers that can appear beneficial to the dreamer but can just as often appear evil, violent, and highly destructive. Snake dreams reveal the potential of the sacred to be both a helpful and an antagonistic force in human life.

One way to appreciate the spiritual dimension of snake dreams is to contrast them with dreams of the dead. If dreams of the dead guide us into a better relationship with the sacred, dreams of snakes confront us with the raw energy, the primal potency, and the antagonistic power of the sacred. Dreams of the dead tend to emphasize the beneficial gains that can come from contacting the sacred; dreams of snakes, by contrast, tend to emphasize the dangerous threats that can come from such contact. The contrast is not absolute, of course, because some snake dreams have quite positive aspects. But on the whole, this type of dream brings the dreamer face to face with the darker, more evil aspects of the sacred.

While pursuing my graduate studies in Chicago I made a weekly visit to a small child-care center, operated by the mother of a good friend of mine. Her English was not especially good, so I helped her by reading stories to the children. Each visit I would read two or three books to them, and then ask each child to share his or her *own* story to the group. The kids would usually improvise a version of one of the books we had just read, or perhaps describe what they'd eaten that morning for breakfast. One day, however, a three year old boy named Sam shared a dream with our little group: he said, in an even but intense voice, "I dreamed that there was a *snake monster* inside grandpa's back, and it broke out and killed grandpa." The other children were fascinated by this brief, powerful dream; after a moment of reflective silence, they all began clamoring to tell their own stories of dangerous snake monsters.

I later learned from my friend that Sam's grandfather had indeed died recently (although she didn't know what caused his death) and that Sam was quite upset by it. She said that Sam had told her the dream earlier in the day, with the same intensity he had expressed during story-time. I've often thought of Sam's dream of the snake monster, and of the ways that death *is* like a snake monster—powerful, mysterious, and ferocious, tearing the people we love away from us forever.

3. Gods

*N*aturally, gods of various kinds appear in spiritually meaning-ful dreams. We have reports of dreams involving deities, super-natural beings, and exalted spiritual leaders from virtually all the world's religious traditions. These are the dreams that modern readers generally identify with spiritual dreams per se: spiritually meaningful dreams are dreams with these characters in them. Unfortunately, this has led to the assumption that dreams without divine beings are therefore not spiritually meaningful.[1] This book will, I hope, work to change that mis-taken assumption. Dreams of gods and other divine beings are not the only dreams that have spiritual dimensions to them. However, this particular type of dream does have a distinctive spiritual quality which deserves attention. As the following examples illustrate, such dreams give people a sense of the *proximity* of the sacred, its *closeness* to the human realm and to the individual dreamer.

> 1) The eleventh-century A.D. Japanese woman known as Lady Sarashina (her real name is not known) recorded a number of dreams in her diary, *As I Crossed a Bridge of Dreams*. Towards the end of her life, after her husband had died and after her hopes for working in the romantic world of the Imperial palace had been dashed, she described the following experience: "Yet we continue to live despite all our suffering. I was greatly worried that my expectations for the future world would also be disappointed, and my only hope was the dream I remembered from the thirteenth night of the Tenth Month of the third year of Tenki. Then I had dreamt that Amida Buddha was standing in the far end of our garden. I could not see him clearly, for a layer of mist

seemed to separate us, but when I peered through the mist I saw that he was about six foot tall and that the lotus pedestal on which he stood was about four *feet* off the ground. He glowed with a golden light, and one of his hands was stretched out, while the other formed a magical sign. He was invisible to everyone but me. I had been greatly impressed but at the same time frightened and did not dare move near my blinds to get a clearer view of him. He had said, "I shall leave now, but later I shall return to fetch you." And it was only I who could hear his voice. Thereafter it was on this dream alone that I set my hopes for salvation."[2]

2) Aelius Aristides was a young author and rhetorician travelling through the second-century A.D. Mediterranean world. He began suffering from numerous physical ills, and so visited temples of the God Asclepius. At these temples Aristides experienced many powerful dreams, which he recorded in his *Sacred Tales*. Here is one of his dreams: He saw a statue with three heads, illuminated by a flame. A paean is sung, and the god's devotees come forward. At that point in the dream, Aristides says, "the god gave the sign of dismissal; he was now in the form in which we see him in his statues. All the others began to go, and I too turned round to go with them, when the god beckoned me to stay. And I, in ecstasy over the honor done me, and over my being chosen above all the rest, cried out: 'One alone!'— meaning of course the god; whereupon he said: 'You are that.' This utterance, O my lord Asclepius, is worth more to me than all this mortal life; no sickness, no joy comes up to it; it has given me both the will and the strength to live."[3]

3) The Chinese writer Liu Hsieh (c. 465–522 A.D.), author of *Wen-hsin tiao-lung (Carving Dragons in the Heart of Literature)*, reported the following dream: "At thirty, I had another dream, in which I saw myself carrying ritual vessels of wood and bamboo, walking behind Confucius.... Waking up early in the morning, I was overjoyed thinking how extraordinary it was for the Sage, not easily accessible to a mortal's eyes, to come into the dream of so undistinguished a person as I. I could not but reflect how the Sage over-towered all mankind in its entire history."[4]

4) St. Martin of Tours, a Christian monk from the fourth century A.D., had a powerful dream experience while still a soldier in the Roman army. As recounted in Severus's *Life of Saint Martin, Bishop and Confessor*, one day "Martin met a poor man who was naked. Martin's clothing was reduced to his armor and his simple military cloak. It was the middle of a winter which had been more severe than usual, and, indeed, many had perished from the extreme cold. Those who had passed that way had been begged by the pitiable pauper to have compassion on him, but all had gone by. Martin, however, filled with God's grace, saw that it was for him...that the suppliant was being reserved. Yet, what should he do? He had nothing except the cloak he was wearing.... Then, drawing the sword which he was wearing, he cut the cloak in two; one part he gave to the pauper; in the other he again dressed himself.... When night had come and he was deep in sleep, Martin beheld Christ, clothed in that part of his own cloak with which he had covered the pauper. He was bidden to look attentively upon the Lord and to recognize the garment he had given. And soon, to the throng of angels standing about, he heard Jesus saying in a clear voice: 'Martin, still a catechumen, has covered me with this cloak.'"[5]

5) In the sixth book of Homer's *Odyssey*, Odysseus has just been washed ashore near the land of the Phaiakians, governed by Alkinoos. While Odysseus slept, his divine ally Athena descended to help him; "on this night the goddess, grey-eyed Athena, entered the palace of Alkinoos to make sure of Odysseus' voyage home. She took her way to a painted bedchamber where a young girl lay fast asleep—so fine in mould and feature that she seemed a goddess—the daughter of Alkinoos, Nausikaa. On either side, as Graces might have slept, her maids were sleeping. The bright doors were shut, but like a sudden stir of wind, Athena moved to the bedside of the girl, and grew visible as the shipman Dymas' daughter, a girl the princess' age, and her dear friend. In this form grey-eyed Athena said to her: 'How so remiss, and yet thy mother's daughter? leaving thy clothes uncared for, Nausikaa, when soon thou must have store of marriage linen, and put thy minstrelsy in wedding dress! Beauty, in these, will make the folk admire, and bring thy father and gentle mother joy. Let us go washing in the shine

of morning! Beside thee will I drub, so wedding chests will brim by evening. Maidenhood must end....' And now Dawn took her own fair throne, awaking the girl in the sweet gown, still charmed by dream."

6) During his teenage years the Mormon Patriarch Joseph F. Smith engaged in missionary work in the Hawaiian Islands. The loneliness and poverty of the work depressed him, until he had a dream that his biographer Francis Gibbons says "served as a beacon throughout the remainder of his life. In the dream, Joseph saw himself hurrying to an appointment, carrying only a small bundle wrapped in a handkerchief. As a large mansion, which was his destination, came into view, he also saw a sign with the word BATH on it. Entering, he washed himself and, opening the bundle, found a pair of clean, white garments, which he put on. He then went to the door of the mansion and, upon knocking, was admitted by the Prophet Joseph Smith, who said to him reprovingly, 'Joseph, you are late,' to which the boy responded, 'Yes, but I am clean—I am clean!'" Later in the dream Joseph F. tried to determine whether his experiences were real or a dream. So when the Prophet told him to bring over a child being held by Joseph F.'s mother, "I carried [the baby] to the Prophet, and as I handed it to him I purposely thrust my hands up against his breast. I felt the warmth.... He smiled at me, as if he comprehended my purpose. He delivered the child to me and I returned it to my mother, laid it on her lap."[6]

7) The Tipu of Mysore, a political and military leader from eighteenth-century Persia, recorded in his journal the following dream: "On the 25th day of the month Rahmani, on Friday, the night of which would be Saturday, the year 1225 from the birth of Muhammed, I dreamed that our lord Muhammed, the Prophet of God, presented me with a turban, saying, 'Tie it on your head, as I have tied mine.' Then his Excellency again presented me a turban, saying, 'Put it on your head,' and I bound that one on also. After that, his Excellency Ahmed did so again a third time, and I obeyed; and on the top of the hill there was a strong castle, and I went and looked at it; when at that moment I awoke, and made an interpretation of my dream, thus, that God and the prophet had bestowed on me the seven climates [the whole world]."[7]

8) The Egyptian Pharaoh Thutmose IV had the following dream experience, as presented in A. Leo Oppenheim's *The Interpretation of Dreams in the Ancient Near East*. One day Thutmose came driving by at midday and he took his rest in the shadow of the great statue of the Sphinx. "Slumber and sleep overcame him at the moment when the sun was at the zenith, (and) he found the majesty of this august god speaking with his own mouth as a father speaks to his son, as follows: 'Behold me, look upon me, my son Thutmose. I will give to you (my) kingly office on earth (as) foremost of the living, and you shall wear the crown of Upper Egypt and the crown of Lower Egypt on the throne of Geb, the Hereditary Prince. To you shall belong the earth in its length and its breadth and (all) that which the eye of the All-Lord illuminates. You shall possess provisions from within the Two Lands (as well as) the great products of every foreign country. For the extent of a long period of years my face (has been turned) to you (and) my heart (devoted) to you. You belong to me. Behold, my state is like (that of) one who is suffering, and all my members are out of joint, (for) the sand of the desert, this (place) on which I am, presses upon me. I have waited to have you do what is in my heart, for I know that you are my son and my champion. Approach! Behold, I am with you. I am your guide.'" Thutmose woke up and recognized that the god had spoken to him.[8]

9) A Zoroastrian priest of seventeenth-century Armenia set down in verse this dream, presented by linguistic historian James R. Russell: "Now, one night as I was deep in slumber, I beheld one whose face was like the Sun, from whom wafted the fragrance of musk and rose water, langorous was that ambergris perfume. I opened my mouth and spoke to him. 'Who are you? Tell me your name.' He said, 'Know that I am the god Mithra, who by the gracious command of the Knower of the Hidden am the overseer of all covenants. I am the guide in the material and spiritual worlds. I shattered the works of Ahreman; I work enmity against the demons and Satan....'"[9]

10) Emanuel Swedenborg was a scientist from eighteenth-century Sweden whose mid-life turn to mysticism led him to produce numerous spiritual texts which had a profound

influence on later Western theological and philosophical thinking. During the period of 1743–1744, the years when he began transforming his life interests from science to religion, Swedenborg kept a journal of his dreams. In this journal he recorded the following dream: "It seemed it was Christ himself with whom I associated as with any other man, without ceremony. He borrowed a little money from another person, some five pfennig. I was sorry that he did not borrow it from me. I took up two [pfennig], of which it seemed I let one drop, and then another also. He asked what it was. I said that I have found two; one may have fallen from him. I gave him them and he received them. In such an innocent manner we seemed to live together, which was the state of innocence."[10]

11) Myoe Shonin was a leader of the Nara Buddhist tradition of Japan's Kamakura period (1173–1232 a.d.). He, like Swedenborg, kept a diary of his dreams, visions, and meditational experiences. His dream diary includes this experience: "I had a dream about a large object which resembled a sheep in the sky. It went through unending transformations. Sometimes it was like a light, sometimes it resembled a human figure. When it was like an aristocrat wearing a cap, it suddenly changed into a commoner who descended to the ground. The priest Girin was there. He looked at it, was disgusted, and detested it. It turned to me and seemed to want to say something. I thought to myself that this was a constellation that had transformed and manifested itself. I thought highly of it. I wanted to resolve my uncertainty [about what it was]. Then it turned to me and said, 'Many [priests] should not accept the faith and offerings of the people.' Then I understood it. I asked it, 'Where will I be reborn next?' It replied, 'In the Trayastrimsas Heaven.' I asked, 'When I am reborn there, will I already be unattached to the five desires and be practicing the Buddha's way?' It replied, 'Yes.' The heavenly being said, 'Shouldn't you keep from burning your head?' I replied, 'Yes.' I thought, my next life will be good. Why do I try to anticipate it? I think it was telling me that I need only do what I must before people in this world. Again I said, 'Will you always protect me like this?' It said, 'Yes.' Then I awoke."[11]

In each of these examples the dreamer experiences a connection, an intimate bonding with the divine being. This intimacy is evident in the rich smells the Zoroastrian priest senses in the presence of Mithra (3.9); in Liu Hsieh's sharing a journey with Confucius (3.3); in Muhammed's bestowing the gift of a turban to the Tipu of Mysore (3.7); in the Sphinx's speaking to Thutmose IV as "a father speaks to a son" (3.8); and in the warm, affectionate conversations Lady Sarafina has with Buddha (3.1), Aristides has with Asclepius (3.2), Swedenborg has with Jesus (3.10), and Myoe has with the heavenly being (3.11).

Related to this experience of intimate connection, many of the dreamers feel specially chosen by the divine beings. Liu Hsieh can't believe so "indistinguished a person as I" has been granted a dream of Confucius. Only Lady Sarafina has the good fortune to see and hear Buddha in her dream, and similarly only Aristides is called forward by Asclepius in his dream. The Tipu of Mysore and Thutmose IV are both specially singled out for divine favor and guidance.

A very important characteristic of these dreams regards the status of the divine beings who appear in them. In all of these dreams the divine beings are relatively close to humans—that is, they are beings who either are human themselves or who stand between humans and the higher gods. Myoe's heavenly being takes the form of a "commoner." Confucius, Buddha, Joseph Smith, and Muhammed were all flesh-and-blood humans. Asclepius was the child of the god Apollo, and Coronis the human daughter of King Phlegyas. Jesus was likewise the child of a divine father and a human mother. The Egyptian sphinx has the head of a man and the body of a lion. And Mithra, the Persian sun god, tells the Zoroastrian priest that he serves the "Knower of the Hidden" in guiding humans through the material and spiritual worlds.

Another way of putting this point is that the beings who appear in these dreams are not the supreme gods, the Lords of the Universe, the great, transcendent creator gods of the world's religious and spiritual traditions.[12] *Deus Otiosus*, to use Eliade's phrase, appears as rarely in dreams as in any other realm of human affairs.[13] The divine beings who appear in dreams are relatively close to the human realm; they stand in a position between the earthly world of humans and the transcendent world of the heavens. Thus, they are able to mediate between the two worlds in an especially effective way.

These examples indicate that the spiritual force of dreams of gods derives from that intense experience of connection with the sacred, that intimate bonding with the greater powers that shape, nurture, and inspire human life. What makes a dream spiritually meaningful is its power to bring people *closer to the sacred*. Dreams of gods, as the examples above illustrate, have this power in abundance. But we have also seen this power amply manifested in dreams of the dead and in snake dreams, and subsequent chapters will demonstrate that this same power is expressed in many other types of dreams.

By now, readers who are familiar with the general trends of modern psychological dream research may have some questions. Haven't psychologists shown that dreams arise out of our unconscious wishes, emotions, and conflicts? Sleep laboratories have found that dreams are generated by the neurological processes characteristic of REM sleep—doesn't this contradict, or at least severely undermine, the idea that dreams bring people into contact with the sacred?

Despite the polemical claims of some researchers, these questions do not have simple answers.[14] Dream researchers have not found a single function for dreaming; rather, dreaming seems to serve a variety of both psychological and physiological functions.[15] One of dreaming's most important psychological functions is its role in helping people deal with situations that are new, strange, confusing, and/or painful. Sleep laboratory researcher Milton Kramer, in a review of various studies of dream function, concludes that "it is clear that the dream is responsive to the significant (emotional) concerns of the dreamer.... It is an orderly event which is structured and reflects important psychological differences, responds to immediate (emotional) influences (concerns), and is significantly related to the waking preoccupations of the dreamer."[16] In her study of the dreams of divorced women, Rosalind Cartwright, another leading sleep laboratory researcher, found strong evidence that dreams promote the psychological integration of troubling or stressful emotional experiences."[17] Psychoanalysts Thomas French and Erika Fromm concluded from their years of clinical research that dreams promote people's efforts to address their most difficult problems in life: "Most dreams are groping to understand problems that cannot yet be adequately grasped."[18] And psychologist Ross Levin, in a sweeping review of recent dream research, emphasizes the power of dreams to create solutions to our problems; the unique psychological and physiological qualities of dreaming "may often lead to highly creative and novel solutions to old conflicts."[19]

Psychological investigators generally agree, then, that dreams serve an *adaptive* function in human life. Dreams help us respond, creatively and effectively, to the most difficult and most troubling emotional problems of our lives.[20]

These researchers speak in strictly psychological terminology; they say nothing directly about spirituality. But I think there are strong correspondences between the "psychological" functions of dreams as demonstrated by modern researchers and the "spiritual" functions of dreams that we have been discussing in these first few chapters. Throughout our history as a species, humans have sought answers to some basic questions about our existence, questions that are best described as spiritual in nature. Humans have wondered why we must suffer pain, illness, misfortune, and death. We have tried to understand the mysteries of love and sexuality. We have searched for moral principles to help us overcome evil and strive toward good. We have speculated about the origins of the universe, the lawfulness of nature, and the destiny of humankind. We have asked about the nature of God, and about God's relationship to humans. These are the sorts of spiritual concerns that have always deeply concerned people. To use modern psychological terminology, these have been our species' "waking preoccupations," our "old conflicts," the "problems that we have not yet adequately grasped." Psychological researchers have found that dreams function to address exactly these kinds of concerns, to seek creative new solutions to our most pressing and difficult problems. Although few modern researchers have made the connection themselves, their findings clearly imply that dreams can function to address *spiritual* concerns. And this, of course, corresponds with our finding in these first few chapters: vivid, powerful dreams relating to basic existential concerns have been experienced by people in many different cultures throughout history. The dreams in this chapter have addressed existential questions about the dreamer's relationship to God, to the gods, to the divine. We stand therefore on solid psychological ground in arguing that dreams serve a spiritual function.

These reflections give us a new perspective on the question of the "realness" of spiritual dreams in general. Reports of spiritual dreams often have a literary, stylized quality, and we may suspect that these aren't *real* dreams, but rather fictions that the alleged dreamers simply made up. Indeed, we have already discussed a number of spiritual dreams that are reported in works of fiction: Achilleus' dream of his dead friend Patroklos in Homer's *Iliad* (1.6), Clytemnestra's dream of the snake biting her breast in Aeschylus' *The Libation Bearers* (2.7), and Nausikaa's dream of the disguised goddess Athena in Homer's *Odyssey* (3.5). However, the line between "real" and "fictional" dreams is not as easy to draw as we might think. Consider two of the classic spiritual dreams of western history, the dream revelations of Abram and Jacob in the Old Testament:

> 12) The twelfth book of Genesis opens with Abram's divine call: "Now the Lord said to Abram, 'Go from your country and your kindred and your father's house to the land I will show you.'" Thus begins Abram's journey to find a land where he and his people can settle, live, and worship God. God comes again and says to Abram, "I am the Lord who brought you from Ur of the Chaldeans, to give you this land to possess." But after enduring many battles and conflicts, and after realizing that he has no child and thus no heir to continue his family line, Abram cannot help but question God's promise. He says, 'O Lord God, how am I to know that I shall possess it?' [God] said to him, 'Bring me a heifer three years old, a she-goat three years old, a ram three years old, a turtledove, and a young pigeon.' And he brought him all these, cut them in two, and laid each half over against the other.... As the sun was going down, a deep sleep fell on Abram; and lo, a dread and great darkness fell upon him. Then the Lord said to Abram, 'Know of a surety that your descendants will be sojourners in a land that is not theirs, and will be slaves there, and they will be oppressed for four hundred years; but I will bring judgement on the nation which they serve, and afterward they shall come out with great possessions. As for yourself, you shall go to your fathers in peace; you shall be buried in good old age.'"[21]

13) Abraham's son Isaac had two sons, Esau and Jacob. As
he lay on his deathbed, Isaac told Esau to come so that Isaac
could bless him. But Jacob tricks Isaac into blessing him
instead of his older brother, a deception which enrages
Esau. To protect himself from Esau's murderous anger,
Jacob leaves his family and travels toward a safer land. In
this way, "Jacob left Beer-sheba, and went toward Haran.
And he came to a certain place, and stayed there that night,
because the sun had set. Taking one of the stones of the
place, he put it under his head and lay down in that place to
sleep. And he dreamed that there was a ladder set up on
the earth, and the top of it reached to heaven; and behold,
the angels of God were ascending and descending on it!
And behold, the Lord stood above it and said, 'I am the
Lord, the God of Abraham your father and the God of
Isaac; the land on which you lie I will give to you and to your
descendants; and your descendants shall be like the dust of
the earth, and you shall spread abroad to the west and to
the east and to the north and to the south; and by you and
your descendants shall all the families of the earth bless
themselves. Behold, I am with you and will keep you
wherever you go, and will bring you back to this land; for I
will not leave you until I have done that of which I have
spoken to you.' Then Jacob awoke from his sleep and said,
'Surely the Lord is in this place; and I did not know it.' And
he was afraid, and said, 'How awesome is this place! This is
none other than the house of God, and this is the gate of
heaven.'"[22]

These dream reports have obviously been shaped by
literary, political, and theological concerns. The two dreams
restate a central theological theme of the Old Testament,
namely God's covenant with the Hebrew people. Moreover, the
dreams serve the important political purpose of establishing
these men's divine credentials as community leaders. And the
nice, neat dialogues between God and the dreamers clearly
betray the editorial hands of the people who compiled the
books of the Old Testament.

It would be foolish to insist that these are "real" dreams.
However, we have good reasons to believe that *despite* all the
literary, political, and theological influences which have so
clearly shaped these dream accounts, these accounts *do*

correspond to "real" dream experiences. Both dreams involve the basic existential question of how humans relate to the divine, a question that is certainly addressed in the dreams of many "real" people. Both dreams are framed by situations that make this existential question a "real," living concern: Abram has just left his home and is now journeying through the wilderness, deeply anxious about his future; Jacob is also out in the wilderness, having shamelessly stolen his father's blessing, and he now fears that his vengeful brother Esau will chase him and do him harm. Both of these dreamers have very good, very "real" reasons for worrying about whether God still favors them or not.

Their dreams provide them with a powerful, vivid confirmation of their intimate connection to God. The dreams reassure Abram and Jacob that God *is* with them and will continue to care for them and their descendants.[23] And Abram's and Jacob's dreams vividly describe the exact kind of emotional intensity that we have found characterizes "real" dreams of gods: a "dread and great darkness" falls upon Abram at the beginning of his dream, and when Jacob awakens he is "afraid" and exclaims, "How awesome is this place!"

Ultimately, we can never know whether or not Abram and Jacob really had these dreams.[24] But if these dreams are nothing more than literary creations, then their authors did a flawless job of grounding the *fictional* dreams in the *real* spiritual potentials of dreaming. Perhaps that is why these spiritual dreams have achieved the status of "classics."[25]

4. Nightmares

We have already seen in dreams of the dead, of snakes, and of gods that sometimes the dreamers are terrified by their experiences. Anggauwane's dream of his dead son reproaching him (1.5), Perpetua's dream of fighting against the serpent grabbing at her feet (2.5), and Abram's "dread"-filled dream of God (3.12) all involve feelings of deep fear and horror. But we should not assume that spiritually meaningful dreams are always happy, cheerful experiences. Revelatory dreams very often take the form of nightmares—dark, harrowing dreams that leave the dreamer trembling with fear.

One way to interpret the spiritual significance of night-mares is to recall again the feelings of ambivalence, of attraction mingled with repulsion, that people have always felt in relation to the sacred. In this view, *all* spiritual dreams can be touched by nightmarish fears, because *all* encounters with the sacred have the potential to disclose the dark, destructive side of spiritual powers and realities.

But in many different cultures people have found certain dreams to be much more frightening than other dreams. These unusually terrifying dreams have a spiritual significance that seems to be distinct from other types of dreams. Nightmares can be warnings that the dreamer is losing, or has already lost, contact with the renewing energies of the sacred.

1) Anthropologist William Morgan, studying the Navaho Indians in the 1920's and 1930's, reported the case of a shaman who suffered from recurrent nightmares. "C, a Shooting Chant shaman, intended to have a Night Chant held for himself. These nine-night ceremonies...are primarily for the curing of sickness.... Last month, he dreamed that

many gods came after him. They tried to drag him away to a mountain. Many *Yei* (who are prominent in the Night Chant) were among these gods. These gods were trying to kill him. Since then, he has had this dream again and again. He asked O [a Navaho diagnostician] what he must do about this dream. O said that the medicines and masks which he handled were too strong; that the gods were trying to kill him. He must have a Night Chant. He told his dream to M [another diagnostician], and this man said what O had said."[1]

2) The Book of Job is the Bible's great meditation on the question of suffering. Job "was blameless and upright, one who feared God, and turned away from evil"; but Satan challenges God to a test of Job's faith. All of Job's children are killed and all his possessions are destroyed, and still Job has faith in God; but after Job is afflicted "with loathsome sores from the sole of his foot to the crown of his head," he finally speaks of his misery and asks God why he must suffer so: "I will not restrain my mouth; I will speak in the anguish of my spirit; I will complain in the bitterness of my soul. Am I the sea, or a sea monster, that thou settest a guard over me? When I say, 'My bed will comfort me, my couch will ease my complaint,' then thou dost scare me with dreams and terrify me with visions, so that I would choose strangling and death rather than my pains." Job's friend Elihu answers him, saying "Behold, in this you are not right. I will answer you. God is greater than man. Why do you contend against him, saying 'He will answer none of my words'? For God speaks in one way, and in two, though man does not perceive it. In a dream, in a vision of the night, when deep sleep falls upon men, while they slumber on their beds, then he opens the ears of men, and terrifies them with warnings, that he may turn man aside from his deed, and cut off pride from man; he keeps back his soul from the Pit, his life from perishing by the sword."[2]

3) Among the Kuma people of the Central Highlands of New Guinea, most of the men report having the following nightmare from time to time: "The Dream Struggle: The dreamer is alone fighting a vast crowd of men whose faces he can see but dimly. They are nearly overpowering him when he manages, with a colossal effort, to brush them all aside with a single gesture and knock them down. But they

spring up and rush at him again. In order to escape them, he spreads his arms like the wings of a bird and tries to fly away. He is not always successful; in one man's experience, the attackers grabbed the dreamer's legs and prevented him from flying." Anthropologist Marie Reay, who studied the Kuma and their dream beliefs in the 1950's, comments that "it is inconceivable for a Kuma to fight alone in reality. He fights with the support of his group, and in order to give his own support to it.... His clan has evidently deserted him in the Dream Struggle, though it would never do this in reality.... I asked the dreamers to identify their assailants, and found that they could not do so.... The figures in the Dream Struggle are dimly seen; there is something familiar about them; they are people the dreamer is used to seeing, but he cannot say who they may be."[3]

4) The ancient Babylonian epic poem *Gilgamesh* opens with a description of the great city of Uruk, over which Gilgamesh rules as king. Gilgamesh is abusing his power— he "does not allow the son to go with his father; day and night he oppresses the weak.... [He] does not let the young woman go to her mother, the girl to the warrior, the bride to the young groom." The people of Uruk pray to the gods for help, and the gods respond by sending Gilgamesh a nightmare: "Gilgamesh rises, speaks to Ninsun his mother to untie his dream. 'Last night, Mother, I saw a dream. There was a star in the heavens. Like a shooting star of Anu [the god of the heavens] it fell on me. I tried to lift it; too much for me. I tried to move it; I could not move it. Uruk, the land, towered over it; the people swarmed around it; the people pressed themselves over it; the men of the city massed above it; companions kissed its feet. I myself hugged him like a wife, and I threw him down at your feet so that you compared him with me.'"[4]

5) Christian missionary Lilian Trotter describes the following nightmare suffered by a woman after her first encounter with a missionary. Trotter tells of how she inadvertently went back to visit a house where the week before the woman living there had told her to leave, "saying she would hear nothing about Jesus. Strangely, I had forgotten it, as we say, when I went in. Her first words were: 'I sent you away last week, I was very wrong. Jesus came to

me that night and frightened me. I dared not open my eyes to look at him. He said: "Why did you not listen? You must listen." His hand was on me. It would have suffocated me if I had not feared and said: "I have had enough, I will listen." I was full of fear, I will listen now.' And listen she did."[5]

6) Josephus tells in *The Antiquities of the Jews* of a Jewish leader named Demetrius, who reads a list of religious laws to an Egyptian king. The king asks why none of the poets or historians have mentioned these wonderful laws, and Demetrius answers that people have feared that if they tried to describe such divine and venerable laws they would be afflicted by God. For example, a man named Theopompos made the attempt to write something about the laws, and his mind became deeply disturbed for thirty days. During a brief pause in the mental torments Theopompus prayed to God for relief, and he "saw in a dream that his distemper befell him while he indulged too great a curiosity about divine matters, and was desirous of publishing them among common men; but when he left off that attempt he recovered his understanding again."[6]

7) A member of the Yir Yoront-speaking Aborigines of Australia reported this dream to anthropologist Lauriston Sharp: "I dreamed a great many *min marl* [ghost shadows] came flying at me, alighted on my back, and wrestled with me." Sharp notes that the group's initiation rites were in progress at the time of this dream, that the dreamer's clan was responsible for its proper conduct, and that his own son was an initiate in the rites. The dreamer said, "this [dream] means that the *pai woror* [initiates] have eaten some tabooed food [and that there will be trouble for those in charge]. *Min marl* are the shadows of dead men; they look like flying foxes and fly like them."[7]

8) In his early fourth-century A.D. *Ecclesiastical History* the church historian Eusebius describes the case of "a certain confessor, Natalius," who had succumbed to the heretical teachings of a rival religious sect: "They persuaded Natalius to be called bishop of this heresy, with a salary, so that he received from them one hundred and fifty denarii a month. Now, when he was with them, he was often warned by the Lord through visions, for our compassionate God and Lord, Jesus Christ, did not wish that one who had been a witness

to His own sufferings [i.e., a confessor] should perish outside the Church. And when he paid rather indifferent attention to the visions, being ensnared by the first position among them [the heretics] and by the shameful covetousness that destroys most men, he at last was scourged by holy angels an entire night and was tormented no little, so that he arose in the morning, put on sackcloth, covered himself with ashes, and with great haste and tears fell down before Zephyrinus, the bishop, rolling at the feet not only of the clergy but also of the laity, and by his tears he moved the compassionate Church of the merciful Christ, and, although he employed much supplication and showed the welts of the stripes which he had received, he was admitted into communion with difficulty."[8]

9) Anthropologist Lydia Degarrod, who has studied the dream beliefs of the Mapuche people of Chile, describes the following case of a young man afflicted by witchcraft. Carlos, thirty-one years old and unmarried, lives with his elderly parents. From his early teens he has suffered frequent nightmares, and because he cannot stand to spend the night alone he sleeps with his parents. Degarrod says that "Carlos' nightmares are characterized by the intense fear that overcomes him afterwards. In some of his nightmares, the *witranalwe* [an evil spirit] appears disguised as a man or a woman. It touches him, enters his bed and sometimes lies on his chest to suffocate him. In other dreams he is chased, or beaten up by several men and usually wakes up screaming." Carlos denies that he has sexual intercourse with the *witranalwe*, although the Mapuche believe that people who have been possessed by these spirits always deny the sexual encounters in their dreams. Shamans were called in to treat Carlos, and they diagnosed him as having a *punkurre*, or night woman, and said that the source of his illness is envy. Degarrod notes that "his paternal aunt was a shaman, who later became a witch. She never got along with Carlos' father due to disputes they had over inherited land. After the death of Carlos' grandfather, the land had passed to Carlos' father and sister, both of whom claimed more than what they received. Before dying, Carlos' aunt cursed him and her brother. She sent an evil spirit in the form of a woman to tempt and harass Carlos, and she cursed him to die an early and lonely death."[9]

10) The plot of great Indian epic *The Ramayana* revolves around a royal succession gone wrong. The aged king Dasaratha, ruler of the city of Ayodhya, plans to step down from his throne and make his eldest son Rama the new king. But one of Dasaratha's wives compels him to crown her son Bharata instead of Rama. In the midst of this succession crisis Bharata experiences the following dream: "Hear the reason for my present sadness! In a dream, my father appeared to me in faded apparel, his hair dishevelled, falling from a mountain peak into a pit of dung! It seemed to me he was wallowing in that sea of dung, drinking oil from the hollow of his hands, bursting into laughter again and again.... And in my dream I saw the ocean dry up and the moon fall on the earth, the world being plunged in darkness.... Finally I beheld a woman dressed in red, a female demon of hideous aspect, who, as if in play, was bearing the king away. This is what I beheld during this terrible night! Assuredly, either I or Rama or the King or Lakshamana [another one of their brothers] are about to die.... My throat is dry; and my mind is uneasy. I see no reason for apprehension and yet I am full of fear; my voice shakes, my features are wan, I am ashamed of myself and yet I do not know the reason."[10]

11) In the Book of Daniel, two nightmares of the Babylonian king Nebuchadnezzar are reported. The second of these nightmares he describes as follows: "I, Nebuchadnezzar, was at ease in my house and prospering in my palace. I had a dream which made me afraid; as I lay in bed the fancies and the visions of my head alarmed me.... The visions of my head as I lay in bed were these: I saw, and behold, a tree in the midst of the earth; and its height was great. The tree grew and became strong, and its top reached to heaven, and it was visible to the end of the whole earth. Its leaves were fair and its fruit abundant, and in it was food for all. The beasts of the field found shade under it, and the birds of the air dwelt in its branches, and all flesh was fed from it. I saw in the visions of my head as I lay in bed, and behold, a watcher, a holy one, came down from heaven. He cried aloud and said thus, 'Hew down the tree and cut off its branches, strip off its leaves and scatter its fruit; let the beasts flee from under it and the birds from its branches. But leave the stump of its roots in the earth, bound with a band of iron and bronze, amid the

tender grass of the field. Let him be wet with the dew of heaven; let his lot be with the beasts in the grass of the earth; let his mind be changed from a man's, and let a beast's mind be given to him; and let seven times pass over him. The sentence is by the decree of the watchers, the decision by the word of the holy ones, to the end that the living may know that the Most High rules the kingdom of men, and gives it to whom he will, and sets over it the lowliest of men.' This dream I, King Nebuchadnezzar, saw." The king's wise men cannot interpret the nightmare, but the Jew Daniel says that the tree symbolizes Nebuchadnezzar himself, who will be struck down by God if he does not practice righteousness. The king refuses, and a year later he goes mad.[11]

The common elements in these nightmares are, of course, their conflict-ridden, often violent content and the feelings of deep fear they evoke in the dreamers. When we look at the sources of these dreams, we see that some of the nightmares are caused by angry spirits: Carlos is afflicted by a *punkurre*, evidently sent by his dead aunt (4.9); the Yir Yoront man is wrestled to the ground in his dream by min marl, the shadows of dead men (4.7). It would be tempting to define nightmares, from a spiritual perspective, as dreams caused by demons or evil spirits, by the "bad guys" of the spiritual world. There is, of course, ample evidence to support such a definition. Moroccan Muslims believe that "false dreams...are caused by the devil, Shitan";[12] the Iban people of western Borneo attribute bad dreams to "the nefarious activities of incubi who are forever abducting the souls of Iban infants";[13] the people of the Ingessana hills of Sudan believe that all frightening dream images are caused by *nengk*, horrible creatures who cause sickness and death.[14]

But when we look at the full range and diversity of people's nightmare experiences we find that the situation is more complex than that. Many of the nightmares considered here are deliberately caused by the gods or by God, that is, by beings who ordinarily promote and defend human well-being. "C," the Navaho shaman, is attacked by a group of gods (4.1), and the Algerian woman is frightened by a stern Jesus (4.5); Gilgamesh's nightmare of the fallen star comes from the gods (4.4); and the terrifying dreams of Job (4.2), Theopompos (4.6), Natalius (4.8), and Nebuchadnezzar (4.11) are all deliberately sent by the Judeo-Christian God. So nightmares cannot be defined by their source: nightmares seem to be caused by demons and gods, by the "bad guys" and the "good guys."

A better way to understand the spiritual significance of nightmares is to look not at *where they came from*, but at *what their effects are*. Nightmares function, in spiritual terms, as signals of a disruption in the dreamer's relationship with the sacred. Nightmares have the effect of a spiritual alarm, alerting people to the dangers of their current activities and pursuits. If dreams serve to bring people closer to the sacred, nightmares function to warn people that they are becoming distant from the sacred.

Looking back at the examples above, we find in some cases that the dreamer has actively done something to create this dangerous breach with the sacred. Natalius makes the mistake of aligning himself with an heretical Christian sect. Gilgamesh has been oppressing and mistreating the people of Uruk. Nebuchadnezzar has arrogantly asserted his individual greatness as king of Babylonia. In these cases, the nightmares warn the dreamers that their actions have led them *away* from the sacred. But in the cases of Theopompos and the Navaho shaman "O," the nightmares warn them that their actions have brought them *improperly close* to the sacred; Theopompos is told that he must restrain his "curiosity about divine matters," and "O" learns that the medicine and masks he has been using are too strong for him to handle safely. Their nightmares show them the dangers of approaching the sacred without proper caution and respect.

In the other examples, the dreamers have not done anything to arouse the wrath of the gods; rather, it is what the dreamers have *failed* to do that brings on the nightmares. The Yir Yoront man has not been diligent enough in preventing the initiates from eating tabooed foods during their initiation rites. The Algerian woman did not heed the words of the Christian missionary, so Jesus comes to her in a frightening dream. The Indian prince Bharata has done little to help resolve Ayodhya's succession crisis (because, perhaps, he secretly wishes to gain the throne, even if it means breaking human and divine law), and thus he has a terrible dream portending death and destruction. And Carlos, the young Mapuche man, has apparently neglected the need to appease the vengeful spirit of his dead aunt, whose curse has caused his incessant nightmares.

Of all the cases we have examined, only Job has done nothing, and failed to do nothing, that would cause his nightmares. Ironically, the explanation given by his friend Elihu applies to all the *other* dreams we have examined in this chapter, but *not* to Job's dream. Elihu tells Job that God sends people nightmares "that he may turn man aside from his deed, and cut off pride from man; he keeps back his soul from the Pit." This is a perfect interpretation of the nightmares of Theopompos, "O," the Algerian woman, Natalius, Gilgamesh, and Nebuchadnezzar—but it is simply wrong in Job's case. Job has committed no impious deeds, nor expressed any undue pride; he has always performed all his religious duties. The intense suffering of the innocent Job brings us back to the view that nightmares express the ambivalent nature of the sacred: nightmares may simply reveal to the dreamer the awesome, transcendent power of the sacred, a power that infinitely exceeds the human capacity for understanding, a power that is, in Nietzsche's haunting phrase, "beyond good and evil." For Job, the only possible interpretation of such an experience is the humble admission that "I had heard of thee by the hearing of the ear, but now my eyes see thee."[15]

So much we learn from studying nightmare reports from various religious and spiritual traditions. Our findings might once again seem suspect because they rely on both "real" and "fictional" dreams. But a brief look at modern psychological research on nightmares indicates that the reports we have been discussing do correspond to "real" nightmare experiences. Sleep laboratory researcher Ernest Hartmann, in his *The Nightmare: The Psychology and Biology of Terrifying Dreams*, says that "the most important result of the laboratory investigations—one that has critical implications for the study of nightmares—is that we now realize that two, or perhaps three, very different phenomena have in the past all been lumped together as 'nightmares.'... Specifically, it is necessary to make a distinction between two quite different biopsychological phenomena—the night terror and the nightmare."[16] Night terrors, Hartmann explains, tend to occur in the first hour or two of sleep, in what is known as stage 4 of nonREM sleep. The subject frequently screams, thrashes about, and experiences a sense of choking and suffocation, as if something is pressing down on the subject's chest. It is difficult to arouse the subject from a night terror, and once awake the subject usually remembers nothing more than a single brief image or scene. Nightmares, by contrast, tend to occur in the second half of the night during REM sleep. They usually involve a long, vivid, and frightening series of images which awaken the subject and which are clearly recalled.[17]

Sleep laboratory researchers may have just discovered these distinctions, but other cultures have apparently known of them for some time. The Kagwahiv of the Brazilian rain forests say that especially intense nightmares are caused by malevolent spirits called *anang*: "the *anang* is often said to throttle (*mobpy-mbopy*) the dreamer. In fact, informants use the phrase "*anang ji jugwy* ("an anang was choking me") almost as a synonym for *anang*-caused dreams."[18] In Newfoundland there are .folk traditions that center on dreams caused by "the Old Hag."

> 12) According to research by David Hufford, these traditions refer "to certain kinds of dreams and dreamlike experiences, all of them unpleasant, which are sometimes seen as pathological. However, most bad dreams are not included under this heading.... Most often Old Hag refers to the following experience: 1) waking up during the night (or occasionally the experience occurs before sleep); 2) hearing and/or seeing something come into the room and approach the bed; 3) being pressed on the chest or strangled and therefore feeling suffocation; 4) being unable to move or cry out until being awakened by someone or finally breaking through the feeling of paralysis."[19]

The Tzintzuntzan people of Mexico make a similar distinction, as noted by anthropologist George Foster:

> 13) The Tzintzuntzan recognized "at least two dream experiences, the simple sueno or dream proper, and the *pesadilla*, or nightmare. The latter...always occurs when the ego is just falling asleep, still half awake and not fully unconscious. Although the content of *pesadillas* is specific and limited, it *is the bodily state* that is critical to the definition. A *pesadilla* is always, and without exception, a terrifying experience, which robs ego of the power of move-

ment and speech, and which leaves him in a cold sweat,
awake.... [The] ego is just falling asleep when a 'something,'
a three-dimensional *bulto* [figure], or perhaps just an *aire*,
an air, identified as death, enters through the door, circles
the room, then sits beside or lies beside the human. One
breathes with difficulty, and often a great cold is felt."[20]

Among the nightmare experiences we have examined in this
chapter, there are many cases that also correspond closely with
the phenomenon of night terrors as studied by sleep laboratory
researchers like Hartmann. Carlos struggles in his dreams with
an evil spirit "who touches him, enters his bed and sometimes
lies on his chest to suffocate him." Gilgamesh anxiously tells his
mother of his paralyzing nightmare: "Like a shooting star of
Anu it fell on me. I tried to lift it; too much for me. I tried to
move it; I could not move it." The Kuma "Dream Struggle"
regularly involves the dreamer being crushed by a group of
dimly-seen warriors, against whom the dreamer struggles to free
himself. In the Algerian woman's frightening dream, Jesus
comes and puts "his hand...on me. It would have suffocated me
if I had not feared and said: 'I have had enough, I will listen.'"

     In each of these examples the dreamer's reported experi-
ence contains many of the primary characteristics that
Hartmann and other scientific dream researchers identify with
night terrors.[21] Again, this does not prove that these were real
dreams. But this does indicate that the nightmare reports we
have been studying are firmly rooted in actual human
experiences.

     Another way to support our findings about the spiritual
significance of nightmares is to look at some of the leading
modern theories about the psychological function of nightmares. Carl Jung argued that dreams and nightmares serve a
compensatory function—"the general function of dreams is to
try to restore our psychological balance by producing dream
material that re-establishes, in a subtle way, the total psychic
equilibrium."[22] Jung believed that nightmares were the psyche's
unsubtle attempts to restore balance to a person whose waking
life has become exceedingly one-sided. And psychoanalyst John
Mack says in *Nightmares and Human Conflict* that nightmares
reflect an adaptive process of striving "to master anxiety and

conflict" in cases of stress, trauma, and developmental crisis; nightmares thus have the potential to promote psychological growth and integration.[23] Jung and Mack are expressing points that many psychological researchers and therapists have confirmed in their clinical work. Nightmares occur in times of extreme conflict; their content reflects, painfully but accurately, the dreamer's emotional experiences and reactions; and their psychological function is to promote a positive, adaptive resolution to the given conflict.[24]

Jung's and Mack's psychological theories help to fill out our understanding of the spiritual dimensions of nightmares. When a person's relationship with the powers of the sacred is thrown into crisis, the first warnings of that danger may come in the form of horrible, terrifying nightmares. To put it in a phrase, nightmares serve as a kind of spiritual warning system. No matter how much people try to ignore or deny the sacred, no matter how much they try to control or manipulate the powers of the divine, at night they learn of the spiritual dangers that threaten them—more than that, they are *forced* to face those dangers, they are shaken to the depths of their souls by frightening images of conflict, violence, and destruction. As horrible and frightening as they may be, nightmares serve a very important, and very *positive*, religious function.

My own nightmares have had a strong and direct influence on my scholarly interst in dreams and spirituality. During adolescence I began suffering horrible nightmares in which dark, evil creatures chased me relentlessly. One of the most frequent, and most frightening, of my pursuers was Darth Vadar, the arch-villain of the movie *Star Wars*. In a deeply visceral way I knew these nightmares meant that something was wrong—wrong in a way that I couldn't help but call "spiritual." During high school and college I read books on psychology, philosophy, comparative religion, the occult, anthropology, on any subject that could tell me something about dreams. As I studied, I noticed that some of my nightmares were changing; small images of light began emerging. The summer before my senior year of college I had this dream:

> I am with, or am a captive of, Darth Vadar. He is in his black
> cape, but I realize his helmet is off, revealing an aged, lined

face and a head of beautiful golden blond hair, about shoulder length. He also wears some soft leather boots, tan. As we walk through his ship he says to me "You have some of the best guerrilla fighters in known space—but you don't have me."

To end this chapter, it should be noted that there are worse things than suffering nightmares—one can have *no dreams at all*. In the twenty-eighth book of 1 Samuel the Hebrew king Saul, facing a large Philistine army, seeks guidance from God; but "the Lord did not answer him, either by dreams, or by Urim [sacred objects used to determine God's will by lots], or by prophets." In desperation, Saul turns to a necromancer to conjure up the spirit of Samuel. When Samuel angrily demands to know why Saul has disturbed him, Saul answers, "I am in great distress; for the Philistines are warring against me, and God has turned away from me and answers me no more, either by prophets or by dreams."[25] And in *Gilgamesh*, the hero asks the gods for a dream to guide Gilgamesh in his journey to find the immortal Utnapishtim: "I lift my head to pray to the moon god Sin: For...a dream I go to the gods in prayer:...preserve me!" But Gilgamesh, who has already suffered many terrifying dreams, does not even receive a nightmare. Here he receives no dream at all: "Though he lay down [to sleep], the dream did not come." The silence from the gods is clearly far more disturbing than were his previous nightmares, as indicated by his enraged, violent reaction upon awakening: "Gilgamesh takes up the axe in his hand; he drew [the weapon] from his belt [and] like an arrow...he fell among them. He struck...smashing them."[26]

To experience a nightmare shows that there is at least a connection with the sacred to be threatened. To have no dreams at all raises the infinitely more awful possibility that one's connection with the sacred has been destroyed entirely.

5. Sexuality

A principal claim of Freud's *The Interpretation of Dreams* is that many dreams reveal hidden conflicts and problems surrounding our sexual lives. Contrary to a popular misconception of psychoanalysis, Freud did not claim that *all* dreams were sexual in nature. While he argued that every dream expresses an unconscious wish—there are no "innocent" dreams[1]—Freud said that dreams may express wishes related to thirst, hunger, sleep, and the need to empty one's bladder or bowels, in addition to sexuality.[2] Contemporary dream researchers have basically confirmed this aspect of Freud's theory, as numerous studies demonstrate that sexual dreams are extremely common, and in many cases extremely disturbing.[3] For example, people often experience dreams of sexual frustration, in which their sexual desires are blocked or disrupted. Even more troubling are the dreams in which the dreamer breaks various sexual "taboos"— engaging in adultery, homosexuality, masturbation, sodomy, incest, rape, sado-masochism, etc. Dream research studies probably understate the frequency of troubling sexual dreams. Some people are so upset by dreams of, say, having sex with a family member that they won't tell the dream to anyone, even a scientific researcher.

Looking at the dream experiences of people from different cultures and historical eras, we find many reports of remarkably vivid dreams involving sexual encounters with gods, demons, and other spirit beings. These dream reports say little about the physical aspects of the sexual act, and focus much more on the dreamers' intense emotional reactions *after* the encounter. At first sight, these dreams all appear to be nightmares, because each one is filled with fear and conflict.[4] But in terms of their spiritual significance, sexual dreams should be distinguished from nightmares. In sexual dreams, the dreamer is in no danger of becoming distant from the sacred; on the contrary, the dreamer experiences an intimate joining with a divine being. What makes these dreams so deeply troubling is that the dreamers, by moving closer to the sacred, move *away* from society and its norms and values. In spiritual terms, sexual dreams seem to reveal a conflict between the dreamer's spiritual yearnings and his or her social duties.

In the following examples, note the many transformations among humans, animals, and gods; these are the same kinds of transformations we have seen throughout the four preceeding chapters.

1) In the Babylonian Talmud, a collection of Jewish teachings dating from 200 B.C. to 300 A.D., erotic dreams are said to be caused by a demon described as "hairy and resembling a goat," and also by a demon named Lilith. In a study of the Talmud's view of dreams, psychoanalyst Sandor Lorand finds that Lilith "attacks those persons who sleep alone in the house. Lilith may take on a masculine or a feminine form. She appears in a female form when approaching men and in a male form when approaching women.... These demons torture the sleeper with erotic feelings, especially during afternoon sleep. The Rabbis of the Talmud made provisions for the dreamer of such erotic dreams so that he may not feel guilty. They declared that the seminal emissions as a result of such dreams were not the responsibility of the dreamer. Rabbi Huna states, 'Even if the emission is connected with feelings of gratification, the dreamer is not responsible, because it was not real sexual intercourse.'"[5]

2) Anthropologist Derek Freeman reports that the Iban people of western Borneo attribute many problems with childbirth to "the nefarious activities of incubi who are forever abducting the souls of Iban infants. The incubus then is ranked among the most malevolent and fearsome of all the spirits with which the Iban are familiar. But mingled with the feelings of fear and hatred which he evokes, is a measure of fascination with the incubus as a consummate lover and an arch philanderer. The evidence for the

presence of an incubus is his appearance in a dream. In such a dream he appears to a woman as a handsome and alluring male whose advances she is quite unable to resist. This, however, is only a guise assumed for the purpose of seduction, for incubi are really animals which, having the power of metamorphosis, may assume human shape at will."[6]

3) In *The Rig Veda*, a collection of Indian religious hymns from 1200–900 B.C., there is the following incantation to help protect the embryo inside a woman's womb: "Let Agni the killer of demons unite with this prayer and expel from here the one whose name is evil, who lies with disease upon your embryo, your womb.... The one who kills the embryo as it settles, as it rests, as it stirs, who wishes to kill it when it is born—we will drive him away from here. The one who spreads apart your two thighs, who lies between the married pair, who licks the inside of your womb—we will drive him away from here. The one who by changing into your brother, or your husband or your lover, lies with you, who wishes to kill your offspring—we will drive him away from here. The one who bewitches you with sleep or darkness and lies with you—we will drive him away from here."[7]

4) Anthropologist Rosalind Shaw finds that among the Temne of West Africa a man who is ill, mentally disturbed, or suffering financial misfortune is often suspected of having formed a sexual relationship in his dreams with a female water spirit called *an-yaron*. If the man remains sexually faithful to her in the waking world, *an-yaron* will help him gain riches; but if he is unfaithful, *an-yaron* will either kill him or make him go insane. Temne women who are suffering from menstrual irregularities or stomach pains or who have had a miscarriage are often diagnosed as having succumbed in dreams to the sexual allures of bush spirits, who frequently appear in the form of the woman's brother.[8]

5) In Muslim regions of Northern Africa there is widespread belief that every person has a spirit double of the opposite sex, a *qarina*, that is generally understood to be a demon or *jinn*. S.M. Zwemer, a Christian missionary, learned that the *qarina* "does not like its particular mortal to get married.... It sleeps with the person and has relations

during sleep as is known by the dreams. This invisible companion of the opposite sex is generally spoken of in Egypt as 'sister' or 'brother.' His or her abode is in quiet shady places, especially under the threshold of the house. The death of one or more children in the family is often attributed to their mother's mate.... It is when a man is overcome with sleep that his *qarina* gets the better of him."[9]

6) In his *Patterns in Comparative Religion* Mircea Eliade refers to a dream of a noblewoman from ancient China: "The father [of Kao-Chu] was called T'ai-kong; his mother was called the venerable Liou. The venerable Liou was one day resting beside a large pool and she dreamt that she met with a god; at that moment there was thunder, lightning, and great darkness; T'ai-kong went to see what was happening and he saw a scaly dragon on top of his wife; as a result she became pregnant and gave birth to Kao-Chu."[10]

7) One of the common dreams of the Kuma people of New Guinea is what anthropologist Marie Reay calls "the Dream of the Strange Girl," which she says is prompted by the people's fear of venereal disease: "They say that the illness comes from an intimate encounter with a bush spirit or *masalai*. The rationale of this illness disposes a man who suffers it to believe that a female bush spirit has tricked him into making love to her by assuming the form of a girl he knows. *The Dream of the Strange Girl*: the dreamer makes love to a strange girl before he discovers that she is really a *masalai* or evil bush spirit masquerading as a human. He is horror-stricken and desperately afraid, but it is too late to avert the consequences of his action." Reay says her male informants claimed that all Kuma men experience this dream from time to time and that the dreamer always awakens with "a cry of discomfort and fear."[11]

8) In his *Oneirocritica* Artemidorus speaks at great length about the meanings of sexual dreams. In one passage he says, "to have sexual intercourse with a god or goddess or to be possessed by a god signifies death for a sick man. For the soul predicts meetings and intercourse with the gods when it is about to abandon the body in which it dwells. But for other men, provided that they have derived pleasure from the intercourse, it signifies assistance from one's superiors. If they did not derive any pleasure from the act, it means

fears and confusion. Intercourse with Artemis, Athena, Hestia, Rhea, Hera, and Hecate, and with these alone, is not auspicious, even if one derives pleasure from it. For the dream prophesies death in the near future for the dreamer. For these goddesses inspire awe and it is my opinion that those who lay a hand upon them will receive no agreeable reward."[12]

9) A shaman of the Goldi people of Siberia told anthropologist Leo Sternberg this story of how he became a shaman: "Once I was asleep on my sick-bed, when a spirit approached me. It was a very beautiful woman. Her figure was very slight, she was no more than half an arshin (71 cm.) tall. Her face and attire were quite as those of one of our Gold women. Her hair fell down to her shoulders in short black tresses.... She said: 'I am the "*ayami*" of your ancestors, the Shamans. I taught them shamaning. Now I am going to teach you. The old shamans have died off, and there is no one to heal people. You are to become a shaman.' Next she said: 'I love you, I have no husband now, you will be my husband and I shall be a wife unto you. I shall give you assistant spirits. You are to heal with their aid, and I shall teach and help you myself. Food will come to us from the people.' I felt dismayed and tried to resist. Then she said: 'If you will not obey me, so much the worse for you. I shall kill you.'" The shaman said that the spirit-woman had been coming to him ever since, sleeping with him like a wife. Sometimes she came as an old woman, sometimes as a frightening wolf, and sometimes as a winged tiger.[13]

10) The native people of the Fijian island of Fuluga are frequently troubled by erotic dream experiences. As anthropologist Barbara Herr reports, these dreams are interpreted in terms of deception by spirits: "*Tevoro* [spirit beings] disguise themselves as familiar, legitimate mates, or as extremely handsome or beautiful strangers, even when they appear as taboo kin. Such dreams are *always* interpreted as really involving not the soul of a non-taboo ancestor. Rather, these are always seen as deriving from the purely malicious (lustful) transformations and deceptions of the "gods" (also called *tevoro*). For women the god is called Tutumatua; for men it's a goddess (actually a pair)

called in Fulaga Yalewa Vuka. There is an explicit conception that such sexual congress may lead to possession
and/or death, and also produces diseases of the sex organs
(everything from fungal infections to Filariasis)." Herr says
the people believe that women can become pregnant from
these sexual encounters, but that miscarriages and
stillbirths usually result.[14]

11) Members of the Hamadsha religious brotherhood of
Morocco frequently have sexual dream encounters with a
she-demon called A'isha Qandisha. As anthropologist
Vincent Crapanzano reports, "belief in A'isha Qandisha is
widespread throughout northern Morocco. She is usually
portrayed as a female *jinn* or *jinniyya*, capable of appearing
as a beauty or a hag, but always with the feet of a camel or
some other hoofed animal. In her ugly aspect, A'isha
Qandisha is black with long, straggly hair, pendulous
breasts, and elongated nipples. She is said to like red and
black.... She is always libidinous, quick-tempered, and ready
to strangle, scratch, or whip anyone who insults her or does
not obey her commands. She demands absolute and
unquestioning obedience from her followers, who are often
called her slaves. Lalla A'isha, as she is sometimes called, is
also said to enter into marriage with men by seducing them
before they discover her identity. She may require them to
wear old and dirty clothes and never cut their hair or
fingernails; she often restricts their sexual activities.... Like
the other *jinn*, A'isha Qandisha often appears in dreams
and other visionary experiences."[15]

Every one of these dream reports involves fear, conflict,
and danger. Temne men are menaced in their dreams by water
spirits, Temne women by bush spirits (5.4); the demon Lilith
"tortures" Jews in their sleep (5.1); the venerable Liou is
mounted by a scaly dragon while thunder and lightning explode
out of the dark skies (5.6); Iban women fear the soul-stealing
incubi of their dreams (5.2); Kuma men awaken from dreams of
"The Strange Girl" with cries of terror (5.7); the Goldi shaman
is threatened with death by the female spirit who comes in his
dreams (5.9).

It seems that fearful, conflict-ridden sexual dreams are a
truly cross-cultural experience. The Freudian view, of course, is

that such dreams function to vent the sexual frustrations people feel in waking life. Many anthropologists have applied this explanation to the sexual dreams of people in other cultures. For example, Derek Freeman says of the Iban people's incubus dreams that "the libidinal impulses of married women, when these women are deprived of the company of their husbands, are more than ordinarily prone to be discharged in incubus-type dreams."[16] Following this psychoanalytic line of interpretation, we could say that Jewish and Christian theologians are so troubled by sexual dreams because their religions teach people to be overly restrictive about sexuality. Saint Augustine of Hippo gives the classic statement in his fifth-century A.D. *Confessions* of this Judeo-Christian concern over sexual dreams:

> 12) Addressing God, Augustine says, "it is truly your command that I should be continent and restrain myself from gratification of corrupt nature, gratification of the eye, the empty pomp of living.... But in my memory...the images of things imprinted upon it by my former habits still linger on. When I am awake they obtrude themselves upon me, though with little strength. But when I dream, they not only give me pleasure but are very much like acquiesence in the act. The power which these illusory images have over my soul and my body is so great that what is no more than a vision can influence me in sleep in a way that reality cannot do when I am awake. Surely it cannot be that when I am asleep I am not myself, O Lord my God?...Yet the difference between waking and sleeping is so great that...I return to a clear conscience when I wake and realize that, because of this difference, I was not responsible for the act, although I am sorry that by some means or other it happened to me."[17]

Some seven hundred years before Augustine, Plato also commented on the unruly sexual desires that burst forth in our dreams. In the ninth book of *The Republic*, Plato argues that such desires pose a grave threat to the stability of any well-ordered society:

> 13) When the rest of the soul, the reasoning, gentle, and ruling part of it, is asleep, then the bestial and savage part, when it has had its fill of food or wine, begins to leap about, pushes sleep aside, and tries to go and gratify its instincts.

You know how in such a state it will dare everything, as though it were freed and released from all shame or discernment. It does not shrink from attempting incestual intercourse, in its dream, with a mother or with any man or god or beast. It is ready for any deed of blood, and there is no unhallowed food it will not eat. In a word, it falls short of no extreme of folly or shamelessness.... [A] terrible, fierce, and lawless class of desires exists in every man, even in those of us who have every appearance of being decent people. Its existence is revealed in dreams.[18]

There is truth to the Freudian explanation (partly anticipated by Plato and Augustine) that frightening sexual dreams are caused by the pressure of unruly sexual desires. One of the great constants of human society is the struggle to restrict, control, and channel people's sexual drives into socially-acceptable forms. Sexual desires are among the most powerful forces in every individual's life; and yet these desires are confronted, and often frustrated, by society's courtship customs, marriage laws, religious teachings, and taboos against incest, adultery, and masturbation. Each society differs in the *types* of controls it imposes on sexuality and in the *severity* of those controls, but every society does devote considerable energy to regulating the sexual behavior of its members. Even modern western society, which prides itself on being so open and enlightened about sexual matters, in fact employs a vast array of technological and cultural mechanisms to oversee, manage, and restrict people's sexuality.[19]

So it is no great mystery why people have dreams of sexual fear, conflict, and danger—the simple experience of living in a society, *any* society, makes it inevitable that each individual will suffer some degree of sexual conflict. This conflict regularly makes itself felt in our dreams.

However, this explanation only helps us to understand the social and psychological dimensions of these dreams. The question of their spiritual significance remains unanswered. What do these dreams reveal of the dreamer's relationship with the *sacred*?

We need to look more carefully at the dreams themselves, which all involve the intimate sexual joining of the dreamer with a spirit being. The dreamer experiences a profound closeness with that spirit being, uniting with it in perhaps *the* primal act of creativity. Many of the world's religious traditions have regarded sexuality as a potent means of encountering the sacred. The Tantric schools of Buddhism have long used techniques of sexual yoga as a path toward enlightenment.[20] Likewise, members of the Jewish mystical tradition of Kabbalism have seen sexual experience as revealing aspects of the sacred.[21] Mircea Eliade says that "sexuality is at one and the same time a physiological activity and a sacrament.... [T]hroughout religious history, sensory activity has been used as a means of participating in the sacred and attaining to the divine."[22] While sexual dreams often emerge out of the dreamer's relations with people in waking life, they may also be emerging out of the dreamer's relationship with the *sacred*. Dreams in which a person experiences an intimate sexual joining with a spirit being can, at one important level, be direct expressions of a passionate connection between the dreamer and the sacred.

A second important characteristic of the dreams above is the powerlessness felt by the dreamer. In each example the dreamer is unable to resist the sexual encounter. Sometimes the dreamer is fooled into surrendering to the spirit beings: A'isha Qandisha "seduces" the members of the Hamadsha brotherhood; the *Tevoro* use "trickery and deception" to have sex with the people of the Fijian island of Fuluga; female bush spirits "trick" Kuma men into making love to them. At other times the dreamer succumbs to frightening threats from the spirit beings: the female spirit tells the Goldi shaman that she will kill him if he does not submit to her; similarly, the female water spirits threaten Temne men with death if they do not remain sexually faithful. However it happens, the dreamer loses control to the spirit being.

This gives us further insight into the spiritual dimensions of sexual dreams. The experience of powerlessness, of being overwhelmed by irresistible energies, is an element of virtually every spiritual experience. Rudolph Otto speaks of the sensation of "absolute overpoweringness" that accompanies all encounters with the sacred.[23] In dreams, the overwhelming rush of passion generated by the sexual encounter expresses, from a spiritual perspective, the tremendous power of the sacred, its numinosity. As many religious traditions have taught, sexual experience can open us to the divine; this is evidently true of sexual dreams no less than of waking life sexual encounters.

In the above examples the fears, conflicts, and dangers surrounding the dream experiences are *not* an integral part of the sexual encounter itself. On the contrary, the dreamer's experience of the sexual act is either ignored or described in positive terms (e.g. the Iban incubi is regarded as "handsome and alluring...a consumate lover," and the *Tevoro* of Fiji appear as "extremely handsome or beautiful strangers"). It is only after the sexual encounter that the fears, conflicts, and dangers usually emerge. The true source of these fears and conflicts, it seems, lies in the dreamer's social world. Dreams of sexual encounters with spirit beings are feared because they pose a danger to the dreamer's social duties and religious beliefs, not because the encounters themselves are negative or unpleasant.

For the women dreamers, the "danger" of sexual dreams is to their fertility and their children. Fulugan women fear that dreams of intercourse with the god Tutumatua will result in miscarriages and stillbirths; Iban women believe that lustful incubi come to steal the souls of their children; Temne women worry that miscarriages and menstrual irregularities are caused by dreams of making love to bush spirits; Indian women pray for protection from incubi who seek to destroy the embryo in their womb. In short, the danger of sexual dreams is that they threaten to disrupt a woman's social duties as a child-bearer.[24] For male dreamers, their sexual dreams pose a danger to their social and religious status. If Temne men are not faithful to the water spirit of their dreams, they will lose their reason and their wealth; members of the Hamadsha religious brotherhood worry that the she-demon A'isha Qandisha will enslave them, controlling all their waking world behavior; the Talmud offers consolation for Jewish men whose sexual dreams make them feel religiously impure; likewise, St. Augustine sees sexual dreams as a threat to his conscience as a God-fearing Christian and Plato regards sexual dreams as outbursts of the violent passions that endanger civil society.

What I am getting at is this: these sexual dreams bring the dreamers *closer* to the sacred in a way that takes them *away* from their social duties and religious beliefs. In these dreams people become intensely, intimately close to the powers of the sacred;

but after this experience, the dreamers become afraid that their experiences will endanger their social responsibilities and religious beliefs in the waking world. The dreamer is caught in a spiritual conflict: by coming closer to the sacred, the dreamer finds himself or herself in a dangerous, anxiety-provoking conflict with society. In the previous chapter we saw that nightmares serve as spiritual warnings that the dreamer's waking world activities are leading him or her to become dangerously distant from the sacred. Here we find that sexual dreams can also be spiritual warnings, but of an opposing type: they indicate that the dreamer is becoming so close to the sacred that his or her waking world connections are in danger. The spiritual significance of sexual nightmares, then, is that they warn dreamers of a conflict between their connection to the sacred and their connection to society.

Many modern psychological researchers have carefully studied the nightmares of sexual abuse victims.[25] This research indicates that such nightmares are often direct and literal reenactments of the abuse. As a result, clinical psychologists are struggling with the very difficult question of whether they should interpret their clients' sexual nightmares "literally," as accurate expressions of sexual abuse that actually happened, or "symbolically," as metaphorical expressions of non-sexual experiences and conflicts. This question is not new to the contemporary era, however. The same problem of trying to discern the relations between dreaming sexuality and waking sexuality is addressed in *The Malleus Malificarum* (*The Witches' Hammer*), the fifteenth-century manual used by the inquisitors of the Roman Catholic Church to detect and hunt down witches. In a chapter that treats "Of the Method by which they [witches] can Inflict Every Sort of Infirmity, generally Ills of the Graver Kind," there is the following description of how the devil can harm innocent men:

> 14) The injury to reputation is shown in the history of the Blessed Jerome, that the devil transformed himself into the appearance of St. Silvanus, Bishop of Nazareth, a friend of St. Jerome. And this devil approached a noble woman by night in her bed and began first to provoke and entice her with lewd words, and then invited her to perform the sinful

act. And when she called out, the devil in the form of the saintly Bishop hid under the woman's bed, and being sought for and found there, he in lickerish language declared lyingly that he was the Bishop Silvanus. On the morrow therefore, when the devil had disappeared, the holy man was scandalously defamed; but his good name was cleared when the devil confessed at the tomb of St. Jerome that he had done this in an assumed body.[26]

Did the devil take the form of Bishop Silvanus to tempt this woman and defame the bishop, or did Bishop Silvanus claim to be possessed by the devil to avoid punishment for his clumsy attempt at seduction? Was this a "real" sexual encounter, or just a "dream"?

6. *Flying*

*A*fter so many dreams filled with fear and violence, it may be a relief to turn now to a type of dream that is almost always regarded as positive, pleasant, and even joyous: flying dreams. The spiritual significance of flying dreams does not derive from the appearance in them of gods, demons, or other spirit beings (although these figures are frequently found in such dreams). Rather, the spiritual power of this type of dream lies in the exhilarating *experience* of flying, in the *wonders* the dreamer discovers during his or her flight, and particularly in the overwhelming *realness* of this experience.

> 1) The fifteenth-century Sufi mystic Shamsoddin Lahiji described the following night vision. One night, after he had finished his evening prayers, Lahiji continued to meditate: "Absorbed in ecstasy, I had a vision. There was a *khangah* [a Sufi lodge], extremely lofty. It was open, and I was inside the *khangah*. Suddenly I saw that I was outside. I saw that the entire universe, in the structure it presents, consists of light. Everything had become one color, and all the atoms of all the beings proclaimed "Ego sum Deus" each in the manner proper to its being and with the force particular to each." Lahiji could not understand what kind of being had made them say this. Suddenly he felt an intoxicating desire to fly in the air, but something like a piece of wood held his feet down: "With violent emotion, I kicked the ground in every possible manner until this piece of wood let go. Like an arrow shooting forth from the bow, but a hundred times stronger, I rose and moved into the distance." Lahihi flew through the heavens and "passed through the moon. Then returning from this state and absence, I found myself again present."[1]

2) Pukutiwara, chief of the Pitjentara Native American tribe, told the following dream to anthropologist Geza Roheim: "I saw the soul of a man. It came like an eaglehawk. It had wings, but also a penis like a man. With the penis as a hook it pulled my soul out by the hair. My soul hung down from the eagle's penis and we flew first toward the east. It was sunrise and the eaglehawk man made a great fire. In this he roasted my soul. My penis became quite hot and he pulled the skin off." The eaglehawk man then took Pukutiwara out of the fire, led him west, and cut him open, taking out his lungs and liver and leaving only his heart. Then "we went further to the west and saw a small child. It was a demon. I saw the child and wanted to throw the *nankara* [magical] stones at it. But my testicles hung down and instead of the stones a man came out of the testicles and his soul stood behind my back. He had a very long *kalu katiti* [the skin hanging down on both sides of the subincised penis] with which he killed the demon child. He gave it to me and I ate it."[2]

3) In *The Night Battles* Carlo Ginzburg describes the benandanti, a small group of men and women from sixteenth and seventeenth century southern Europe who, because they were born with a caul, were considered "good witches." In their dreams the benandanti fought ritual battles against witches and wizards who threatened the harvest. The Holy Inquisition investigated these claims for evidence of devil-worship, and Ginzburg describes the Inquisitors' questioning in 1618 of a woman named Maria Panzona: Maria told the Inquisitors that she went riding on a cock, "in other words on a spirit which had assumed the form of a cock, and we travelled a great distance, into the valley of Josephat, and the spirit only went, not the body, which remained behind in bed, as if dead." The Inquisitors became skeptical and asked how she could see the cock flying away with her spirit, if her body remained behind in bed as if dead? Ginzburg says, "Maria did not understand: 'How should I know?' was her reply. This was not disrespect on her part, but a simple inability to comprehend. She had believed, and still did—and she said so herself—that her spirit could leave the body, and return to it, but she did not know 'through what power.'"[3]

4) Artemidorus recorded the following dream in his second century A.D. *Interpretation of Dreams:* "A man who was living in Rome dreamt that he flew around the city near the rooftops and that he was elated by his adept flying. And all those who looked at him were struck with admiration. But as a result of certain pain and palpitations of the heart, he stopped flying and hid in shame."[4]

5) Emanuel Swedenborg recorded the following experience in his dream journal: "July 1–2 [1744]. Something very wonderful happened to me. I came into strong shudderings, as when Christ showed me the divine grace; one followed the other, ten or fifteen in number. I waited in expectation of being thrown on my face as the former time, but this did not occur. With the last shudder I was lifted up and with my hands I felt a back. I laid hold of the whole back, as well as put my hands under to the breast in front. Straightaway it laid itself down, and I saw in front the countenance also, but this very obscurely.... This was in a vision when I was neither waking nor sleeping, for I had all my thoughts together. It was the inward man separated from the outward that knew this. When I was quite awake, similar shudders came over me several times. It must have been a holy angel, because I was not thrown on my face. What it could mean our Lord knows best."[5]

6) A young woman of the Melpa people of the New Guinea highlands reported this dream to anthropologist Andrew Strathern: "She dreamt that Jesus had come back to earth and was taking his people with him. Saved people were flying off and leaving her behind while she struggled to make her wings work, hopping around. Eventually she got them going and took off, anxious not to miss out on the Rapture."[6]

7) The fourth century B.C. Chinese philosopher Chuang-tzu concludes his work *Ch'i-wu lun* (*Discussion on Making All Things Equal*) with the famous story of Chuang Chou's butterfly dream: "Once Chuang Chou dreamed he was a butterfly, a butterfly flitting and fluttering around, happy with himself and doing as he pleased. He didn't know he was Chuang Chou. Suddenly he woke up and there he was, solid and unmistakable Chuang Chou. But he didn't know if he was Chuang Chou who had dreamed he was a butterfly, or a butterfly dreaming he was Chuang Chou."[7]

8) Among the Ojibwa people of the Great Lakes region of North America, each individual gained the help of certain spirit beings by performing ritual dream fasts, usually during adolescence. An Ojibwa boy told anthropologist Irving Hallowell of this dream, which the boy had during his dream fast: a *pawagan*, or spirit being, said to the boy "'Grandchild, I think you are strong enough now to go with me.' Then the *pawagan* began dancing and, as he danced, he turned into what looked like a golden eagle, that is, the Master of this species. Glancing down at his own body, the boy noticed that it was covered with feathers. The Great Eagle spread its wings and flew off toward the south. The [boy] then spread his wings and followed." Hallowell comments that "in later life the boy will recall that in his dream fast he himself became transformed into a bird.... [T]he Master of the Golden Eagles became one of the boy's tutelaries, or 'guardian spirits,' for life."[8]

9) A Mohave man named Robert Martin told anthropologist A.L. Kroeber this dream, which occurred during an epidemic of influenza among Martin's people in 1918: "I was flying, soaring along with my arms spread, and saw the earth opening and boiling up, with people lying dead, scattered around. I came down close to it, but rose again and flew on.—An old kinsman later told me it was a good dream because I was up and out of the death and destruction."[9]

10) Flying dreams play an important role in the religious life of the Aboriginal people of Jigalong, Western Australia. According to anthropologist Robert Tonkinson, "all Jigalong Aborigines share an unquestioning belief in the reality of dream-spirits, *badundjari*, which are said to leave the body during dreams and travel about, flying from place to place.... The dream-spirit is usually described as resembling an eaglehawk, except that a man's legs become its wings, his testicles its eyes and his anus its mouth. Thus it travels back to front, they say, as a protective device when it descends into the sometimes dangerous interiors of increase centres and other spirit-filled sites." Most Jigalong people who go or are taken *badundjari* seek to visit their home areas, where the spirits are known to be friendly. They may even get to see the exploits of their ancestral heroes, engaging in battles, rituals, and other mythic activities. such as fights or

ritual performances. "Aborigines who awake after dreams in which they saw themselves elsewhere are convinced that they travelled there in dream-spirit form."[10]

There are clearly many sharp differences that distinguish these dreams from each other. *How* the dreamer flies, the particular *mode* by which the dreamer moves through the air, is different in each dream.[11] Lahiji shoots up into the heavens like an arrow (6.1); Pukutiwara is dragged away by the penis-hook of a spirit being (6.2); the benandanti Maria rides atop a cock (6.3), Swedenborg is lifted out of his bed (6.5), and the Ojibwa boy grows feathers and turns into an eagle (6.8). There are also important differences in what the dreamers see and where they go when they fly. The Mohave man Robert Martin looks down on a plague-ridden earth (6.9); the Aboriginal people of Jigalong fly across the desert to view their ancestral lands (6.10); the Melpa woman strives to fly with Jesus upward, toward heaven (6.6).

We should not blithely disregard the important differences among these dreams, differences that render each dream a distinct experience with unique meanings for the given dreamer. But neither should we overlook the many remarkable similarities either. To begin with, these dreams all have a revelatory quality: whatever the dreamer encounters during his or her flight, it is amazing, astounding, and wondrous. Pukutiwara journeys to the four quarters of the world; Chuang Chou discovers a wholly different mode of existence, as a butterfly; the structure of "the entire universe" is disclosed to Lahiji; the Ojibwa boy encounters his "guardian spirit"; the people of Jigalong visit the spirit realms of their ancestral heroes; the Roman man soars over his home city, the center of ancient civilization, "elated by his adept flying"; Swedenborg embraces a "holy angel"; Maria and the other benandanti engage in ritual combat with evil witches and wizards; Robert Martin sees "the earth opening and boiling up"; the Melpa woman meets Jesus, leading people to salvation. Each of these dreams of flying brings the dreamer into contact with great spiritual wonders; each of these dreams reveals an aspect of the sacred.

A second common element in the dream reports above regards the physical condition of the dreamer during the flight.

Although they focus on different details, every one of these dream accounts specifically mentions the dreamer's body and his or her physical experiences while flying. The Melpa woman hops up and down, flapping her wings in an effort to get up in the air; similarly, Lahiji must struggle free from the wood holding his feet down, recalling the Christian martyr Perpetua's dream struggle to kick away the serpent that kept her from climbing up the ladder to heaven (3.5). Swedenborg describes laying his hands on the back of the angel that lifted him up, and Pukutiwara tells of his soul being pulled out by the hair. Robert Martin says he fell close to the ground but then rose up again, while the Roman man must stop his flight because of "pain and palpitations of the heart." The benandanti Maria emphasizes that during her flight her body "remained behind in bed, as if dead," and Chuang Chou awakes suddenly from his butterfly dream, acutely conscious of being his usual, "solid and unmistakable" self. The dream-spirits of the Aborigines of Jigalong appear like an eaglehawk, except that "a man's legs become its wings, his testicles its eyes and his anus its mouth."[12]

In many of the above examples the dreamers try to convey the powerful sense of *realness* they felt in their flying experiences.[13] The benandanti Maria did not know "through what power" her experiences occurred, but she insists to the skeptical inquisitors that her spirit really flew even as her body remained in bed. Swedenborg says his experience occurred in "a vision when I was neither waking nor sleeping," but he can fathom little more than that; "what it could mean our Lord knows best." Lahiji's flight to the heavens occurs late at night, when he was praying and "absorbed in ecstasy," apparently in a state between a dream and a vision; in this state he gets a glimpse of the ultimate structure of reality itself. Chuang Chou wakes from his butterfly dream and suddenly wonders which life is real, that of Chuang Chou or that of the butterfly. When the Aborigines of Jigalong awake from their dream journeys to spirit realms they "are convinced that they traveled there in dream-spirit form." These dreams are so striking, and the bodily sensations in them are so intensely vibrant, that the dreamers awaken with a certainty that they have experienced something *real*. Although they may not be able to explain their dreams in rational terms, they are nevertheless convinced that they have encountered forces that lie far beyond the grasp of ordinary consciousness.

Western skeptics have viewed such dream reports as evidence that pre-modern people lack the ability to distinguish between "reality" and "illusion."[14] For example, the developmental psychologists Bernard Kaplan and Heinz Werner claim that "the relative lack of differentiation between dreams and actuality, as is found in psychosis and in some preliterate societies...betokens a condition of developmental primitivity as compared to the polarity between subject and object found in [modern western] reflective thinking."[15]

However, the dream reports above indicate that the boundaries between "reality" and "illusion" are not always as clear and certain as some westerners may believe. The spiritual significance of flying dreams lies precisely here, in the profound challenge they present to our conventional beliefs about waking "reality." Flying dreams provide incredibly vivid experiences of spiritual realms and forces that lie beyond our waking world; they provide experiential proof that the sacred exists and that we partake of its power.

As we have seen in many of the above examples, such dreams can utterly change the way the dreamer views the nature of reality. Eliade has said that "the images of 'flight' and 'ascension,' so frequently appearing in the worlds of dream and imagination, become perfectly intelligible only at the level of mysticism and metaphysics, where they clearly express the ideas of *freedom* and *transcendence*."[16] Flying dreams, in Eliade's view, reveal the spiritual potential in all humans to break free from profane, mortal life and enter into the transcendent realm of the sacred.

Along similar lines, cultural historian Hans Peter Duerr argues in his book *Dreamtime* that people who experience "flying" in dreams and other ecstatic phenomena

> are persons who are able to *dissolve* "within themselves" the boundary between civilization and wilderness, who can step across the fence separating their "civilization side" from their "wilderness side." It is not so much that we fly. What happens instead is that our ordinary "ego boundaries" evaporate and so it is entirely possible that *we* suddenly

encounter ourselves at places where our "everyday body," whose boundaries are no longer identical with our person, is *not* to be found. Such an expansion of our person can easily be described as "flying."[17]

If we follow Eliade and Duerr in their analyses, we will no longer explain away reports of revelatory flying dreams as the failure of "pre-modern" people to distinguish reality from illusion. Rather, we will begin to see flying dreams as having the power to transform a person's understanding of waking reality and of the spiritual forces that lie beyond the boundaries of waking reality.

I am always struck by how often people ask me about their flying dreams. It seems that whenever I give a talk or lecture on dreams someone describes an amazing, incredibly realistic experience of flying in a dream and asks me what it means. Given that people in our society take words like "spiritual," "religious", and "sacred" in so many different ways, I usually avoid using these terms. Instead, I try to emphasize the *vivid experiences* of freedom, power, and ecstasy that so often come with such dreams. I have found this to be an effective way of highlighting the spiritual power of flying dreams to people who have *felt* this power in their own dreams but who are skeptical about all things "religious." Even when dreams of flying contain no special spirit beings and involve no fantastic journeys to otherworldly realms, they still possess a genuinely spiritual dimension. Flying dreams have a transcendent quality that marks them as religiously significant, a quality that appears in mystical dream visions like Lahiji's flight into the heavens as well as in seemingly "secular" experiences like the Roman man's dream of simply being "elated by his adept flying."

The spiritual wonder that people feel toward such dream experiences is eloquently expressed in anthropologist Mubuy Mubay Mpier's account of dreams among the Yansi people of Zaire. Mpier says:

11) The dream as a phenomenon is regarded by the Yansi as extraordinary.... The attitude of admiration is most evident in the conversations of the elders. Gathered in the shade of a tree to deliberate upon a dispute, or in a house, or perhaps casually engaged in making ropes or basket work, they

recount their dreams. During these conversations perhaps one of them will exclaim, 'God is strangely entertaining! He has even made these things we call dreams.' The dream, though difficult to define, is nevertheless an object of admiration. Yansi say it takes wings from a bird and gives them to a man; it paralyses the legs of a man standing before a lorry which is bearing down upon him at great speed; it gives a beard to a small infant; it puts the living and the dead into face to face relationships. Dream life is marvelous: the dreamer is transported to a world which is inaccessible in waking life.[18]

7. Lucidity

*L*ucid dreams are those dreams in which the dreamer becomes aware, during the dream, that he or she is dreaming. We have already encountered some examples of lucid dreaming, particularly in the last chapter. The flying dreams of Emanual Swedenborg (6.5), Shamsoddin Lahiji (6.1), and Maria Panzona (6.3) all involved some degree of lucidity; these dreamers felt they were in a kind of reality or state of consciousness *between* sleeping and waking.[1] Lucid dreaming was "discovered," in western scientific terms, in the late 1970s. Psychologists like Stephen LaBerge and Jayne Gackenbach have taught us a great deal about the psychological and physiological aspects of this type of dream.[2] Just as importantly, independent research by people like Celia Green, George Gillespie, Ken Kelzer, Patricia Garfield, and others has enriched our understanding of the experiential aspects of lucid dreaming.[3] All of these researchers have offered provocative thoughts about the *spiritual* dimensions of lucid dreams. Gackenbach, for example, argues that if we want to understand the phenomenon of lucid dreaming we must develop a theoretical model that "will not only have to embrace waking consciousness but also altered and higher states of consciousness."[4]

For modern westerners the experience of lucid dreaming seems to be relatively rare, although people often say the few lucid dreams they have experienced have been the most amazing, exhilarating dreams of their lives. Interestingly, I have heard many people report that they had lucid dreams while they were children, but that as they grew up they "lost" this ability to become aware within their dreams.

As the following set of examples indicates, lucid dreams

have been reported in various cultures throughout history. These examples reveal the great diversity of lucid dream experiences and attitudes toward lucid dreaming. The spiritual impact of these dreams comes not from any specific *content*, but rather from the extraordinary *power of vision* that people gain: lucid dreams enable the dreamers to perceive important new aspects of reality, and thus to transform ordinary waking consciousness.

1) Among the Makiritare, who live in the highlands of southern Venezuela, the dreams of shamans are different from the dreams of ordinary people. As anthropologist David Guss reports, "instead of the *akato* or [spirit] double leaving the body at will, the shaman 'takes' his double out of his body. It is an act of volition and for this reason the double of the shaman is transformed and given the special name of *damodede*. *Damodede*...is the shaman's *akato*, which is different from that of ordinary people because it is consciously controlled by its master. The shaman's dream is a conscious dream.... It is an 'awakened dream' in every sense of the word, wherein the dreamer's double is at all times being directed by the dreamer himself."[5]

2) Girolamo Cardano was a philosopher, physician, and astrologer from renaissance Italy who wrote a number of works on dreams. He reported this account of a lucid dream: "In my sleep I saw my friend. I asked him to extend his hand to me.... At that moment I thought I woke up. I imagined being awake and reflected on my dream. I was relieved that the deceased was not threatening me.... I imagined that I awoke from my second dream, although I actually went on sleeping. I did not remember anything about the previous dream."[6]

3) Confucian philosopher Wei Hsiang-shu, of the Chi'ing dynasty (early eighteenth century A.D.), wrote that "to be able to hold one's own while dreaming is a sign of consummate scholarship. Such an ability ensures orderliness in the management of important affairs. My own experience has attested to this." Roberto Ong, commenting on this passage in *Dream Interpretation in Ancient China*, says it "suggests the idea that if we but had the right frame of mind, it might even be possible for us to manipulate the

content of our dreams.... [T]o the orthodox Confucian, the human mind is by nature rational. It is imperative that we behave according to the dictates of reason and lead a virtuous life."[7]

4) A man from the Kwakiutl tribe of North America reported this dream to anthropologists Franz Boaz and A. Hunt: "I dreamed I was going sealing near Mapegem. There I got many seals. I came home here to Fort Rupert. Immediately I singed the seals. After I was through singeing I butchered them. Then I found a quartz crystal in the stomach of a large seal. Then I had a treasure. Then I hid it in the woods. Then I gave a feast to the Kwague tribes with the seals. After I had given the feast I lay down. Then I dreamed that I was asleep. A man came and sat down by my side, toward the middle of the house. Then he said, 'You must now lie down with your wife for four years, else you will be unlucky, for you have received your treasure, the quartz crystal from me.' Thus the man spoke to me. Then I awoke."[8]

5) Milarepa, the eleventh-century yogin and poet, is one of the most famous Tibetan Buddhist saints. In his biography, *The Life of Milarepa*, he describes the experiences he had at the advanced stages of his spiritual practice: "During the day I had the sensation of being able to change my body at will and of levitating through space and of performing miracles. At night in my dreams I could freely and without obstacles explore the entire universe from one end to the other. And, transforming myself into hundreds of different material and spiritual bodies, I visited all the Buddha realms and listened to the teachings there. Also, I could preach the Dharma to a multitude of beings. My body could be both in flames and spouting water. Having thus obtained inconceivably miraculous powers, I meditated joyfully and with heightened spirit."[9]

6) The seventeenth-century philosopher René Descartes, one of the leading figures of the enlightenment, had a series of three dreams in 1619 that he recorded in his unpublished notebook, *Olympica*; recent scholarship indicates that these three dreams had a profound effect on Descartes' life and philosophical world-view. In the third of these dreams, Descartes experiences a degree of lucidity.

According to his biographer Adrien Baillet, in this dream Descartes suddenly found a book on his table, without knowing who had put it there. Descartes opened the book and "saw that it was a Dictionary, which delighted him, because he hoped that it might be very useful to him. At the same moment, he noticed that another book came to hand which was no less new to him. He did not know from whence it had come. He discovered that it was a collection of poems by different authors, entitled *Corpus Poetarum*. He was curious to read some of it, and, opening the book, he chanced upon this verse: What way in life shall I follow? Just then he noticed a man whom he did not know. This unknown man gave him a piece of poetry that began with these words: Yes and No. The man recommended it to him as an excellent piece. M. Descartes told him that he knew this verse: it was one of the *Idylls* of Ausonius included in the big anthology of poetry on the table...." Then, the books and the man disappeared, although Descartes did not immediately wake up. Rather, Baillet says, Descartes reflected on the dream while still dreaming: "It is a most remarkable thing that, wondering whether what he had seen was a dream or a vision, he not only decided that it was a dream while he was still asleep but also interpreted it before he was fully awake. He judged that the Dictionary could only mean all the Sciences gathered together and that the anthology of the poets entitled the *Corpous Poetarum* represented in particular and in a more distinct way the union of Philosophy and Wisdom.... Monsieur Descartes continued to interpret his dream while asleep, thinking that the piece of verse on the uncertainty of what sort of life one should choose, beginning 'What way in life shall I follow?' represented the good advice of a wise person or even of Moral Theology. Thereupon, uncertain whether he was dreaming or thinking, he awoke and calmly continued to interpret the dream in the same sense."[10]

7) In *The Art of Dreaming*, anthropologist Carlos Castaneda learns to "intend" greater dream awareness from his teacher don Juan, a sorcerer of the Yaqui people of northern Mexico. Don Juan explains that "sorcerers view dreaming as an extremely sophisticated art...the art of displacing the assemblage point [of each individual's energy body] at will from its habitual position in order to enhance and enlarge

the scope of what can be perceived." Castaneda is skeptical, so don Juan strikes him on the back to induce artificially a "dreaming" condition: "I believed he had instantaneously put me to sleep, and I dreamt that I found myself walking with him on a wide avenue lined with trees in some unknown city. It was such a vivid dream, and I was so aware of everything, that I immediately tried to orient myself by reading signs and looking at people.... [Then] a certainty hit me like a blow: this was not a dream at all; we were in a reality beyond what I know to be real. I turned to face don Juan.... The next instant, I was back where I had started from: don Juan's house. I was lying on a straw mat, curled up on my side.... 'Where were we, don Juan?' I asked. 'Was it all a dream? A hypnotic state?' 'It wasn't a dream,' he replied. 'It was dreaming. I helped you reach the second attention so that you would understand intending as a subject not for your reason but for your energy body."[11]

8) According to research conducted by Kilton Stewart, the Senoi people of the Malay Peninsula actively cultivated lucid dreaming as a psychological and spiritual discipline: "The Senoi [person] believes that any human being, with the aid of his fellows, can outface, master, and actually utilize all beings and forces in the dream universe. His experience leads him to believe that, if you cooperate with your fellows or oppose them with good will in the day time, their images will help you in your dreams, and that every person should be the supreme ruler and master of his own dream or spiritual universe, and can demand and receive the help and cooperation of all the forces there.... The Senoi believe and teach that the dreamer—the 'I' of the dream—should always advance and attack in the teeth of danger, calling on the dream images of his fellows if necessary, but fighting by himself until they arrive. In bad dreams the Senoi believe real friends will never attack the dreamer or refuse help. If any dream character who looks like a friend is hostile or uncooperative in a dream, he is only wearing the mask of a friend."[12]

9) In a letter to a friend who had asked him about dreams and the soul's existence after death, St. Augustine of Hippo describes the dream experience of a man named Gennadius. Gennadius had also been wondering about the

afterlife, when he had a dream in which a young man showed him a beautiful city, filled with hymns being sung to the saints. The next night Gennadius had a second dream, in which "the youth inquired whether it was in sleep or when awake that he had seen [the city]. Gennadius answered: 'In sleep.' The youth then said: 'You remember it well; it is true that you saw these things in sleep, but I would have you know that even now you are seeing in sleep.' Hearing this, Gennadius was persuaded of its truth, and in his reply declared that he believed it. Then his teacher went on to say: 'Where is your body now?' He answered: 'In my bed.' 'Do you know,' said the youth, 'that the eyes in this body of yours are now bound and closed, and at rest, and that with these eyes you are seeing nothing?' He answered: 'I know it.' 'What, then,' said the youth, 'are the eyes with which you see me?' He, unable to discover what to answer to this, was silent. While he hesitated, the youth unfolded to him what he was endeavoring to teach him by these questions, and forthwith said: 'As while you are asleep and lying on your bed these eyes of your body are now unemployed and doing nothing, and yet you have eyes with which you behold me, and enjoy this vision, so, after your death, while your bodily eyes shall be wholly inactive, there shall be in you a life by which you shall still live, and a faculty of perception by which you shall still perceive. Beware, therefore, after this of harboring doubts as to whether the life of man shall continue after death.'" Augustine concludes the story by saying that Gennadius never again doubted the reality of the afterlife. Augustine then asks his friend, "By whom was he [Gennadius] taught this but by the merciful, providential care of God?"[13]

We see in these examples that there are many different degrees of lucidity in dreams.[14] In some cases, the dreamer achieves a total awareness of being in the dream state. The lucid dream of Gennadius has a "young man" carefully demonstrating to Gennadius that he is sleeping and yet conscious (7.9); the Chinese philosopher Wei Hsiang-shu indicates that he has been able to "hold his own," to maintain his rational self-awareness, against the deceptive fancies of dreaming (7.3); and Castaneda realizes with both amazement and terror that he has left the ordinary boundaries of waking and dreaming realities (7.7). In other cases, the dreamer achieves not simply awareness, but a power to change, guide, and control the dream. The Makiritare shamans are able to control the dream journeys of their spirit doubles (7.1); the Tibetan saint Milarepa has the power to fly and perform various wonders in his dreams (7.5); and the Senoi cultivate the ability to become "supreme ruler and master" of their dreams (7.8). In still other cases, the dreamer develops only limited degrees of awareness and power. Girolamo Cardano "wakes up" within his dream, but does not know that he is still dreaming (7.2); Descartes has a relatively "normal" dream, then becomes conscious and interprets it while still dreaming (7.6); and the Kwakiutl man dreams that he goes to sleep, and watches as his sleeping self receives a visit from a spirit being (7.4).

Lucid dream experiences can also have many different spiritual values to the dreamer. Milarepa finds lucid dreaming to be an excellent means of learning Buddhist teachings about the nature of reality. The Makiritare shamans use lucid dream journeys in the service of their work as healers, diviners, and defenders against evil spirits; likewise, don Juan portrays the "art of dreaming" as a means of training Yaqui sorcerers and entering into the "second attention." The lucid dream of Gennadius serves as an unforgettable lesson in the Christian doctrine of the immortal soul; similarly, the partly lucid dream of the Kwakiutl man is the occasion for him to receive an important gift from a spiritual guide. For Wei Hsiang-shu, lucid dreaming demonstrates the power of reason to rule even in the realm of dreams. The Senoi use lucid dreams as a way of confronting and conquering their dream antagonists. Descartes' lucid dream evidently played an important role in his decision to pursue a life as a philosopher.

But as diverse as these reports of lucid dreams may be, the one important feature they share is a vivid clarity that distinguishes them from other dreams. Lucid dreams tend to be remarkably powerful experiences; very much like flying dreams, they make a strong, often unforgettable impression on the dreamer. Becoming lucid within a dream gives the dreamer an opportunity to grasp spiritual truths and relate to sacred powers with an extreme degree of clarity, intensity, and experiential force. As the examples above indicate, there is no distinctive spiritual content to lucid dreams. On the contrary, the lucid dreams we have discussed relate to very diverse spiritual world-views—Christianity, Tibetan Buddhism, Confucianism, and the spiritual traditions of several different native cultures. This point, that lucid dreams *in themselves* teach no particular spiritual notions, is most bluntly demonstrated by the lucid dream experience of philosopher Thomas Reid:

> 10) Reid, an eighteenth-century Scottish philosopher, recalled in a letter to a friend that when he was a teenager he suffered from horrible, recurrent nightmares. As Peretz Lavie and J. Allan Hobson tell the story in their article "Origin of Dreams," Reid used lucid dreaming to stop the nightmares: "In order to combat these dreams, Reid decided to attempt to modify them by the power of will. He went to bed repeating to himself that these were only dreams that did not put him in any real danger. After many fruitless attempts, he succeeded in awakening from sleep while dreaming and thus terminated the nightmare. Shortly thereafter Reid stopped remembering any dreams and was subjectively dreamless for almost 40 years."[15]

There is no awesome spiritual revelation with this lucid dream experience. Reid's case indicates that lucid dreaming can be quite non-spiritual and can actually serve in an effort to eliminate the experience of dreaming entirely.

The phenomenon of lucid dreaming overthrows our culture's common-sense belief that human life can be divided into two separate states of existence, waking consciousness and sleeping unconsciousness. Lucid dreams have aspects of *both*, and thus seem to reveal entirely new realms of human awareness and perception. This raises some intriguing philosophical questions: if we can become self-aware in our dreams, what does this say about the developmental potentials of human consciousness? What does this say about our abilities to perceive "reality" in both the waking world and the dreaming world?

Unfortunately, the modern study of lucid dreaming has been clouded by a great deal of controversy and debate. Many western scholars have taken a dim view toward the subject because some of the claims made by lucid dreaming popularizers have been poorly reasoned and sloppily documented. For example, Kilton Stewart's research on the Senoi has been attacked as a happy fiction. He is charged with attributing to the Senoi dream practices that they never actually performed.[16] Likewise, Carlos Castaneda's writings on the teachings of don Juan have been challenged as total fabrications, pleasing to read but without any real basis in fact. And religion scholars have questioned the notion that lucid dreaming can be a way for modern westerners to have spiritual experiences identical to those of Tibetan Buddhists.[17]

As is usually the case in such controversies, the truth lies somewhere in the middle, between the idealistic popularizers and the academic debunkers. Kilton Stewart and Carlos Castaneda probably did rework their anthropological data—perhaps too much so—to make their findings accessible to non-academic audiences.[18] But at this point, the comparative method we have used in this book can be of some help. When we look at Stewart's and Castaneda's writings in the typological context of other instances of lucid dreams through history, we find that their claims are not utterly outrageous; they are not beyond the pale of what is possible in human dream experience. On the contrary, Stewart and Castaneda are describing a type of dream experience that does indeed occur in various cultural settings and historical eras. We may challenge certain anthropological details in the stories that Stewart and Castaneda have told us, but we cannot for this reason alone dismiss everything they say. Spiritually powerful lucid dreams have been reported from cultures all around the world. It is possible, of course, that Stewart and Castaneda knew of these other lucid dream reports and falsely attributed similar phenomena to the Senoi and the Yaqui peoples, respectively. But my sense is that the writings of Stewart and Castaneda are, despite their academic weaknesses, genuine reports of spiritually significant lucid dream experiences.

The interest of modern westerners in lucid dreaming stems from the same interest people throughout history have always had in this type of dream: lucid dreams bring people close, with remarkable clarity and intensity, to sacred powers, truths, and realities. It is certainly foolish for modern westerners to think their lucid dreams can, for example, transform them into Tibetan Buddhists. The religious teachings of Tibetan Buddhism grew out of a historical and cultural environment that is radically different from the western world of the 1990s; spiritual doctrines and practices are not like clothes that we can just slip into whenever the exotic colors strike our fancy. In the introduction to *Dream Yoga and the Practice of Natural Light*, Namkhai Norbu makes this point from the Tibetan Buddhist perspective:

> 11) There is no doubt that lucid dreams and clarity experiences are fascinating occurrences which seemingly have positive benefits for self-esteem, integration of personality, and overcoming of fear. It is also critical to place their occurrence within the context of the quest for spiritual transformation or enlightenment. Insofar as a culture such as [that of the west] tends to value experience for experience's sake, there is the danger of missing the forest for the trees. One lama from the Tibetan Buddhist tradition likened the pursuit of lucid dream experience to mere play and games except when it arises as the by-product of an individual's development of meditative clarity through the Dzogchen night practice of the white light or Tantric dream yoga. Although there does seem to be relative value in lucid dream experience, from the Buddhist perspective its usefulness is limited unless the individual knows how to apply the lucid awareness in the after-death states of the Chonyid and Sipa Bardos.[19]

The mere experience of lucid dreaming does not make one a Tibetan Buddhist; to become a Tibetan Buddhist requires a deep devotion to a system of very sophisticated spiritual practices, of which lucid dreaming is only one element.

The most sensible conclusion, then, is that the intense spiritual clarity generated by lucid dream experiences can take many different forms, none of which is automatically "better" or more "advanced" than the others. When a dreamer becomes lucid during a dream, he or she becomes open to especially powerful religious experiences. Lucidity can heighten the intensity of the spiritual discoveries to be made in the dream state, making clear that which is but dimly perceived in the waking world. For modern westerners interested in lucid dreams, the greatest significance of becoming more spiritually aware in the dream world may be in prompting us to become more spiritually aware in our *waking* world—in the advanced capitalist society of the turn-of-the-millennium west.[20]

8. Creativity

*J*orge Luis Borges once called dreaming "the most ancient aesthetic activity" of humankind. Throughout history dreams have been directly related to creative endeavors that are directly religious or that have a strongly spiritual quality. As the examples below illustrate, people have frequently reported dreams that inspired the creation of religious shrines, songs, masks, paintings, and written texts. People have also described dreams that guided the creation and performance of religious rituals. These "creative dreams" reveal another important feature of spiritually significant dreams: *the impulse toward expression.* In this chapter, and in several of the coming chapters, we will see the different ways that people have sought to express their spiritual dream experiences, to give form to those experiences, to connect the sacred power of their dreams with the concerns, problems, and conflicts of their waking lives.

> 1) The veneration of Muslim *awliya*, saints or holy men who act as intercessors between the divine and human realms, is widespread throughout the Islamic world. According to ethnographer M. Geijbels, there are in Pakistan alone hundreds of shrines devoted to the worship of particular saints: "The shrines in Pakistan are either tombs of deceased saints, places where a living saint resides, or a combination of the two.... The saint's tomb is either an actual or an empty tomb.... Since famous saints sometimes have tombs in different places, some tombs are actually empty but the saint is considered to be there as *shaykh mu'ashshir*, i.e., a saint who has revealed, 'indicated,' in a dream to a 'holy man' that he wants to be venerated in a particular place. It is believed that the saint's spiritual power

is present there just as much as in the real tomb. Such an empty tomb is called *mashhad*, 'a place where testimomy is given,' namely, of the saint's power."[1]

2) Berthold Laufer's article "Inspirational Dreams in Eastern Asia" presents an account of dreams inspiring religious art. The Arhats, or Lo-han in Chinese, are the supreme disciples of the Buddha and are regarded as the most powerful guardians of the Buddhist religion. According to Laufer, the Arhats have roughly the same place in Chinese religion and art as the apostles have in Christianity, and portraits and statues of them are widely revered in China. "The creator of the Arhat types was a Buddhist monk, Kwan Hiu, who lived from A.D. 832 to 912.... In his biography it is said, 'Every time he desired to paint one of the venerable saints, he first recited a prayer, and then in his dreams obtained the respective figure of the Arhat. Awakening, he fixed this dream picture in his mind and painted it accordingly, so that his portraits did not conform to the customary standard.'...When people marveled at his pictures and interrogated him, he replied, 'I paint what I see in my dreams.' In honor of this artist, a temple was erected at She (in Hui-chou fu, An-hui-Province), called the 'Hall of the Arhats Corresponding to Dreams.'"[2]

3) King Nabonidus, who ruled the Babylonian empire from 555–539 B.C., reported that in the first year of his rule he had the following dream: "Marduk, the Great Lord, and Sin, the luminary of heaven and earth, stood (there) both; Marduk said to me: 'Nabonidus, king of Babylon, bring bricks on your own chariot (drawn by your own) horse, (re)build the temple...and let Sin, the Great Lord, take up his dwelling there!'" In the dream Nabonidus expresses concern, because his enemy the Medes have laid siege to the very temple that the gods have ordered him to rebuild, and their army is large and powerful. "But Marduk said to me: 'The [Medes] of whom you spoke, they, their country and (all) the kings, their allies, shall cease to exist!'"[3]

4) For the Xavante Indians of the central Brazilian plateau, a major element in male initiation rites is receiving dream songs from ascestral spirits. As anthropologist Laura Graham describes it, the senior men perform a series of

rites to prepare the young men "to receive their own *da-nore* [songs] through dreams. In his dreams an individual sees and hears the 'always living' [ancestral spirits] sing and dance *da-nore*. All the men I spoke with report that after dreaming a song, the dreamer wakes and sings the song through softly one time. They say a man 'sings quietly so as not to forget....' He then repeats the song loudly to etch it indelibly in his memory. At this point, the Xavante consider the dreamer to be the 'owner' of the song. At the next appropriate opportunity the dreamer will call the members of his age-set together and teach it to the members of his group. In teaching and then performing *da-nore*, the dreamed-song, initially an expression of inner experience becomes the property of the group. In the process, the song dreamer's individual identity is gradually absorbed into the group. His expression of individual inner experience becomes an expression of group, or collective, experience."[4]

5) The East Cree people who live along James Bay, Quebec continually seek help in their dreams from powerful spirit beings, to guide them in their hunting activities. According to anthropologists Regina Flannery and Mary Elizabeth Chambers, "The East Cree believed that a hunter's success in securing any form of game was ultimately dependent on the consent of the animals who, in friendship to man, allowed themselves to be taken, and of the spirits believed to influence their behavior, distribution, and availability. Dreams were the vehicle for communication with these spirits [*powatakanak*].... The *powatakanak* [gave] songs, various kinds of hunting charms and paraphernalia, and designs for the decoration of hunting clothing and equipment that would enhance the hunter's power to attract game. As the Cree said, 'Everything a man uses in hunting, he has to dream it first.' Hunting songs were the ubiquitous 'gifts' bestowed in dreams. A man received a song when he dreamed he heard 'someone' singing as he comes to him.... On waking, he began to sing just like he has been dreaming, and might sing for several hours to fix it in his memory.... Dreams were the inspiration for decorative motifs of special hunting clothing and equipment that would be pleasing to the animals so that they might more easily be subdued.... The aid of dream-visitors was framed in terms of friendships established with the spirit-persons who may

operate as intermediaries with the game animals sought by man.... Through the avenue of dream visitations, all hunters had access to the spirits most directly related to hunting success. The rites carried out in reciprocity for their aid in securing game required the active participation and cooperation of all members of the group."[5]

6) Shortly after the death of Socrates his pupil Phaedo gave an account to a group of friends of their teacher's last hours. Phaedo reported that Socrates was asked why he had suddenly begun composing lyrics in prison, "when you had never done anything of the kind before." Socrates answered, "I did it in the attempt to discover the meaning of certain dreams, and to clear my conscience, in case this was the art which I had been told to practice. It is like this, you see. In the course of my life I have often had the same dream, appearing in different forms at different times, but always saying the same thing, 'Socrates, practice and cultivate the arts.' In the past I used to think that it was impelling and exhorting me to do what I was actually doing; I mean that the dream, like a spectator encouraging a runner in a race, was urging me on to do what I was doing already, that is, practicing the arts, because philosophy is the greatest of the arts, and I was practicing it. But ever since my trial, while the festival of the god has been delaying my execution, I have felt that perhaps it might be this popular form of art that the dream intended me to practice, in which case I ought to practice it and not disobey. I thought it would be safer not to take my departure before I had cleared my conscience by writing poetry and so obeying the dream. I began with some verses in honor of the god whose festival it was. When I had finished my hymn, I reflected that a poet, if he is to be worthy of the name, ought to work on imaginative themes, not descriptive ones, and I was not good at inventing stories. So I availed myself of some of Aesop's fables which were ready to hand and familiar to me, and I versified the first of them that suggested themselves."[6]

7) M.C. Jedrej reports that among the people of the Ingessana Hills of Sudan two of their main religious festivals, *Sak* and *Poinj*, are organized according to the dreams of the *bao i semk*, the man who governs an important

ritual center. The *bao i semk* "will be approached in a dream by his father and others among his ancestors who were his predecessors, that is those who, when they were alive, were responsible for identifying the precise day of the festival and regarded as the custodians of the temple. In the dream they will say to him: 'announce the festival tomorrow.'" Jedrej goes on to say that for the Ingessana people dreams serve to allow ordinarily invisible beings, *nengk* (ghosts), *meithet* (ancestors) and *tel* (god) to communicate with the living, giving them advice, counsel, and warnings. When these beings demand that a ritual be performed in their honor, the people of the community quickly comply so as to insure good and prosperous relations with the spirit world.[7]

8) Dreams played an important role in the spiritual lives of medieval Jews, and Monford Harris provides the an account of a religious text inspired by a dream. Rabbi Moses (ben Jacob) of Coucy, whose book the *SeMaG* was finished in 1250, says in the introduction to that work that many people had requested that he compile a code of Jewish law, but he had been reluctant because of his own ignorance of such matters. But then, he says, "there came to me a vision in a dream. 'Arise, compose a book, concerning Torah, in two parts.'" Rabbi Moses says he pondered the dream, and concluded that the "two parts" meant a book containing the positive commandments in one section and the negative commandments in a second section. He was again reluctant to write about the negative commandments, when another dream came to him, in which he was told, "'You have forgotten the primary matter.' And I attended to it [the dream] in the morning, and, behold, it is indeed a major foundation of piety. Consequently, I composed it.... And the Lord God knows that I do not falsify on the matter of the dream visions. And the Lord knows that I have mentioned them only so that Israel be strengthened in Torah and admonition."[8]

9) Anthropologist Michele Stephen summarizes the ways in which dreams have inspired religious creativity in various Melanesian cultures: "Inventions and innovations of all kinds are revealed in dreams to specialists, and to ordinary men and women. Magical charms may be revealed to the Tangu in dreams. Among the Koita, according to Seligman,

'Charms are sometimes found by means of dreams. Under these circumstances it is the spirits (sua) of dead Koita who send the dream and who usually indicate where the charm is to be sought and for what it is to be used.' Roro and Mekeo sorcerers employ dreams to enable them to find a 'snake stone' which gives them power to control deadly snakes. Kiwai magicians have new types of charms and spells revealed to them in dreams. The Kyaka may obtain cult stones accidentally or by purchasing or stealing, but also through dreams. Masks and other carved representations of spirits displayed in men's houses and paraded in ceremonies may be inspired by dreams; new songs and dances may originate in the same way."[9]

These examples reveal the intimate relationship that has always existed between dreams, the sacred, and creativity. In each of the above cases, dreams provide the inspiration for specific creative acts that have strong spiritual value for the dreamer. An important, and easily overlooked, feature of these creative dreams is their connection to the dreamer's *community*— the dreams have strong spiritual value not only for the dreamer, but also for the people of his or her community. The Pakistani shrines (8.1), whose locations are often determined by the dreams of holy men, give all Muslims the opportunity to worship the given saints. The lyrics of Socrates (8.6), which he composed during his final days of life because of a recurrent dream, are an object of deep wonder and amazement to his students. Kwan Hiu's dream-based paintings of Buddhist Arhats (8.6) were revered among the Chinese as truly sacred art. The dream of King Nabonidus (8.3) prompts him to restore a religious temple, thus fulfilling one of the primary duties a Babylonian ruler owed his people, the maintenance of good relations with the gods. Each song dreamed by a Xavante male (8.4) contributes to the group's collective store of dream songs, or *da-nore*. The aim of Rabbi Moses' commentary on the Torah, which he wrote in response to a dream (8.8), is to strengthen the faith of the Jewish people. The creative expressions generated by these dreams do more than bring the individual dreamer closer to the sacred; they also serve to enrich the spiritual lives of the dreamer's community as well.

At first glance, it seems that dream experiences provide

people with a direct channel to pure creative energies. The examples we have examined from various cultures and historical eras do indeed suggest that dreams represent a primal source of creativity. But some dream researchers argue that the relationship between dreams and creativity is more complex than that. For example, Freud argues vigorously in *The Interpretation of Dreams* that dreams themselves display no special creativity; they simply draw upon the ready-made creative expressions to be found in the dreamer's culture. He claims that "there is no necessity to assume that any peculiar symbolizing activity of the mind is operating in the dream-work, but that dreams make use of any symbolizations which are already present in unconscious thinking."[10] Anthropologist George Devereux adds to Freud's argument on this point. He carefully studied the practices of Mohave shamans, whose dreams allegedly inspire the creation of myths, songs, and curing rituals. Devereux found that the *reverse* is actually the case, that the shamans are constantly studying traditional myths, songs, and rituals in waking life, all of which become the "day-residue" for *subsequent* dreams: "although Mohave shamans and singers are supposed to acquire their knowledge in dream, they actually learn it in waking life and then have dreams which condense or allude to this body of knowledge."[11] Freud and Devereux grant that dreams and artistic creativity are *related*; they just deny that dreams are the primal source of such creativity. In their view, dreams are secondary reflections of creative expressions that already exist in the dreamer's culture.

Freud's and Devereux's argument certainly accounts for important elements of the dream reports we have examined above. The Xavante males who receive special songs in their dreams (8.4) have, like Devereux's Mohave shamans, regularly heard similar songs in waking life. Likewise, the hunting songs and gear that the East Cree derive from their dreams (8.5) are also clearly influenced by hunting traditions that are well-known in their culture. And if we follow this skeptical line of reasoning even further, we must be suspicious of the claims that dreams have inspired the founding of Islamic shrines in Pakistan (8.1), the instigation of Ingessana rituals (8.7), and the rebuilding of Babylonian temples (8.3). Each of these creative acts could easily be explained by referring to the waking life political interests of the dreamers—in each case the alleged "dream" has the effect of substantiating the person's religious authority and thus legitimating his political power.

Some anthropologists have suggested that this question should not be cast in "either-or" terms; they argue that dreams are both a primal source of creativity and a reflection of the social, historical, and political forces at work in the dreamer's community. Dorothy Eggan speaks of "an interaction" between the dreamer's individual psyche and his or her cultural world; Laura Graham uses the term "dialogic dreams" to indicate the lively interplay in dreams between the unconscious and culture; and Greg Urban and Patricia Kent see "a two-way street" of culture influencing dreaming and dreaming influencing culture.[12] The argument of these anthropologists gives us a much more sophisticated understanding of dream-related creativity.[13] As we found in the examples above, the creative expressions generated by people's dreams contribute to the spiritual welfare of the dreamer's community. And as Freud and Devereux rightly point out, the dreamer's culture always wields a strong influence on his or her dreams. There is clearly a "dialogue" at work between the individual and his or her community, with dreams as the medium.

But what this "dialogical" approach neglects is the central role of the sacred in these dreams. As so often happens in modern dream research, the spiritual elements of dream experiences are ignored, dismissed, or "explained" in reductionistic terms. If we can suspend our biases and accept these spiritual elements as integral to the dream reports, we find that the "dialogue" at work here involves not just the individual and the community, but the sacred as well. Rather than a two-way street, we find evidence of a *three*-way street, an interplay between the individual, the community, *and* the realm of spiritual powers. The individual's dreams and dream-related creative expressions are the mediators of that interaction, the shared space in which that three-way dialogue occurs.[14]

The following three examples offer illustrations of this creative interplay between the individual, the community, and the sacred *by means of* the individual's dreams:

10) Among the Aboriginal people of Jigalong, Western Australia, Robert Tonkinson describes a type of ritual

called *badundjaridjanu*, "from the dream-spirit", which derives from the dream-spirit journeys of the Aboriginal elders. This ritual has a central place in the spiritual life of the Aborigines of Jigalong. Every few years, Tonkinson says, a new *badundjari* is composed: "It originates when one of the elders, most often a native doctor who is known to undertake dream-spirit journeys frequently, goes *badundjari* and in the course of his trip is taken by spirit children (*djidjigargal*) who show him songs and dances generally involving spirit beings or creatures in totemic form. He may also see a fight or some spectacular magical happening, which he remembers when he wakes up." If, upon awakening, the elder believes his experience is significant enough, he will share the dream-spirit journey with others, sing the song that was given to him, and ask for interpretations. Themes and images are developed, usually relating to the community's myths of ancestors and spirit beings. "Later, other men report their dream-spirit journeys and experiences to an informal group, among whom there are native doctors who usually compose the bulk of the songs that will form the series for the ritual. More and more songs are added to the original one, and men describe the dances and sacred objects that they have seen. Rough sketches of the objects are made in the sand or on paper, dance steps are demonstrated and copied, and the overall ritual sequence falls into shape." Tonkinson says that although all dream-spirit rituals are similar in their basic structures, each one has unique songs, tunes, dances, and body decorations. The rituals are not restricted to the elders alone, but eventually include men, women, uninitiated youths, and children—the whole community.[15]

11) The *Mabube* weavers among the Tukulor people of Africa continually draw upon dreams for inspiration, guidance, and technical advice regarding their craft. The myths of the *Mabube* portray the weavers' belief that their craft originated in the spirit world. The mythical ancestor Beram is supposed to have seen in a dream one night an image of a loom frame. Beram did not know what the dream image was, so he asked his father to explain it to him. His father consulted the *jinn*, who described to him the use of the loom; he then showed Beram how to weave on the loom. As anthropologist Roy Dilley reports, the present-day

practices of Mabube weavers parallel this origin myth: "They see themselves to be enacting the deeds of the ancestors, whose example provides a model for the explanation and elaboration of their practices and experiences, particularly in the way they regard dreams. Thus, just as Beram and his father had difficulties over the operation of the loom that were solved by recourse to the *jinn*, so a weaver today facing an aspect of weaving he cannot solve for himself often finds its solution in a dream visited upon him by the *jinn*." Dilley says that dreams often provide a source of inspiration for creating new cloth designs, color combinations, and weaving techniques; likewise, in dreams the *jinn* teach weavers magical formulae, incantations, and various lessons regarding the mystical dimensions of weaving. Dreams, Dilley says, mediate between the human and the spiritual realms; they are "a vehicle for the tranmission of weaving expertise and lore from the world of spirit to the world of men."[16]

12) The Dream-Guessing Rite of the Iroquois Native Americans is a three day ceremony held in midwinter. The purpose of the rite, according to anthropologist Harold Blau, is "to alleviate symptoms, cure afflicted minds, guess dreams, and fulfill the desires of the individual." It begins with the members of one moiety house walking over to the cabins of the opposite moiety and asking to have their dreams guessed and fulfilled—with the dreams being proposed to the assembled group in the form of riddles. "These riddles are stylized and are clues to the assembly as to the subject of the dream. Clues may be understood more readily if one is familiar with legendary accounts of various societies and spirit forces. Single sentence riddles are proposed: 'It whistled in the wind,' may refer to a corn husk spirit. Likewise, 'It has holes, yet it catches,' may refer to a lacrosse stick net. The people take delight in attempting to guess the dream from the clue given.... The [Iroquois at] Onondaga today, in guessing dreams, promise to present to the dreamer the item guessed, if correct.... The tremendous and genuine joy displayed when a dream is ultimately guessed is quite understandable. Some of the more difficult or unusual dreams may take many guesses before a successful solution is ventured.... It is interesting to note...that as part of this general complex, the 'dreams' of

the False Face Society [a community of spirit beings] are
later guessed, and the 'dreams' of the Creator as well...The
Dream Guessing Rite is a method of satisfying the underlying Iroquois need to have their desires fulfilled, and to act
as agents in fulfilling the desires of others. Their dreams
must be guessed, because these represent a disturbing
element. The people *must* help in fulfilling the desires of
others, because of *hadaenidaseh*, the cooperative spirit of
helping one another, a cardinal principle in Iroquois
society."[17]

In each of these examples the "creative dreams" of
individuals serve as *mediators* between the individuals, his or her
community, and the sacred. The dream-inspired creative expressions—the rites, songs, dances, and cloth patterns—open the way
to an interplay between them, deepening and strengthening
their mutual relationship. A remarkable feature of these three
cases is the direct and explicit influence of the dreamer's
culture on his or her dreams. The dreams of the people of
Jigalong involve myths and spirit beings "whose characteristics
are well known"; the *Mabube* weavers have dreams that are
directly modeled on the dreams of their mythical ancestors; and
the Iroquois share their dreams with each other in forms that
are highly stylized by long cultural traditions. There is no need
for Freud and Devereux to ferret out the carefully masked
influences of the dreamer's culture—here those influences are
blatant, and, more importantly, *deliberate*.[18] The dreamer's
culture is actively working to guide his or her dreams, to
cultivate them, to enhance their spiritual power. Freud,
Devereux, and many other modern dream researchers seem to
assume that cultural influences serve only to limit and constrain
the individual's dreams. But these examples indicate that an
individual's culture can help to *stimulate* his or her dreams,
guiding them in directions that promote a remarkably rich
interplay between the dreamer, the culture, and the sacred.[19]

The individual's effort to create something from his or her
dreams is an effort to bring the sacred *into* the dreamer's
community, *into* the broader waking world. When this effort
succeeds, the result is a powerful, dynamic integration of the
individual, the community, and the sacred.

9. Healing

*T*he healing traditions of many different cultures have relied heavily on dreams in helping to cure people of their ills and sufferings. Shamans, diviners, herbalists, and witch doctors have looked to dreams for insights into the causes of sickness and for indications of what specific treatments should be used in a given case. Of course the same is essentially true of many modern psychotherapists, who rely on dreams as an important resource in their healing efforts. Therapists look to dreams for insights into the unconscious anxieties, conflicts, and complexes that trouble their patients. Jung, for example, said he made it a rule to "take dreams as diagnostically valuable facts" that could provide crucial information on the patient's illness.[1]

The great difference between "native" healing traditions and western psychotherapy is that the latter conceptualizes dreams in psychological terms—dreams are windows onto psychodynamic malfunctions that have disturbed the patient's mind. Most healing traditions outside the west, however, regard the healing power of dreams in spiritual terms. In their view, dreams bring the patient and/or the healer closer to the renewing energies of the sacred. The closer the ill person is brought to the sacred, the more his or her suffering is relieved.

For many years western psychotherapists dismissed non-western healing practices as the sad superstitions of people who have no knowledge of modern medical science. But recently the limitations of western therapeutic techniques have become obvious; people are looking for alternatives to expensive hospital treatments, dubious "miracle drugs" and endless therapy sessions. In this context, a more careful examination of the relationship between dreams, healing, and spirituality can be of value. The following examples demonstrate that, far from foolish superstitions, the dream-oriented healing methods of many non-western healing traditions have actually provided an effective means of relieving people's sufferings.

1) In *Shamans, Mystics, and Doctors* Indian psychoanalyst Sudhir Kakar describes the healing practices of an elderly man named Baba, a devout Muslim who treated his patients in a mosque in the Indian city of Patteshah. Baba was visited by a young man named Sundar, who told Baba he was suffering from seizures and attacks of numbness. "'What do you see in your dreams?' Baba asked his standard opening question. Sundar hesitated for a moment before replying that he had many kinds of dreams. 'Do you see a woman, a man, a child, a snake or a monkey or any wild animal in your dreams?' Baba clarified.... [Sundar told] of a recurrent dream that he has had since childhood. 'I am sleeping on my bed when a shadow attacks me. I fight against the shadow but fall down from the bed. My mother picks me up. When I wake up I feel tense, as if I have been in a fight.'...'Aha, the shadow is a bala [demon] that is attacking you,' Baba pronounced confidently. He then asked for the bottle of water that Sundar had brought with him and closed his eyes for some meditative moments. His lips moved soundlessly as he silently recited the required Koranic verses while he held the bottle in his hands. Intermittently, he opened his eyes, blew forcefully on the water, and then continued his silent recitation. 'Drink a little water from this daily,' he said after he had finished the ritual. 'Come back next week when I'll "read" another bottle for you.'" Kakar, who had earlier tried (with little success) to treat Sundar with psychoanalytic therapy, says, "as far as a quick cure of this particular patient's symptoms is concerned, I must admit that the score stands: demonology, 1; psychology, 0."[2]

2) Among the Turkic peoples of Central Asia, shamanic healers are called *baxsi*. According to anthropologists Micheline and Pierre Centlivres and Mark Slobin, "the *baxsi* is primarily an exorcist. He is supposed to drive away the evil spirit which has possessed a patient and thereby caused his illness.... When a patient suffers from an ailment of unknown origin which has resisted the usual charms and

medications, his family may summon the *baxsi*, who arrives at sunset with his *gobuz* [horsehair fiddle] wrapped in soft flannel. The *baxsi* begins the seance with the sacrifice of a *kabut* (bluish) goat. A portion of the meat is consumed the same evening, but the best pieces belong to the *baxsi*, who removes them the next morning. The meat that is eaten immediately is boiled in a closed pot; when it is cooked, the *baxsi* lifts the lid and distributes the pieces. He spends the night in the patient's house unless his own home is nearby. During the night he receives a dream. This and the chewing of the goat's flesh, according to our informants, has a divinatory value which enables the *baxsi* to diagnose the ailment and select the appropriate therapy. Not until the next morning does he actually enter the presence of the patient."[3]

3) The *n'anga*, traditional healers among the Zezuru people of Zimbabwe, are considered to be intermediaries between the human community and the community of the "shades," the various spirit beings that influence Zezuru life. Anthropologist Pamela Reynolds found that Zezuru believe the shades "use healers' dreams to reach the community in order to diagnose patients, to foretell the future, to call for the redress of neglect, to caution against immoral behavior, and to make connections between the past and the present." Healers who rely on the guidance of the shades say that they derive their healing techniques from dreams. Reynolds tells of one example in which a sixteen-year-old girl told her mother's mother (an old and widely respected healer) that she had dreamed of a particular herb. Her grandmother then instructed her how to use the herb as a medicine against witches, venereal diseases, and stomach pains.[4]

4) Some healers of the Manumanua people of Goodenough Island have the ability to use their dreams in the service of curing ills. Anthropologist Michael Young describes the case of a healer named Kimaola: "Kimaola relied heavily upon dreams to assist him with diagnosis. In Kalauna belief, a person's spirit becomes detached from the body during sleep, and dreams are held to be the spirit's nocturnal experiences. But only Kimaola and one or two other men of knowledge could control their spirits' movements and

hence their dream experience. It is well known how he acquired this faculty. Before his father died he instructed Kimaola to break his coconut-shell drinking cup and bury half with his body; the other half Kimaola was to keep by his pillow while he slept. His father promised to guide his dream travel and show him secrets hidden from mortal eyes. Subsequently, any ailing person, on the payment of a fee, could request Kimaola to dream why he or she was sick and what course of action to take to restore health."[5]

5) In Namkhai Norbu's account of the role of dreams in the Tibetan Dzogchen practices, he describes the diagnostic value of dreams. Some dreams are believed to be caused by karma, and these dreams correspond to the three categories of existence: relating to the body, to energy or speech, and to the mind. "In the tradition of Tibetan medicine, a physician who is conducting an investigation as to the origin of an illness will also consider to which of the three existences the sick person's dreams relate. With this information, he or she can discover the real condition and situation of the body, energy, and the mind of the sick person." Norbu also says that dreams may be emanations of "karmic traces" from the dreamer's past lives, from youth, and/or from the recent past. To the extent that illnesses are due to such karmic traces manifesting in the present, dreams can provide valuable clues to diagnosis and treatment. Norbu says, "the method of examining dreams becomes one of the most important means for analyzing and discovering the principal and secondary causes of the problem."[6]

6) The Yuma, a Native American people who lived along the Colorado River and now reside in a reservation in southeastern California, believed that their healing traditions were taught to humans in dream revelations. Anthropologist John Harrington recorded this "Yuma Account of Origins" from Joe Homer, a Yuma *sumatc* (professional dreamer): "The people asked Kumastamxo [the younger of the two great gods of the Yuma], 'If we fall sick, who will cure us?' 'Men who have been instructed,' said Kumastamxo. 'We do not believe that,' said the people, 'for when you get sick, you cannot even cure yourself.' Kumastamxo called all the Yuma men into the darkhouse.

'You are my favorite people,' said he, 'and I will tell you all secrets.' He then made a dust-storm arise in the east. It covered up the sun. It became like night. 'Now sleep,' said Kumastamxo. Dreams came. One man noticed that Kumastamxo's eyes were sore. He rubbed spittle on them and cured them. Another man saw that Kumastamxo had rheumatism. He found the pain and pressed it out. To another man Kumastamxo appeared to have diarrhea. Kumastamxo sang, and this man sang with him, till it became cured. When a man talked wrongly, Kumastamxo stopped him, and asked another man to talk. 'Most of you fellows talk right,' he said, 'and will be great doctors. If a man gets sick, let him call a Yuma doctor.'" Harrington notes that for the Yuma, "'doctor' (*kwasidhe*) and 'dreamer' (*sumatc*) are synonymous."[7]

7) Sinologist Roberto Ong reports that all the way into contemporary times, Chinese medical authorities have regarded dreams as indicators of internal bodily conditions. Ong refers to a text called *Huang-ti nei-ching su-wne* (*The Yellow Emperor's Inner Canon: Plain Questions*), which explains the cosmological principles guiding Chinese medical practice: "'Thus do we know that when the Yin thrives, one dreams of wading through great [bodies of] water in fear. When the Yang thrives, one dreams of great fire burning and scorching. And when both Yin and Yang thrive, then occur dreams of killing and maiming each other.... Overfed, one dreams of giving. Famished, one dreams of taking. When the breath of the liver thrives, one dreams of being angry. When the breath of the lungs thrives, one dreams of crying.'"[8]

8) The native people of the Hawaiian Islands frequently relied on dreams for guidance in healing. Anthropologist E.S. Craighill Handy describes an instance in which "an elderly native woman, who for years had suffered from a chronic organic disorder, dreamed that an ancient Hawaiian wearing the *malo* (loincloth), whom she took to be an ancestor (*kapuna*) of her family, came to her and prescribed a decoction of certain herbs and certain other measures." The woman did as she was told, and says she was cured. She would not, however, reveal the precise nature of the treatment, for such a dream revelation is

regarded as a treasured secret. Handy also offers the following account from a native doctor, "a medical *kahuna* named Ka-wai-lii-lii": "'I was not taught to diagnose by feeling with the hands [*haha*, one of the traditional methods of physical diagnosis]. I received my knowledge through dreams. I was taught the recipes and the methods of treating the sick, to diagnose, and whatever else that the dreams revealed in this way.'"[9]

9) In M.L. Daneel's work on the Southern Shona Independent Churches he presents the following dream reported by a member of the First Ethiopian Church: "I suffered from ear-ache since my youth. Nobody could heal it. I went to *nganga* and hospitals, even to European doctors in South Africa. Yet my ear never healed properly. Back from South Africa, I had a dream. A man clad in white garments entered my house with a torch. He asked me what my greatest wish was. I told him: 'To be healed.' He spat on the floor, mixed the spittle with some sand and inserted it into my ear. It was then that the worm which had troubled me came out of my ear. I took it and crushed it. The next morning when I washed my face the pus came out through my nose, and I could hear once more with this ear which had been deaf for some time. I told my wife what had happened. She said: 'It must be God who has healed you.' My friends advised me to start worshipping God because it was He who had healed me."[10]

10) Aelius Aristides, a Roman orator from the second century A.D., is perhaps the most famous recipient of healing advice via dreams. In his *Sacred Discourses* he describes the various ills he suffered (toothaches, earaches, fits of asthma, and attacks of fever) and the numerous dreams he had of the god Asclepius, giving him medical advice and spiritual counsel. Among the dream prescriptions are these: Asclepius commands Aristides to take a cold bath; to smear mud by the Sacred Well and bathe there; to smear mud on himself and run in a circle around the Temple three times; to go to the hearth of his foster fathers and pray before the statue of Zeus there. Aristides says, "I almost got rid of all my disease, save that when the god [Asclepius] gave me signs and changed my [medical] regimen, I myself was ready to act in this way, but

the evil counsel of my comrades prevailed, who pretending to wisdom and seeming to have a certain cleverness in these matters, explained my dreams rather unnaturally and said that the god expressly indicated that it was necessary to keep to the same things.... By experience I learned well that I was right.... For whenever the god prescribed and clearly stated them, the same regimen and the same things brought to my body and to my spirit salvation and strength and comfort and ease and high spirits, and every good thing. But when some other person advised me and missed the intention of the god, they brought everything opposite to this. How is this not the greatest sign of the god's power?"[11]

These examples show that dreams have historically served two key roles in healing. First is a diagnostic role: dreams can give people a clearer picture of what the given illness is, what precisely is causing the person to be sick. Second is a therapeutic role: dreams can give people specific remedies and treatments that will remove the illness and heal the sick person. In all of these examples, the diagnoses and the therapies emerge out of spiritual realities and powers. The Indian healer Baba (9.1), the Afghan baxsi (9.2) and the Makiritare shamans (9.3) do battle with the hostile spirits that have afflicted their patients. The Zezuru *n'anga* (9.3), the Yuma doctor-dreamers (9.5), the native Hawaiians (9.8), Kimaolo (9.4), and Aristides (9.10) all receive healing advice from gods, ancestors, or spirit beings in their dreams. The physicians of Tibet (9.5) and of China (9.7) draw upon the religious doctrines of karma and Yin-Yang correspondences, respectively, to help interpret the medical significance of their patients' dreams.

In these examples there is no sharp, absolute distinction between "naturalistic" and "spiritual" healing. People throughout history have used *both* approaches to healing their ills—they have seen no contradiction in using medicines *and* rituals to treat a sick person.

One way to understand the effectiveness of spiritual healing methods is to recognize and appreciate the very strong, very positive emotional effects they have on people. Most illnesses cause, in addition to physical suffering, a terrible amount of emotional suffering. Sick people often feel weak, vulnerable, and powerless; their illness has removed them from their daily lives, and perhaps left them isolated from their social group; they may be confused about why this particular disease or injury has happened to them, why they must suffer so horribly; and, finally, they may be worried about death—serious illnesses force people to face their own mortality, the fact that someday they will die. Naturalistic treatments may help with people's physical pains, but when used in isolation they do nothing to ease the deep emotional suffering that illnesses generate.

Methods of spiritual healing have the specific effect of relieving the anxieties and negative emotions that arise with almost every illness. The basic premise of spiritual healing methods is that becoming closer to the sacred *heals*. The sufferings of a sick person can be soothed, and even cured, by striving to relate the person ever more closely to the powers of the spiritual world. Becoming closer to the sacred renews the sick person's hope, confidence, and emotional vitality; it replaces the person's debilitating feelings of isolation and despair with a powerful sense of security, integration, and spiritual community. Jerome Frank, in *Healing and Persuasion: A Comparative Study of Psychotherapy*, comments: "methods of primitive healing involve an interplay between patient, healer, [social] group, and the world of the supernatural; this serves to raise the patient's expectancy of cure, help him to harmonize his inner conflicts, reintegrate him with his group and the spirit world, supply a conceptual framework to aid this, and stir him emotionally."[12] Becoming closer to the sacred renews people, revitalizes them, and thus genuinely helps to heal their ills.[13]

When we consider reports of healing *dreams* in this general context, we can better appreciate their intimate connection with spirituality. For example, the Indian healer Baba interprets Sundar's recurrent dreams of struggling with a shadow as evidence of possession by a *bala* (9.1). *Balas* are a type of *jinn*, those spirit beings that in Islamic spirituality are believed to have frequent, and often mischievous, relations with humans. Baba's interpretation thus renders Sundar's illness spiritually meaningful; Sundar now understands that his suffering is an instance of the cosmic, eternal struggle between Allah and the devil. By means of Sundar's dreams Baba is able to reconnect Sundar to the sacred, thereby giving Sundar the resources to overcome his fears, regain his sense of confidence and vitality, and heal his illness.

The spiritually-oriented dream interpretations made by Tibetan and Chinese doctors (9.5 and 9.7) serve the same purpose. When their patients report dreams, these doctors make sense of the dreams by referring to religious conceptions. The Tibetan physicians look at an ill person's dreams for evidence of "karmic causes originating in youth or even in a past life," causes which underlie the illness; similarly, the Chinese doctors probe the dreams for signs that the sick person is suffering from an imbalance of the cosmological principles of Yin and Yang. These interpretations locate the dream, and the sick person, in a spiritual context; by means of the dream the physicians re-establish the sick person's relationship with the sacred, and thus open a channel for the healing powers of the sacred to work on the illness.

The specific healing treatments that are revealed in dreams also have this effect. The Hawaiian woman who is visited in a dream by "an ancient Hawaiian wearing the *malo*" (9.8) is brought, by virtue of this dream, into a closer relationship with the sacred. She is no longer powerless against her illness because she *knows*, thanks to her dream, that a spirit being is actively helping her. By obeying the ancient Hawaiian—by gathering the herbs and performing the various healing measures that he prescribes—the woman places her sickness within a spiritual context, a context in which she can find the means to combat her pains and anxieties. The sufferings of Aelius Aristides are relieved in an identical fashion (9.10). The god Asclepius regularly appears in his dreams to prescribe treatments, give advice, and offer consolation. Aristides cherishes these dream visitations (unlike the reticent Hawaiian woman, he describes his dreams in copious detail) because they are vivid, tangible evidence that he is close to the sacred. Aristides finds that when he ignores the god's instructions, his suffering worsens; but when he obeys Asclepius, when he strives to stay close to the god, he gets better.

Finally, we see the same essential process at work in the dream revelations experienced by professional healers. The healing powers of the Afghan *baxsi* (9.2), the Zezuru *n'anga* (9.3), Kimaola (9.4), the Yuma doctor-dreamers (9.6), and the

Hawaiian *kahuna* (9.8) are rooted in their especially close connection with spiritual powers and realities. They possess the ability to heal people *because* they have regular and intimate relations with the spiritual world. Thus, the specific treatments these professional healers learn in their dreams serve as powerful vehicles for bringing their patients closer to the sacred. Here the process is not as direct as in the examples of Aristides and the Hawaiian woman, dreamers who were themselves the patients, but the ultimate effect is the same: a connection is made between a sick person and the sacred via dreams, a connection that heals.

The experience of illness, disease, and suffering is one of the great universals of human existence. Throughout history, people have relied on dreams to help ease their sufferings and cure their ills. From a spiritual perspective, dreams have the power to heal illness because they renew and revitalize people's relationship to God, to the gods, to the forces of the spiritual world. Frequently, the very experience of this renewed relationship is enough to relieve an ill person's sufferings.

10. Prophecy

*O*ne especially widespread type of spiritual dream experience is the prophetic dream, a dream which gives a glimpse of the future, of destiny, of providence.[1] Whether the prophetic power of dreams is attributed to the gods, to the travels of the dreamer's soul, or to some other supernatural force, there is a nearly universal belief that dreams can reveal aspects of the future. Indeed, this belief is alive and well in contemporary American society, to judge by the countless "dream books" to be found at liquor stores, newsstands, and twenty-four hour convenience marts around the country. I've collected a number of these manuals, with titles like "Dr. Pryor's Lucky Number Master Dream Book," "Dream Your Lucky Lottery Numbers," and "The Lucky Star Dream Book, by Prof. Konje." As their titles indicate, these books aim primarily at helping people predict winning lottery numbers based on their dreams. For example, Prof. Konje's booklet offers these interpretations:

> Ants—To dream of ants denotes money in abundance. To dream that they bite you denotes good business relationship on the following day. 230.
>
> Maid—To dream that you are a maid denotes bad luck on the following day. 765.
>
> Sailing—To dream that you sail on a smooth stream or sea denotes riches and good health. 517.[2]

Serious skepticism may begin to arise for some readers at this point. We may well accept that people have had dreams of snakes, of gods, and of flying; we may even grant that people have had dreams that "healed" them of their sufferings. But can dreams really foretell the future? The notion is so ridiculously irrational that it hardly seems worth discussing. However, if we set aside the question of lotteries and focus instead on a careful examination of various cross-cultural and historical examples, we may actually find some good reasons for granting a prophetic power to dreams.

1) In *Witchcraft, Oracles, and Magic among the Azande* (a people living between the Nile and Congo rivers in central Africa), anthropologist E.E. Evans-Pritchard comments that "Azande speak of dreams as oracles, for they reveal hidden things (*soroka*). In a sense all dreams foretell events, but some more clearly than others.... When the dream is oracular it will then prophesy the future truly and warn a man of impending danger and tell him of fortune to come.... Azande distinguish between witchcraft-dreams and oracular dreams; usually, a bad dream, i.e. a nightmare, is a witchcraft-dream and a pleasant one an oracular dream. Nevertheless, all dreams are in a sense oracular: a bad dream is regarded as both an actual experience of witchcraft and a prognostication of misfortune, for if a man is being bewitched it is obviously likely that some mis-fortune will follow.... The dream is a shadow cast by witchcraft before the event it is about to produce—in a sense has already produced, though at the time the dreamer does not know what it is."[3]

2) In Richard J. Smith's *Fortune-Tellers and Philosophers*, a survey of divination in traditional Chinese society, he demonstrates that all sectors of Chinese society attached great importance to dream divination. "The tradition of dreams as harbingers of future events had a long and distinguished pedigree in China. The Confucian classics contain a number of references to dream divination.... 'Dreams have their fulfillments' (*meng you zheng ye*) went a well-known Qing dynasty proverb. And because dream prophecies often seemed to come true, whether unsolicited or not, they, like other omens, easily acquired explicitly political implications. Thus, when an individual named Zhi Tianbao made predictions concerning the length of the Qianlong emperor's reign based on dream revelations...the pronouncements were treated like a curse, and both Zhi and his disciple, Zhang Jiuxiao, were executed."[4]

3) Among the Kagwahiv of Brazil dreams are seen as predicting, among other things, sickness, death, and success in hunting. Waud Kracke notes that "dreams are not only told on a regular basis in Kagwahiv society, but are earnestly discussed to ascertain what they 'mean'; what event or development they augur, or what state of the spiritual surround they reflect. Dreams foretell the future, either literally or by way of an extensive list of metaphorically or metonymically based formulae.... Dreams, like myths, are sources of significant information about the nature of the world and the spiritual beings in it, and, like myths, they are to be shared, puzzled out, and understood."[5]

4) *The Zohar* (*"The Book of Splendor"*), a Jewish mystical text probably dating from the thirteenth and fourteenth centuries, contains this passage: "Nothing takes place in the world but what has previously been made known, either by means of a dream, or by means of a proclamation, for it has been affirmed that before any event comes to pass in the world, it is first announced in heaven, whence it is proclaimed to the world. Thus Scripture states, 'For the Lord God will do nothing but he reveals His counsel unto His servants the prophets' (Amos 3:7). This refers to the time when there were yet prophets in the world; when the prophets were no more, they were succeeded by the sages. And, in our time, when the sages too are no longer among us, that which is still to come is revealed in dreams, or, if not in dreams, through the medium of the birds of the heavens."[6]

5) The Hupdu Maku Indians live in the rainforests along the border between Brazil and Colombia. According to anthropologist Howard Reid, "most Hupdu said that when a person is asleep and dreams, his or her soul may depart from its host body and is able to travel freely in time and space to the many different levels of the Cosmos. In this stage the soul perceives things which can be translated by means of the appropriate interpretation to tell one about some future event or explain some present state in terms of causation in the past (as is often the case for sickness and death), or simply provide unknown, hidden information about the present such as the whereabouts of animals in the forest. However the vast majority of dreams are concerned with predicting the future, and the standard format used

when explaining dreams to me was, 'if we dream this before, that will happen.' In this sense, dreams are concerned with bringing to light forces and events which are latent in the Cosmos, but not perceivable to the waking self."[7]

6) According to Buddhist legends, Buddha's mother Queen Maya had this dream shortly before giving birth: "The four great kings, it seemed, raised her together with the bed, and taking her to the Himalayas set her on the Manosila tableland...beneath a great sal-tree seven leagues high.... Then their queens came and took her to the Anatatta lake, bathed her to remove human stain, robed her in heavenly clothing, anointed her with perfumes, and bedecked her with divine flowers. Not far away in a silver mountain, and thereon a golden mansion, there they prepared a divine bed with its head to the east, and laid her upon it. Now the Bodhisatta [Buddha] became a white elephant. Not far from there is a golden mountain, and going there he descended from it, alighted on the silver mountain, approaching it from the direction of the north. In his trunk...like a silver rope, he held a white lotus, then trumpeting he entered the golden mansion, made a rightwise circle, three times around his mother's bed, smote her right side, and appeared to enter her womb. Thus when the moon was in the lunar mansion, he received a new existence."[8]

7) In his *On Divination*, the Roman orator and philosopher Cicero (second century A.D.) compiles numerous prophetic dream reports from ancient Greek and Roman cultures (in the course of attacking superstitious beliefs in divination). Among the reports is this one of a man named Simonides "who, having found the dead body of a man who was a stranger to him lying in the road, buried it. Having performed this office, he was about to embark in a ship, when the man whom he had buried appeared to him in a dream at night, and warned him not to undertake the voyage, for that if he did he would perish by shipwreck. Therefore, he returned home again, but all the other people who sailed in that vessel were lost."[9]

8) The New Testament book of Matthew opens with a recounting of the birth of Jesus: "Now the birth of Jesus Christ took place in this way. When his mother Mary had been betrothed to Joseph, before they came together she

was found to be with child of the Holy Spirit; and her husband Joseph, being a just man and unwilling to put her to shame, resolved to divorce her quietly. But as he considered this, behold, an angel of the Lord appeared to him in a dream, saying, 'Joseph, son of David, do not fear to take Mary as your wife, for that which is conceived in her is of the Holy Spirit; she will bear a son, and you shall call his name Jesus, for he will save his people from their sins.'... When Joseph woke from sleep, he did as the angel of the Lord commanded him; he took his wife, but knew her not until she had borne a son; and he called his name Jesus."[10]

9) Before St. Augustine converted to Christianity, his mother Monica (who was already a Christian) worried about the future of her son's soul. As Augustine recounts in his *Confessions*, God sent her the following dream: "She dreamed that she was standing on a wooden rule, and coming towards her in a halo of splendour she saw a young man who smiled at her in joy, although she herself was sad and quite consumed with grief. He asked her the reason for her sorrow and her daily tears, not because he did not know, but because he had something to tell her, for this is what happens in visions. When she replied that her tears were for the soul I had lost, he told her to take heart for, if she looked carefully, she would see that where she was, there also was I. And when she looked, she saw me standing beside her on the same rule." Augustine says that "the dream had given new spirit to her hope."[11]

10) Among the Blackfoot Indians of North America, dreams were regarded as important omens relating to success or failure in battle. According to ethnographer G.B. Grinell, "a dream, especially if it is a strong one—that is, if the dream is very clear and vivid—is almost always obeyed. As dreams start them on the war path, so, if a dream threatening bad luck comes to a member of a war party even if in the enemy's country and just about to make an attack on a camp, the party is likely to turn about and go home without making any hostile demonstrations."[12]

11) The Second Book of the Maccabees, one of the books of the Old Testament Apocrypha, tells the history of the Jewish people in the early second century B.C. When the Jews were being threatened by a large army, their leader

Maccabeus "cheered them all by relating a dream, a sort of vision, which was worthy of belief. What he saw was this: Onias, who had been high priest, a noble and good man...was praying with outstretched hands for the whole body of Jews. Then likewise a man appeared, distinguished by his gray hair and dignity, and of marvelous majesty and authority. And Onias spoke, saying, 'This is a man who loves the brethren and prays much for the people and the holy city, Jeremiah, the prophet of God.' Jeremiah stretched out his right hand and gave to Judas [Maccabeus] a golden sword, and as he gave it he addressed him thus: 'Take this holy sword, a gift from God, with which you will strike down your adversaries.' Encouraged by the words of [Maccabeus]...they determined not to carry on a campaign but to attack bravely."[13]

12) Roberto Ong describes the legend that Confucius had a dream foretelling his own death: Confucius arose one morning and started singing a mournful song. When a disciple entered his room, Confucius told him about the ways in which funeral rites were performed in previous dynasties. Under the Yin dynasty the rites were performed between the two pillars of the hall. "'Some nights ago,' the Master went on, 'I dreamed that I was sitting between the two pillars, with the sacrificial offerings in full view. Since sage-kings do not arise, who on earth will honor me? I am dying, I suppose.' After this, he lay ill for seven days and died."[14]

13) Among the native people of the island of Tikopia (near the Solomon Islands), dreams reveal future events with regard to "the pursuit of fishing, and the sphere of birth, sickness, and death." Regarding birth dreams, anthropologist Raymond Firth says that "a woman dreams that she goes to the stream, fills her water-bottles, and puts them in a kit on her back. It is believed that this indicates she will conceive and bear a girl-child. Or if she goes out fishing with a *kuti*, a small scoop-net used on the reef by women, then the same interpretation is attached. Dreams of a similar type associated with pursuits of sea-fishing portend the conception of a man-child."[15]

14) The early fourth-century Christian leader Gregory of Nyssa had the following prophetic dream, as described in historian Patricia Cox Miller's *Dreams in Late Antiquity*:

"Gregory of Nyssa was on the road with the intent of visiting his sister at the community of celibate women that she had established on the family estate at Annesi. He had not seen Macrina for many years, and when he was only one day's travel away from her convent, he had a worrisome dream. In his biography of his sister, he wrote, 'I saw in dream a vision that made me apprehensive for the future. It seemed that I was holding in my hands the relics of martyrs, and there flowed from them such a bright beam of light, like that from a spotless mirror placed facing the sun, that my eyes were blinded by its brilliance. This vision occurred three times during that night, and although I was not able to interpret clearly the enigma of the dream, I nonetheless sensed some sorrow for my soul....' While traveling the next day, Gregory learned that Macrina was seriously ill; in fact, when he arrived, she was laid out on the ground, dying.... [Gregory wrote] 'What I had seen seemed to unravel the enigma of the dream. The sight set before me was in truth the remains of a holy martyr, the remains of one who had been dead to sin, but shining with the presence of the Holy Spirit.'"[16]

15) In Plato's *Crito*, Socrates is held in an Athenian prison, as the city waits for the return of a boat that will signal the time for his trial and execution. His friend Crito awakens Socrates just before dawn, and Socrates says he does not think the boat will arrive that day. The dialogue ensues: "Crito: Why do you suppose not? Socrates: I will tell you. I am to die on the day after the ship arrives, am I not? Crito: That is what the authorities say. Socrates: Then I do not think it will come today, but tomorrow. I am counting on a dream I had a little while ago in the night, so it seems to be fortunate that you did not wake me. Crito: And what was the dream? Socrates: A fair and beautiful woman, clad in white, seemed to come to me, and call me and say, 'O Socrates—On the third day shall you fertile Phthia reach.' [A quote from Homer's *Iliad*, 9.363] Crito: What a strange dream, Socrates! Socrates: But its meaning is clear, at least to me, Crito."[17]

These prophetic dreams relate to events or activities that concern the dreamers in a direct and strongly emotional way. Many of the examples involve parents dreaming of childbirth and children, something that has an obviously great emotional importance to the dreamers. Queen Maya has a rapturous dream of her son Buddha entering her womb (10.6); Joseph is told in a dream that his son, whom he must name Jesus, will be his people's savior (10.8); Monica's dream reassures her that her son Augustine will one day join her in the Christian faith (10.9); and the Tikopians find omens in their dreams indicating whether they are pregnant with girls or with boys (10.13).[18] Many of the other dream reports are tied to the life-and-death circumstances of war and battle. The Blackfoot Indians look to their dreams for insights into the future success or failure of their war parties (10.10), and Maccabeus' dream comes on the eve of a major military confrontation (10.11).[19] The reports from so-called "hunter and gatherer" cultures—the Kagwahiv (10.3), the Azande (10.1), the Hupdu Maku (10.5), and the Tikopians (10.13)—present prophetic dreams related to the all-important economic activities of tracking game and catching fish. Prophetic dreams in these cultures also relate to illness and death, something we find as well in other examples: Simonides is warned in a dream by the spirit of a dead person to avoid embarking on a ship that will sink, killing all its passengers (10.7); Confucius has a dream indicating that the time for his death has arrived (10.12), Socrates has a similar dream that informs him his execution is three days hence (10.15), and Gregory of Nyssa finds the death of his sister Macrina foretold in a dream (10.14).

To put the point in different terms, prophetic dreams are not concerned with trivial, inconsequential affairs. Rather, they address the *most* important, *most* consequential matters of the dreamers' lives: birth, war, food, illness, death. This list of the primary subjects of prophetic dreams discloses another common characteristic— these are phenomena that are in large part beyond human control. Bearing children, fighting battles, finding food, overcoming illness, and facing death are all experiences that humans would very much like to control, and energetically try to control, but ultimately do not control. Throughout history people have framed this dilemma in spiritual terms: such matters are ultimately controlled by forces of the sacred. Dreams, as we have seen in this chapter, are widely regarded as an excellent means of perceiving those forces, learning about them, and anticipating their future effects on waking life. Here is yet another way in which dreams serve to bring people closer to those transcendent powers that create, shape, sustain, and at times destroy human life.

However, this analysis may only give rise to further skepticism: doesn't this show that supposedly "prophetic" dreams merely reflect the childish, frustrated fantasies of people who lack the scientific knowledge and technological powers we enjoy in the modern west? People may wish that dreams could give them insights into future events over which they have little control—but wishing does not make it so. We might also object that many of these alleged dream prophecies appear to have been fabricated by the dreamers. After all, in earlier chapters we saw that dream reports are frequently altered in order to conform to the literary, political, and/or theological interests of the dreamer. Looking at the dream reports in this chapter we might suspect, for example, that the Jewish leader Maccabeus (10.11) carefully edited his dream of Onias and Jeremiah to enhance its encouraging "prophecy." We may even suspect that he had no such dream at all, and simply made it up to provide a rousing speech to his troops.

Still another explanation of the widespread belief in prophetic dreams points to the logically fallacious process of "retrospective interpretation." Anthropologist F.E. Williams found evidence of this in his study of the dream beliefs of various cultures in Papuan New Guinea.[20] For example, the people of a particular village told Williams of a man who had dreamed of copulating with a dog. Soon afterward the man died, and the people concluded that the horrible dream had in fact foretold the death. Williams comments:

> such cases of retrospective interpretation suggest a means by which a prophetic significance comes to be attached to dreams in general. The striking dream and the striking event which follows it come to be associated. If the one does not actually cause, then it at least foretells the other. And if one dream is thus proved to have prophetic significance, why not all?[21]

This tendency to interpret dreams in the light of subsequent events makes it quite easy, as Williams suggests, to believe that certain dreams have "predicted" the future.[22] Gregory of Nyssa's dream of the shining relics, which he only interpreted as foretelling his sister's death *after* he discovered that she was mortally ill, could be regarded as an instance of such faulty reasoning.

There can be no doubt that all of these elements—wishful thinking, subtle or not-so-subtle editing, retrospective inter-preting—have helped to encourage belief in prophetic dreams. However, modern dream research has found increasing evidence that dreams do indeed look toward the future. As discussed in chapter 3, many researchers believe that dreams serve a fundamentally *adaptive* function, helping people respond to the most difficult and troubling emotional problems of their daily lives. In the course of serving this adaptive function, dreams regularly address events, prospects, and possibilities that lie in the dreamer's *future*. C.G. Jung refers to the "prospective function" of dreams, in which various percep-tions, thoughts, memories, and feelings are brought together and used to envision the dreamer's future. Jung says that in many dreams we find "an anticipation in the unconscious of future conscious achievements, something like a preliminary exercise or sketch, or a plan roughed out in advance."[23] Similarly, Thomas French and Erika Fromm speak of dreams as addressing the "focal conflicts" of our lives, those conflicts that are most pressing and yet most difficult to resolve. French and Fromm argue that dreams are "groping to understand problems that cannot yet be adequately grasped," and striving toward possible solutions that we may achieve in the future.[24] And Rosalind Cartwright, in her book *Crisis Dreaming*, describes numerous dreams that anticipate in various ways people's upcoming encounters with childbirth, illness, and death. She concludes that "dreams review the experiences that give rise to strong feelings and match them to related images from the past. They enable us to revise our pictures of our present selves and to rehearse our responses to future challenges."[25]

I would summarize modern psychological research on this point by saying that *in dreams we wonder about the future*. In our dreams we anticipate the future, envision it, ponder it, play with it, worry about it, rehearse it. Dreams are especially involved with aspects of the future that are of strong emotional concern to us, that pertain to particularly troubling, unsettling, or exciting prospects, and that lie just beyond the reach of our control. Dreams draw upon both experiences from the past and realities in the present to imagine possibilities for the future. Charles Dickens got it essentially right in *A Christmas Carol*, when he has Ebenezer Scrooge experience dream visitations from the ghosts of Christmas Past, Christmas Present, and Christmas Yet to Come.[26]

One of the earliest philosophical evaluations of the phenomenon of prophetic dreams came in Aristotle's short treatise, *On Prophesying by Dreams*.[27] Aristotle is often cited as an arch-rationalist regarding dreams, the first person to use logical analysis to dispel the irrational superstitions surrounding the subject. Aristotle's treatment of prophetic dreams is remarkably fair and balanced, and his arguments remain compelling 2,300 years later. Aristotle says that prophetic dreams can be regarded in three different ways. They may be *causes*, *tokens*, or *coincidences*.[28] Dream prophecies may indeed be the cause of future actions, Aristotle argues, for matters of importance in our waking lives regularly appear in our dreams; and just as waking life influences dreams, "conversely, it must happen that the movements set up first in sleep should also prove to be starting-points of actions to be performed in the daytime."[29] Aristotle also states that dream prophecies are frequently tokens (we might say symbols) of events to come in the future. He refers to dreams that reveal the imminent onset of an illness, before the person has become consciously aware of being sick.[30] Aristotle says that in the quiet of sleep we become aware of slight "movements" and "beginnings" that are lost to us in the bustle of daily life; "in conclusion, it is manifest that these beginnings must be more evident in sleeping than in waking moments."[31]

Having granted all this, Aristotle still believes that "most [so-called prophetic] dreams are, however, to be classed as mere coincidences,"[32] especially those that are "extravagant," or that involve matters with no direct connection to the dreamer. It happens all the time, he argues, that people mistakenly connect two events that are in fact unrelated; people make the same logical error when they connect a striking dream to a striking, but actually unrelated, event that comes after the dream (i.e. retrospective interpretation).

Aristotle's conclusion, then, is quite skeptical toward the majority of prophetic dream reports. But at the same time, he is careful not to deny the possible legitimacy of *some* of these reports. He says:

> as to the divination which takes place in sleep, and is said to be based on dreams, we cannot lightly either dismiss it with contempt or give it implicit confidence. The fact that all persons, or many, suppose dreams to possess a special significance, tends to inspire us with belief in it [such divination], as founded on the testimony of experience; and indeed that divination in dreams should, as regards some subjects, be genuine, is not incredible, for it has a show of reason; from which one might form a like opinion also respecting all other dreams. Yet the fact of our seeing no probable cause to account for such divination tends to inspire us with distrust."[33]

This strikes me as the most reasonable attitude to take. *Most* "prophetic" dreams are probably mere coincidences; we have no compelling evidence that dreams can predict, say, winning lottery numbers with any reliability. However, Aristotle concludes that it is reasonable to accept that *some* dreams truly do reveal aspects of the future, aspects that we cannot perceive by ordinary conscious means.

Such an attitude of open-mindedness is necessary if we want to begin understanding the uncanny, almost frightening revelations that come in some prophetic dreams. For example, a young woman I know ("Pam") told me that one night she had a dream in which her college roommate was in terrible danger. Pam's roommate lived in another city, and they had not been in touch with each other for some time; but the dream was so vivid that when Pam woke up she immediately tried to telephone her roommate. After many hours of unsuccessful calling, Pam finally reached the roommate's boyfriend, who told her that the roommate had tried to commit suicide the night before, and was now in the hospital.

We could insist on a skeptical explanation for Pam's dream—maybe it was nothing more than a wild coincidence; maybe she knew somewhere in her mind that her friend was in trouble; maybe she just made the whole thing up. But at a certain point, such stubborn skepticism becomes a mere fig leaf used to cover naked ignorance. The fact is, conventional western psychological theories simply cannot explain extraordinary dreams like Pam's. A more open-minded, "Aristotelian" position would be that dreams seem to have the potential (especially in times of crisis) to give us special powers of perception and to connect us with forces and realities that transcend ordinary waking consciousness.[34] The testimony of dreamers throughout history and the findings of modern psychological researchers both provide evidence in support of this position.

11. Rituals

A natural reaction to spiritual dream experiences is to seek *more* of them. Rather than passively waiting for revelatory dreams, people throughout history have used rituals to solicit, evoke, or induce spiritually meaningful dreams. The most common ritual methods are 1) regulating one's diet and social contacts prior to the night of the desired dream, 2) performing purification ceremonies and reciting prayers just before sleeping, and 3) going to sleep in a special posture and/or location. Western scholars refer to these practices collectively as rituals of dream *incubation*, a term which stems from the Greek word *incubatio*, or "sleeping in" (e.g. a temple or shrine).

In recent years a number of popular psychology books have been written which give instructions on how modern westerners can incubate dreams for themselves.[1] People are often amazed to find that this *really works*: if you use these incubation techniques and focus your pre-sleep attention on a waking life concern, your dreams will usually respond by addressing that particular concern. This has led people to believe that they can systematically "program" their dreams for fun and profit. But what is often lost in this oneiric gold rush is an appreciation for the spiritual context in which dream incubation has traditionally been practiced. The following cross-cultural and historical examples illustrate the ways that rituals of dream incubation have involved respectful, reverential appeals to the powers of the sacred. The prospective dreamers may be motivated by various "worldly" concerns to perform these rituals, but the ultimate goal of dream incubation is always a spiritual one: to become closer to the sacred, to bring the renewing energies of the sacred more fully into the dreamer's waking world.

1) The Yansi people, who live along the Kwilu and Inzia rivers in central Africa, incubate dreams for various communal purposes. According to anthropologist Mubuy Mubay Mpier, the Yansi seek dreams as commentaries on their current and future activities (e.g., hunting, making a journey, performing a ritual). For example, when twins are born a special rite must be performed to integrate them into the clan: "In order to identify the day for the ceremony the clan elders pass the night out in the open under the stars. In the morning all the dreams of the night are recalled and carefully interpreted to learn how the dead are disposed towards the ceremony, for they are supposed to participate with the living whenever the clan comes together." During the ceremonies themselves, the elders monitor their dreams for signs of the success or failure of the ritual.[2]

2) The fifth century B.C. Greek historian Herodotus writes in his *History* of the Egyptian king Sethos, who neglected his country's warrior class. When a large enemy army threatened the land, the Egyptian warriors refused to help Sethos: "On this the monarch, greatly distressed, entered into the inner sanctuary, and, before the image of the god, bewailed the fate which impended over him. As he wept he fell asleep, and dreamed that the god came and stood at his side, bidding him be of good cheer, and go boldly forth to meet the Arabian host, which would do him no hurt, as he himself [the god] would send those who should help him. Sethos, then, relying on the dream, collected such of the Egyptians as were willing to follow him...." Sethos and his troops won the next day's battle, and to commemorate the victory he erected a stone statue of himself, with the inscription, "'Look on me, and learn to reverence the gods.'"[3]

3) John Wesley (1703–1791), the English theologian and founder of Methodism, had a partly spiritual, partly romantic relationship with a woman named Grace Murray. In *John Wesley's Last Love*, a personal manuscript he wrote describing his troubled feelings over the relationship, Wesley tells of how he prayed one night for a vision from God that would help him resolve his troubles: "I dream'd I saw a Man bring out G.M. [Grace Murray], who told her, she was condemn'd to die: And that all things were now in

readiness, for the Execution of that Sentence. She spoke not one word, or shew'd any Reluctance, but walk'd up with him to ye place. The Sentence was executed, without her stirring either hand or foot. I look'd at her, till I saw her face turn black. Then, I cd not bear it, but went away. But I return'd quickly, & desir'd she might be cut down. She was then laid upon a bed. I sat by mourning over her. She came to herself & began to speak, & I awaked."[4]

4) In *Islam in West Africa* J. Spencer Trimingham portrays the Islamic method of evoking dreams, called *istikhara*: "A common form of *istikhara* ('asking favor of heaven') is the following. The cleric advises his client to recite certain Qur'anic phrases after each *rak'a* of the next ritual prayer, then shielding his mouth with his hand to whisper his request. After that he must lie down to sleep where he will not be disturbed, on the right side, placing his right hand under his ear. He receives the answer in the form of a dream which the cleric interprets. More commonly the cleric does the dreaming on behalf of his client. He prays two *rak'as*, incorporating a *sura* [verse from the Koran] appropriate to the request, recites a *dhikr* of one of the names of god until he is almost asleep when he makes his request, and continues with the *dhikr* until he falls asleep. A Hausa or Songhay cleric, when called in to prescribe for an illness, often sleeps on his Book of Divination in order to ascertain the cause of the illness and its cure. Similarly, if a new spirit is suspected of having settled in a house he sleeps on his book to discover who it is, and, if it is 'black', performs the rites necessary to drive it away."[5]

5) In Berthold Laufer's article on "Inspirational Dreams in Eastern Asia," he reports that dream incubation, or "temple sleep," was widely practiced in China: "Every town has a tutelary god styled 'the father of the walls and moats' and worshipped in a special temple.... The city god cares for the welfare of the inhabitants under his jurisdiction, and is the mediator between this and the other life.... The worship of city gods reached its climax toward the end of the fourteenth century under the first emperor of the Ming dynasty. At that time it was obligatory for all officials of higher ranks when entering a walled city to pass the first night in the temple of the city god, in order to receive his

instructions in a dream. In the case of a difficult point in law judges will spend the night in the city god's temple, in the hope that the god will appear to them in a dream and enlighten them on the case in question.... The temple sleep is always preceded by bathing and fasting, and the official betakes himself to the temple in a solemn procession. Sometimes a written petition is burnt before the altar of the god with proper ritual, and then the official retires to rest in an adjoining room."[6]

6) Roberto Ong offers an account of the continuing practice of dream incubation in modern-day China. Each year at the winter solstice people meet at nightfall, despite the cold and frost, to seek dreams. They approach the temple of the Arch-God of Walls and Moats of All-under-Heaven, bringing candles, incense, and blankets with them. "On entering the temple, the dream seekers light up their incense and candles. After going through the prescribed ritual of kneeling thrice and kowtowing nine times, they spread out their blankets and bedding and fall asleep in a peaceful frame of mind."[7]

7) Among the Aguaruna people of northern Peru, dream revelations are considered necessary for a successful career as warrior and hunter. Anthropologist Michael F. Brown says that "the dream experience most highly esteemed by Aguaruna men is the establishment of contact with an ancient warrior soul (*ajutap*). The dream is essential for any warrior who hopes to survive combat. Because of the dream's importance, men are willing to undergo the most extreme hardships—weeks of enduring a restricted diet, lonely vigils deep in the forest, and frequent use of psychotropic plants—to obtain it.... [A] man remembers the privations he suffered during the vision quest: 'I took a lot of *datem* [a hallucinogen] and continually went to a forest shelter. I also took *baikua* [another hallucinogen]. My mother served me bland manioc soup because one can't drink much manioc beer. I took more *datem*, one day, then another. And when I felt exhausted, ready to die, I left it for a while. When looking for a vision, one can't eat chicken with manioc, or boiled peccary or the fish *kagka* and *wakampi*...[and a] young man can't have intercourse or play around with women.'"[8]

8) The Jewish "dream question" ritual, *she'elat chalom*, focused on learning the answer to a particular theological question from an incubated dream. Joel Covitz has translated the following version of this rite from a seventeenth century Jewish encyclopedia: "Fast for one day. Upon completion of the fast, purify yourself by going to the *mikveh* [ritual immersion]. That night, refrain from eating meat or drinking wine.... Before retiring, wash your hands. Recite the Shema [bedtime prayer] as usual, and then intone silently the following three verses.... [A large number of scriptural passages are given to be read.] After completing this prayer, be cautious and refrain from any kind of conversation. Sleep on the left side. Sleep alone in your bed and alone in the house, and be careful to have clean underwear, bed, and sheets. Be careful not to allow your hands to stray below your navel, and do not touch your body. Honor your home by keeping it clean and free from foul odors and anything impure. Above all, one should guard oneself from women and nocturnal pollution. The customary practice is to compose this request [the dream question] in writing and read from it. After completing everything that has been mentioned, you should then place the request and the prayer under your pillow and concentrate your thoughts upon the request, so that you will fall asleep while contemplating the formulation."[9]

9) As we have already noted in discussing the dreams of Aelius Aristides, the practice of dream incubation at the temples of Asclepius, the Greek god of healing, flourished throughout the Mediterranean world in the second and third centuries A.D. Jungian analyst C.A. Meier gives a good account of dream incubation at the Asclepian temple at Epidaurus, Greece: "The place is beatifully situated far out in the country with a *via sacra* five miles long connecting it with the port. Its buildings are world famous for their beauty.... The place swarms with harmless snakes. Lots of trees, predominantly Oriental plane trees, and a plentiful supply of water are found in the sanctuary. Near the entrance are six stone stelae with inscriptions telling the case histories of more than a hundred cures that had become famous.... As a patient you would readily be admitted to the sacred precinct unless you were moribund or a pregnant woman near confinement, as the sanctuary

had to be kept ritually pure from death and birth. After having performed certain purificatory rites, ablutions, and preliminary sacrifices, you would go to sleep on your *kline* in the *abaton* or *adyton*, 'the place not to be entered by the unbidden.'... Apparently he [the patient] was always cured if in his dream he experienced an epiphany of Asclepius."[10]

10) Despite skepticism by church officials, early Christians frequently engaged in dream incubation. As historian Steven Oberhelman describes it, incubation was practiced in churches, shrines of martyrs and saints, and former pagan temples that had been transformed into Christian holy sites. "The Asclepian sanctuary on the south slope of the acropolis in Athens was converted in the fifth or sixth century into the healing shrine of Cosmas and Damian. These saint-physicians conducted business just as Asclepius had done: they came in person in a dream, bringing unguents and medical instruments, and then either cured the suppliant during sleep or gave instructions for a cure that the patient was to follow on wakening."[11]

11) Dick Mahwee, a middle-aged shaman among the Paviotso people of the Pyramid lake reservation in Nevada, gave the following account to anthropologist Willard Park of a vision quest he made to a cave known as a source of shamanic power: "There is a mountain below Dayton [Nevada]. Men go to the cave on this mountain to get power. Women never go into this cave. They [men] get their power in dreams. I went there when I was about twenty-five. I stayed in the cave all night. When I got inside I said what I wanted. I said I wanted to be a shaman and cure sick people." Mahwee lay down and the floor, and soon heard the sounds of animals going through the cave. He knew that they were testing his bravery, so he continued to lie still. "Then a tall slender man stood in front of me. He said, 'You want to be a shaman. You must do as I tell you. First get your eagle feathers and do what I tell you with them. You have chosen this and it may be hard for you. Do that, otherwise you will have a hard time. At the bottom of this cliff there is some water. Bathe in it and paint yourself with white paint. Don't be impatient but wait for my instructions.' I did what he told me and I learned my songs and how to cure the sick when this tall man came to me in

dreams. He helps me doctor people and tells me what to do."[12]

12) In *Melanesian Religion* G.W. Trompf describes a collective dream incubation ritual used by the Mendi people of the New Guinea southern highlands: The Mendi "organize impressive collective dream-sessions in times of crisis.... After a death by supposed sorcery, to illustrate, the bereaved kinsfolk lie in a line under a 'dream shelter' on a mountain-top. They are tied together by the arms and across the chest with cordyline and sleep under the supervision of a 'dream master,' who tugs at the rope during the night—to wake everyone—when one of the sleepers shows signs of having experienced something disturbing. Traditionally, the corpses of the recent dead were deposited in nearby graves on the heights; a bamboo tube was inserted throught the earth to a buried person's skull, and the living would whisper down questions about his or her death before the dream sessions began."[13]

As these examples illustrate, the particular goals that motivate people to incubate dreams have varied widely. Often the aim is to gain divine help in healing illnesses, as with the Muslim practitioners of *istikhara* (11.4), the supplicants at the temples of Asclepius (11.9), the early Christians (11.10), and the Paviotso man Dick Mahwee (11.11). Another common goal is to receive guidance from the gods or spirit beings regarding a problem facing the community. The clan elders of the Yansi (11.1) incubate dreams when they desire help from the dead in dealing with religious, political, or legal matters. Similarly, the Chinese of the Ming dynasty (11.6) used dream incubation as an integral part of their judicial and governmental procedures. The Egyptian king Sethos (11.2) was prompted by an invading army to sleep in the god's temple. And after a troubling death Mendi kinsfolk (11.12) sleep together on mountain-tops, waking each other during the night to seek dream answers from the dead. People have also practiced dream incubation for more personal reasons. Aguaruna men (11.7) seek dream visions to become more powerful warriors, Jews rely on *she'elat chalom* (11.8) to answer theological questions, and John Wesley (11.3) prayed to God for help in resolving his feelings over a romantic relationship.

The examples above also illustrate how the particular means by which people have sought to incubate dreams are highly varied as well. In the Muslim ritual of *istikhara*, the person must recite various prayers from the Koran and must sleep "on the right side, placing his right hand under his ear." Aguaruna warriors sharply restrict their diets, spend days alone in the forest, and consume huge portions of psychotropic plants. Visitors to the beautiful temples of Asclepius "performed certain purificatory rites, ablutions, and preliminary sacrifices" before going to sleep. And Jews seeking answers to a "dream question" were required to fast for a day, pray, wear clean clothes, and sleep alone "on the left side," carefully guarding themselves from "nocturnal pollution."

People resort to dream incubation when they need support, guidance, and encouragement from the spiritual realm in order to deal with an urgent, pressing concern—a health crisis, a military threat, a judicial conflict, an obsessively troubling romantic affair. In his *Oneirocritica* Artemidorus warns, "you must remember that whenever you ask for a dream, you must not...put before the gods a question that is prompted by mere curiosity."[14] The fundamental aim of virtually all dream incubation practices is to gain the help of spiritual powers, to do whatever it takes to bring those powers directly to bear on a vital problem in the dreamer's life.

This sheds light on a basic feature of the various methods, techniques, and strategies that people have employed to evoke special dreams. As diverse as these methods are, they all work to *separate* the dreamer from the ordinary human world. Many methods of dream incubation require the person to sleep alone, far away from other people; and even in cases where dreams are sought by groups of people sleeping together (the Yansi, the contemporary Chinese, the worshipers of Asclepius, the Mendi), these groups are themselves separated from the rest of the community. Likewise, the purifications and dietary restrictions so often required serve to take the prospective dreamers away from "profane" life, detaching them from ordinary human society. And once the people seeking a revelatory dream have become well separated from the profane world, the focus moves to becoming as closely *connected* to the sacred as possible. The various sacrifices, readings, and prayers the people are required to perform all function to carry them toward the spiritual powers whose aid they are so energetically seeking.

This basic feature of all methods of dream incubation, the dynamic of trying to become separated from the profane and connected to the sacred, is best illustrated by the choice of locations for incubating a dream. When people are actively seeking a special, revelatory dream, they go to sleep in a place that is far removed from the human world and extremely close to the world of the sacred. Thus, people try to incubate dreams at tombs or graves, where the powerful, ever-present ancestors are buried; in caves, openings into the dark depths of the earth; in temples, shrines, and sanctuaries of the gods; and in the wilderness, where the spirits rule and where the stars shine brightly above. Dream incubation practices from all over the world share this very simple, very straightforward logic: if you want to have a dream encounter with the sacred, your best chance is to sleep in a place that's *close to the sacred*, where the sacred has been known to manifest itself.

Some Jewish and Christian theologians have expressed deep skepticism about dream incubation. This skepticism first appears in the Old Testament book of Isaiah, where the prophet records God's denunciation of the unfaithful people "who sit in tombs, and spend the night in secret places," praying for dream revelations from other gods.[15] St. Jerome (347–419 A.D.) condemned those "who sit in the graves and the temples of idols where they are accustomed to stretch out on the skins of sacrificial animals in order to know the future by dreams, abominations which are still practiced today in the temples of Aescylapius."[16] Benedict Pererius, a sixteenth-century Jesuit priest, wrote that the stories about Asclepius and other pagan deities appearing in people's dreams only prove that "the devil at one time was wont in many instances to sport with the mortal races, blinded by impiety, with this kind of dreams."[17]

The basic theological argument against dream incubation seems to be this: the Judeo-Christian God, as a transcendent, omnipotent deity, cannot be beckoned by humans who simply perform a few ritual procedures and sleep in a temple. It is God who initiates contact with humans, not vice versa; the devil is more likely to heed such calls than is the Lord. Thus, any human effort to evoke a dream revelation from God is impious and worthy of condemnation.[18]

Such arguments do not sqare with the historical evidence, however. Dream incubation has rarely been regarded as a mechanical process—as if performing ritual A automatically produced divine response B. Those who practice dream incubation are *appealing* for a revelatory dream, *asking* if God will respond to their petition; it always remains in God's power to answer, or not answer, these requests. Only in the strictest Judeo-Christian theologies can such appeals be seen as disrespectful to God's majesty. The countless Jews and Christians who have engaged in this practice through history have evidently found no contradiction between the effort to incubate a dream and the sincerity of their monotheistic faith.

The theological arguments against dream incubation may, in fact, be masking a different concern, a *political* concern. Dream incubation offers people relatively "direct" access to God, angels, and saints, circumventing the control of religious officials and thus threatening their authority. The spiritual insights and revelations that come through dreams do not always conform to the official dogmas of religious orthodoxics. Dreams tend to be iconoclastic—they challenge conventional religious beliefs and practices, provoking people to question their present spiritual condition. But this does not mean that dreams inevitably take people away from their religious tradition. It might surprise those skeptical Jewish and Christian theologians, but the iconoclastic thrust of dreams frequently strengthens people's religious faith. As we will find in the next two chapters, on the role of dreams in initiations and in conversions, dreams often have the effect of bonding people ever more closely to "official" religious traditions and institutions. A Christian, for example, may follow the church's basic teachings—but after having a numinous dream encounter with Jesus, that person suddenly *believes* in those teachings with infinitely greater passion and conviction than before. Such a dream challenges the superficial adherence to church doctrines, and brings real energy to the person's spiritual life; such a dream replaces mere conformity with genuine faith.

In this regard, dreams definitely do represent a threat to those religious beliefs and practices that fail to provide people with real, living spiritual sustenance. But as many religious leaders (including many Jews and Christians) have recognized, dreams also provide the members of established religious traditions with a powerful source of true spiritual vitality. In a spiritual sense, then, the practice of dream incubation is an act of worship, an expression of reverence toward the sacred and a respectful effort to become more closely connected to its power.

12. Initiation

*I*n his classic study *The Rites of Passage*, anthropologist Arnold Van Gennep describes the common structures that underlie initiation rituals found in many different cultures around the world.[1] Van Gennep argues that the basic goal of initiation rituals is to *transform* an individual, to move the initiate from one level of social and religious existence to another. This ritual movement requires the initiate to enter into a special threshold realm "betwixt and between" the two levels, a realm where the initiate meets and is transformed by the sacred. According to Van Gennep, rites of passage generally involve three distinct phases: a *separation* from the individual's ordinary, daily community, a *transition* into a sacred or "liminal" realm, and an *incorporation* back into the community.

Dreams have played a very prominent role in the initiation rituals of various cultures. Specifically, dreaming has provided a powerful means of bringing the initiate into that liminal realm where he or she is spiritually transformed. Whether the individual is being initiated into a new religious office like shaman, healer, or diviner, or is being initiated into a new spiritual community, tradition, or church, the transition to that new social and religious position can be forcefully propelled by a dream experience.

1) In his study of the puberty dream fast rite practiced among the Ojibwa and Ottawa peoples of North America, anthropologist Paul Radin recounts the experience of an Ojibwa man named Agabegijik: Agabegijik says that one spring, when he was "a half-grown lad" his grandfather told him it was time to be taken to the forest, to fast so that Agabegijik could learn something of his future and his

131

calling. His grandfather took him by the hand and led him deep into the forest. He selected a tall red pine tree and prepared a bed in the branches for Agabegijik, where he lay down for his fast. In the first year of seeking a revelatory dream Agabegijik failed, but in the second year he succeeded after eight nights of trying. He began to hear strange rustlings in the branches, and then a man began speaking to him: "Art thou afraid, my son?' 'No,' I replied; 'I no longer fear.' 'Why art thou here in this tree?' 'To fast.' 'Why dost thou fast?' 'To gain strength, and know my life.' 'That is good; for it agrees excellently with what is now being done for thee elsewhere, and with the message I bring thee. This very night a consultation has been held about thee and thy welfare; and I have come to tell thee that the decision was most favorable. I am ordered to invite thee to see and hear this for thyself. Follow me....' When he ordered me to follow him, I rose from my bed easily and of my own accord, like a spirit rising from the grave, and followed him through the air.... [I]t seemed to me as if we were ascending a lofty mountain, ever higher and higher, eastward...." Agabegijik goes on to have a series of adventures in his dream, which climax in an ascent to a beautiful place in the sky where four white-haired men instruct him in various healing methods.[2]

2) Among the Sambia of New Guinea, "the dreams of a child foretell a shaman's calling, and, moreover, they may be interpreted as the first indication of it." Anthropologist Gilbert Herdt gives this report from "the most powerful living female shaman, Kwinjinaambi": "'When I was a girl (*tai*, pre-menses), I had no husband yet. I had a dream. I saw my deceased mother. She said to me: "If you want to *kwolyu* (individual healing ceremony), you must gather these leaves—*yum'i'u* and *aalut'nbi*." It was at the time of my brother's (lineal brother, a medium and novice shaman) first stage initiation. I woke up. These leaves were adhering to my skin; I do not know how they got there. I knew then that I could become a *kwooluku* [shaman]. My father, Wangamiko, said to everyone: "My sons will not become a *kwooluku*; Kwinjinaambi will."'" Herdt comments that, "the dream was not only a personal revelation for her, it subsequently represented a 'charter' for her shamanistic powers by the community at large. Her deceased mother

had been a well-known shaman. The dream revealed that her daughter would assume her powers; and her father— himself a leading fightman—not only suggested to the girl that she would become a shaman but thus interpreted the dream for the community."[3]

3) Shaikh Ahmad Ahsa'i (1753–1826) was the leader of an Islamic reform movement that resisted the legalism of Shi'ite theology and promoted the experience of spiritual "reawakening." As the scholar of Islam Henri Corbin reports, Shaikh Ahmad had a number of visionary dreams during his adolescence. First was a vision of a young man, holding a book, who taught Shaikh Ahmad the proper interpretation of two verses from the Koran. Another night he saw himself, in a visionary state, walking into a mosque and meeting three deeply revered Islamic leaders. After this Shaikh Ahmad experienced a series of visionary dreams: "'In the Heavens, in Paradise, in a suprasensible world, and in the barzakh, I saw strange and wonderful dreams, figures and colors which dazzle the intelligence.'" Corbin comments, "these dreams can be very exactly described as 'initiatory': which they are to the point that doctrines later developed in many writings are inseparable from the teachings thus received in dreams. These visionary experiences reached their high point when Shaikh Ahmad saw the tenth Imam in a dream holding a bundle of papers. These were the *ijazat* (authorizations to teach) which each of the twelve Imams bestowed on him."[4]

4) *The Golden Ass*, the tale written by the second-century A.D. Roman writer Apuleius, recounts the unfortunate story of Lucius, a cheerful young man who becomes romantically involved with a witch. Lucius watches her turn herself into a bird, and he desires to do the same; but when he rubs himself with the magic ointment, he is transformed not into a bird, but into an ass. In this form Lucius experiences a long series of painful, humiliating misadventures. The night before he is to be led by his captors into an arena filled with wild beasts, Lucius prays for help from "the risen Goddess...Queen of Heaven," who appears as Venus, Isis, Ceres, and many other divine forms. The Goddess comes to him in a dream, and says to Lucius, "behold, I am come to you in your calamity. I am come with

solace and aid.... Hearken therefore with care unto what I bid. Eternal religion has dedicated to me the day which will be born from the womb of this present darkness. Tomorrow my priests will offer to me the first fruits of the year's navigation.... You must await this ceremony without anxiety and without wandering thoughts. For the priest at my suggestion will carry in the procession a crown of roses attached to the sistrum in his right hand; and you must unhesitatingly push your way through the crowd, join the procession, and trust in my good will. Approach close to the priest as if you meant to kiss his hand, and gently crop the roses. Instantly you will slough the hide of this beast on which I have long looked with abhorrence.... Only remember, and keep the remembrance fast in your heart's deep core, that all the remaining days of your life must be dedicated to me, and that nothing can release you from this service but death. Neither is it aught but just that you should devote your life to her who redeems you back into humanity. You shall live blessed. You shall live glorious under my guidance." Lucius awakens, does as the Goddess instructs, and is transformed back into human form. After this he experiences further dreams which complete his initiation into the mysteries of the Goddess.[5]

5) For the Temne people of the Guinea Coast of West Africa, dreams are crucial in the training of "diviners," ritual specialists who mediate between the community and the spirit world for the purposes of healing, prophecy, and communication with the ancestors. According to anthropologist Rosalind Shaw, no one can be a diviner unless he or she has had an initiatory dream in which a spirit or ancestor (usually a close relative of the same sex) comes and forms a special bond with the dreamer. A Temne diviner named Pa Ahmadu describes how he had come to use river-pebble divination (*an-bere*): "I had no training: I got the knowledge from God. While I slept, I dreamt that a spirit tied me up and said we should do this work together. When I woke up the next morning, I could do it, and gave an egg to the spirit." A woman diviner named Ya Mabinti tells how her dead aunt taught her in a dream how to practice a divining technique using cowrie shells: "In the first dream my aunt showed me how to use the cowries. I woke up and started doing it. Then I was in *ro-mere* ["the place of

dreams"], and I saw these cowries first in a heap, then a circle. When I woke up, I was afraid." Shaw says that for some Temne diviners the dream serves as a spontaneous "call," in which the diviner receives all the training required. For other diviners, significant dreams come at the climax of their training and apprenticeship.[6]

6) The Musama Disco Christo Church (MDCC) of central Ghana was founded in the 1920s as an offshoot of Methodist missionary efforts in Africa. According to theologian John S. Pobee, "the MDCC puts a high premium on dreams, visions, and trances. One characteristic feature of the MDCC is the adoption of so-called heavenly names in response to a dream, a vision or trance. The name of their holy city, Mozano, is a heavenly name received in a dream. It means 'my own town.' The founder and first leader of the church, Akoboha I, adopted the name of Prophet Jemiseham Jehu-Appiah in obedience to a vision. His wife, Hannah Barnes, was similarly renamed Akatitibi Natholomoa, i.e., Queen mother. Each member of the church gets a new name at baptism.... Priests and other religious leaders, like Akoboha I himself and medicine men, are called by dreams.... [T]he MDCC's penchant for dreams, visions and trances represents a spirituality that is at once biblical and indigenous. The God and Father of Jesus Christ continues to speak to Africans through dreams, visions and trances that are to be heeded. They form the basis for the coming into being of the MDCC and its mission in the world, thus legitimizing the MDCC's mission."[7]

7) The professional healers, or witch doctors, of the Diegueno Indians of Southern California experience a series of dreams which train them in their calling. Anthropologists Gertrude Toffelmier and Katharine Luomala describe the first of these dreams, the "*Toalache* Name Dream": "The initiate's dreams of his *toloache* or medicine name which he keeps for the remainder of his life is one of the most important events in the career of any witch doctor. Our informant stated that the name is always conferred in the following way: during some part of the initiation...his teacher asks him to select a name that he would like to carry with him always as a sort of descriptive badge of his real personality.... The candidate begins to

concentrate on the selection of a name and in the next dream which he has while in the brush enclosure, an appropriate name comes to him." The other dreams are 2) the "ERuR Dream," or "circle dream," in which the initiate dreams of "putting his arms around the world with the fingers touching, a symbol of all-embracing knowledge"; 3) the "Guardian Animal Dream", introducing him to the animal that will guide him on hunting trips; 4) the "Cosmogonic Dream", in which he meets "*Synioxau*, 'the hunter's grandmother' and the first woman in the world"; and 5) the "Magic Rocks Dream," revealing to the initiate the magical rocks that will enable him to interpret subsequent dreams.[8]

8) Gregory of Nazianzen was a leader of the Christian Church in the fourth century A.D. who wrote a number of theological poems. In these poems he describes the role of his dreams in bringing him into the church: "And God summoned me from boyhood in my nocturnal dreams, and I arrived at the very goals of wisdom." According to theologian Morton Kelsey, the main spiritual beliefs that guided Gregory's life were first revealed and reinforced by his dreams. "In the story of one of them he told how chastity embraced him as two maidens who came to him with warmth and affection. When he asked who they were, they replied: Temperance and Virginity. Then they asked him to mix his mind with theirs, his torch with their torch, so that they might place him near the light of the immortal Trinity." This dream, which Gregory said "was the hidden spark that set his whole life aflame for God," prompted him to renounce marriage and adopt an ascetic way of life."[9]

9) In his book *Shamanism: Archaic Techniques of Ecstasy*, Mircea Eliade reports on the place of dream experiences in the initiations of central and northeast Asian shamans: "[U]sually sicknesses, dreams, and ecstasies in themselves constitute an initiation; that is, they transform the profane, pre-'choice' individual into a technician of the sacred." Eliade says that the traditional pattern of initiation ceremonies (suffering, death, resurrection) is found in all the ecstatic experiences that determine a shaman's future vocation; often the candidate suffers horrible bodily mutilations in the process of these initiatory experiences.

According to one shaman's account, "the 'devils' keep the candidate's soul until he has learned all their wisdom. During all this time the candidate lies sick. His soul is transformed into a bird or some other animal or even into a man.... [Eliade concludes] the shaman's instruction often takes place in dreams. It is in dreams that the pure sacred life is entered and direct relations with the gods, spirits, and ancestral souls are re-established."[10]

10) Throughout the history of Sufi mysticism, people have entered into the faith by means of an initiatory dream experience. Anthropologist Katherine Ewing describes the phenomenon of initiation dreams in modern Pakistan, at a time when many people are struggling with the cultural conflicts of the postcolonial situation. She says that these conflicts between traditional and modern ways of life have led some Pakistanis to look to their dreams for guidance, inspiration, and a sense of cultural identity. Ewing goes on to tell the story of a man named Ahmad Sahib, who became a Sufi as a result of a special dream, which "'was very vivid, as if it actually happened. I dreamed of a basement room, with a street passing outside at the level of the ventilators. It was a long narrow room with a low table and a carpet. There was food on the table. I was at the door waiting for a guest to arrive, sitting cross-legged in a spirit of great expectation. Then I saw two people coming, and they stood on the stairs. One was my *pir* [Sufi teacher and healer]. I didn't know him. The other was very saintly, tall, fair, with curved eyebrows and a white turban. Both were dressed in white, with black shawls, as the Prophet wore. I suddenly realized that these were the people I had been waiting for. I was awe-struck. I couldn't move. They came and sat at the low table. My *pir* beckoned to me and told me to sit with them. I crawled up to them on hands and knees, with great respect. The saint was one side, my *pir* was in the center, and I sat on the other side. My *pir* said to the saint, "This is my son. Take a good look at him." The food on the table was *dal* [lentils], curried spinach, and *chapatis* [flat wheat bread]. The saint took a morsel of *chapati*, dipped it into the spinach and *dal*, and then put it into my mouth. I ate it, and as the morsel went down my throat, both of them disappeared. I ran up the road, like a madman on the public street, shouting and crying for them. I knew that

they were my life. Then I saw a telephone booth and a thick
telephone directory. I flipped through it as if I were
searching for his number. I was saying Khwaja Mu'inuddin
Chishti [founder of the Chisti order of sufis in India, d.
1236] over and over again. When I awoke I was actually
saying this.'" After this dream Ahmad Sahib searched for
the *pir* who had appeared in his dream, finding him twelve
years later and becoming his *khalifa* [designated spiritual
successor].[11]

In some of these examples the dreamers are youths—
Agabegijik (12.1), Kwinjinaambi (12.2), Shaikh Ahmad (12.3),
Lucius (12.4), and Gregory of Nazianzen (12.8)— suggesting that
one dimension of their initiations involves a transformation from
childhood to adulthood. But in the other examples the dreamers'
ages are apparently irrelevant to their initiatory experiences.
Some of the dreamers are formal candidates seeking initiation
into well-defined spiritual traditions: Agabegijik is engaged in a
ritual dream fast that all Ojibwa youths must perform (12.1), and
the *"Toalache* Name Dream" comes to candidates seeking to
become healers among the Diegueno Indians (12.7). Like the
initiatory dream of the Paviotso man Dick Mahwee (11.11), their
dreams are the products of dream incubation rituals. Other
dreamers, while not "initiates" in a formal sense, nevertheless
hope for dreams that will spiritually transform them: Ahmad
Sahib (12.10), the new members of the MDCC (12.6), and Lucius
(12.4) all fervently desire dreams that will initiate them into a
new realm of religious existence. But in many of the examples
above, the initiatory dream comes quite unexpectedly. The
dreams of the Sambia shaman Kwinjinaambi (12.2), of Shaikh
Ahmad (12.3), of the Temne diviners (12.5), of Gregory of
Nanzianzen (12.8), and of the Yakut shamans (12.9) serve both as
calls to initiation and as the initiation itself—the dream alone is
sufficient to transport the surprised individual from one level of
social and religious existence to another.

However, if the various *dreamers* here do not share any one
distinctive characteristic, we do find some common elements in
the *contents* of their dreams. In almost every instance the dream
involves an encounter between the dreamer and a powerful
spirit being, often a revered ancestor or teacher. Many of these
dream encounters, like those we discussed in earlier chapters,

have a profoundly intimate quality—the dreamer becomes closely, personally related to the spirit being. Kwinjinaambi meets her dead mother, who presents her with certain medicinal leaves; Gregory of Nazianzen is embraced with "warmth and affection" by the two maidens Temperance and Virginity, and mingles his mind and his torch with theirs; Shaikh Ahmad receives the special attentions of the great Muslim Imams; and both Agabegijik and Ahmad Sahib are greeted as "son" by friendly spirit beings. Even in the torturous dreams suffered by the Yakut shamans, the demons become intimately, if horribly, related to the dreamer.[12]

A second common element in these dreams is the transmission of special teachings and instructions regarding the dreamer's new spiritual life. The Diegueno healers and the new members of the MDCC receive special names in their dreams, names which mark their spiritual transformation. Agabegijik, Kwinjinaambi, and the Temne diviners are taught specific healing techniques by spirit beings in their dreams. And the dreams of Shaikh Ahmad, Lucius, Gregory, the Yakut shamans, and Ahmad Sahib provide them with valuable instructions about the religious traditions into which they are entering.

Considered in the light of Van Gennep's analysis in *The Rites of Passage*, the dream reports in this chapter all possess the three basic elements of separation, transition, and incorporation that he identifies in rites of initiation. Simply going to sleep effects a sharp separation of the individual from the ordinary social world; and going to sleep in a temple or wilderness area, after performing various rituals and saying certain prayers, makes that separation all the more dramatic. The experience of dreaming is a transitional state *par excellence*— it is a threshold space outside of, or in the margins between, the structures which govern our day-to-day life. Dreaming is a liminal realm where the initiate may directly encounter, and be transformed by, the sacred. And in terms of the third element of Van Gennep's analysis, each of these dream reports portrays a very strong and successful incorporation of the initiate into a spiritual or religious tradition.[13] The spiritually-transformed initiate is welcomed back into a community that recognizes his or her new, changed status. The initiate is no longer an "ordinary" person, but a shaman, a healer, a disciple, a full member of the church.

Every night when we go to sleep we separate ourselves from ordinary waking society and enter into the liminal world of our dreams, where the sacred is a powerful, living presence. Going to sleep and dreaming has deep structural parallels to many different spiritual practices: praying inside a temple or sanctuary, ecstatic dancing and singing, consuming psychotropic drugs, journeying into the wilderness in quest of visions. In each case, the individual leaves the profane world and enters into a transitional realm where he or she may be transformed by an encounter with the sacred. Dreaming is, by its very nature, an ideal setting for experiences of spiritual initiation.[14]

All of this raises an interesting question: Does modern western culture provide any resources for *incorporating* people who have transformative dream experiences? In the dream examples above, the dreamers lived in cultures where their spiritual dreams were recognized, respected, and appreciated; the cultures acknowledged the dreams as transformative experiences, and helped to reintegrate the dreamers back into the community. Does this sort of spiritual reintegration of a newly transformed dreamer into a community ever occur in modern western culture?

It does, but only sporadically.[15] Some churches, synagogues, and religious associations regard dreams as legitimate means of relating to the divine. Many 12-step programs and support groups accept the valuable role of dreams in spiritual guidance and healing. Members of the art community, including writers, painters, and musicians, often appreciate the profoundly creative powers that emerge in dreams. And of course, many schools of psychology consider dreams as a primary channel to the individual's unconscious self. The training of prospective Freudian and Jungian therapists involves a careful analysis of their own dreams, an experience that literally initiates them into their new position as members of a special community of psychological healers.

But for the most part, modern western culture does not accord dreams the same high degree of respect that they are given in many other cultures. Aside from those scattered instances just mentioned, there are few communal efforts at helping to incorporate people who have had extraordinary, spiritually-charged dream experiences—helping people to make sense of these dreams, and channeling their energies into the life of the community. My guess is that many modern westerners have had profoundly spiritual dreams and have, for lack of cultural support, interest, or "rites of incorporation," simply forgotten them.

13. *Conversion*

*W*e have already seen considerable evidence of the role of dreams in converting people to the Christian faith. Dreams in which Jesus, usually dressed in shining white clothes, appears and beckons the dreamer to join him have frequently been described by historians and missionaries.[1] The most famous of these conversion dreams was experienced by the Roman emperor Constantine in the early fourth century A.D. Right before leading his troops into battle, Constantine dreamed that Christ appeared to him and showed him a cross of light (the *labarum*); Christ told Constantine that this heavenly image would provide a safeguard against all his enemies.[2] As a consequence of this dream, Constantine made Christianity the official religion of the empire.

But dreams leading to a spiritual conversion—that is, to the adoption of a new faith, way of life, system of belief, and/or mode of relating to the sacred[3]—are not exclusive to Christianity. Such "conversion dreams" can be found in many different cultures through history. However, when we examine these dream reports we find once again cause for deep skepticism. To put it bluntly, the dreams sound *fake*—they sound like stories made up by the alleged dreamers and/or those who recorded the dreams, stories intended to give an aura of heavenly sanction to decisions made for more earthly reasons. For example, many historians suspect that Constantine in fact fabricated his remarkably convenient "dream" as a means of expanding and legitimating his political power.[4]

We can never determine the "reality" of any particular dream experience; we can never know whether Constantine "really" dreamed of Christ presenting him with a cross of light.

But we *can* determine that dreams truly do have a powerful capacity to transform a person's spiritual life, and we *can* develop a solid, well-reasoned understanding of that capacity. As the following examples illustrate, conversion dreams work to *integrate* psychological, cultural, and spiritual elements in such a way that the dreamer is thoroughly transformed. By means of these dreams, the sacred becomes a more vital, immediate presence in the dreamer's life.

1) The Aladura church is a Christian revitalization movement among the Yoruba people of western Nigeria. As J.D.Y. Peel describes in his research on the movement, many Aladura members convert because of dreams. One man gave Peel the following account: "On the night of my dream I was ready to go to bed at 9 o'clock p.m. after dinner but in the bedroom a thought suddenly sprang to my mind and I heard a soft commanding voice saying 'spread an ordinary mat on bare ground in your bedroom and sleep on it this night, do not sleep on your bed....'" The man obeyed the voice, and during the night had a revelatory vision. "I then saw a hefty, very tall and giant-like man standing about forty feet away from where I stood at the junction of a two-forked road. He did not speak to me at all but his attitude to me challenged me to a duel with him if I considered myself to combat him." A crowd gathered around the man and the giant, to see who would win the battle. The man held up magical charms and recited traditional African chants of power to protect himself, but they had no effect on the giant. Then, "providentially, a flickering thought came to my mind as before this revelation and I heard a small voice saying 'recite Psalm 121.'... I summoned up the little courage left in me and started to recite the 121st Psalm.... At once, on hearing this psalm, the giant stopped dead, stepped backwards, retreating slowly at first and taking to his heels, ran away without looking back.... It was then I heard a distinct voice from above my head saying, 'the giant-like man is the typical devil, if reciting a Psalm smatteringly could rescue you from his grips and certain death, won't you from now on divest yourself of charms, juju, incantations and all evil trappings and cling to Almighty God alone, trusting in Him in all your prayers for all purposes.'"[5]

2) Although the fourth-century Christian leader Jerome was highly skeptical of dream incubation rituals (see chapter 11), his own religious life was deeply changed by a dream. Born into a Christian family but educated in the Greek and Roman classics, Jerome could not reconcile his Christian faith with his love of the classics. One night, while he was extremely sick, Jerome had a dream in which he was suddenly "caught up in the spirit" and taken before the "judgement seat of the Judge." The light was so brilliant that Jerome immediately threw himself to the ground. He was asked who he was, and he answered "I am a Christian." But the Judge replied, "Thou liest, thou art a follower of Cicero and not of Christ. For 'where thy treasure is, there will thy heart be also.'" Jerome then silently endured the torturous strokes of the lash that the Judge had ordered be given to him. After this harsh scourging the angelic bystanders prayed that the Judge have pity on Jerome's youth and give him an opportunity to repent of his sins—"He might still, they urged, inflict torture on me, should I ever again read the works of Gentiles." Jerome then swore an oath and said, "Lord, if ever again I possess worldly books, or if ever again I read such, I have denied Thee." With this oath, Jerome was dismissed by the heavenly tribunal. Then, he says, "I returned to the upper world, and, to the surprise of all, I opened upon them eyes so drenched with tears that my distress served to convince even the credulous. And that this was no sleep nor idle dream, such as those by which we are often mocked, I call to witness the tribunal before which I lay, and the terrible judgement which I feared.... I profess that my shoulders were black and blue, that I felt the bruises long after I awoke from my sleep, and that thenceforth I read the books of God with a zeal greater than I had previously given to the books of men."[6]

3) A very interesting account of the ambiguous role of dreams in conversion comes from the Baptist missionary Kenneth Osborne, who worked among the people of the New Guinea Highlands. Osborne describes the founding of a "Christian Graveyard Cult" in 1967: "Pyanjuwa, a local school teacher and prominent church leader, received a vision early one morning, when Christ appeared in bright clothing and told him to clear the undergrowth from the old graveyard not far from the church. In subsequent visions he

was given directions to plant shrubs and lawns, and to begin dawn services in the cemetery. The services became very popular and were held twice weekly, drawing people from other churches for a radius of about five miles.... His strong belief in the reality of dreams and visions is one of the focal points of the movement.... [Pyanjuwa] had also decided to help analyze and interpret dreams for other people. He explained that as belief in direction through dreams and visions was very common among his people he had instituted this 'advice service' to try and guard against wrong teaching and unwise action coming into the community through dreams.... There can be little doubt that Pyanjuwa is finding ways to make Christianity more meaningful to his people...[and] that the movement is responsible for a great deal of new enthusiasm in the churches.... A meeting of the Church District Executive was convened to discuss the new movement. Many of the pastors saw it as an exciting new possibility for renewal in the churches, but others saw the dangers of incorporating beliefs from the old religion, especially in regard to ancestor spirits. It was decided not to encourage the spread of the cult until the church leaders had time to observe its fruits."[7]

4) Members of the True Church of God, an evangelistic, fundamentalist Christian church which originated in eastern Nigeria in 1953, regard dreams as a primary source of conversion. As reported by sociologist Richard Curley, "a typical convert is introduced to the church when he is faced with a critical problem which cannot be solved by conventional means.... Perhaps the clearest indication of a person's religious commitment is a vision which comes to him in the form of a dream." Curley illustrates the conversion process with the example of an Igbo woman named Victoria, thirty years old and the mother of three children. Victoria grew up in eastern Nigeria, to Roman Catholic parents, and she attended the Catholic church and a Catholic missionary school. "Soon after the birth of a second child she began to be sickly and prone to nervous disorders.... [O]ne night her husband brought her to a prayer meeting of the True Church of God. The church is well known for its policy on medicines, and many people in [the region] believe that the church has effective healing powers. In any case church members prayed over Victoria

on seven or eight separate occasions, and she soon found herself getting up to dance. On the night before she was to be baptized she dreamt that she had been driven from her father's house and sent to wander in the bush. She saw herself as a lame person walking through a dense forest in eastern Nigeria where she encountered numerous snakes but had nothing to eat except berries and water. Then one day a light appeared and guided her to a clearing which abounded with her favourite foods. Her lameness disappeared, and while she was drinking water from a clear pool she saw an image of God, who told her to renounce all of her medicines and follow the rules of the True Church as strictly as possible. She was baptized the following day, when she recounted the dream to the assembled congregation, which received it enthusiastically."[8]

5) Anthropologist Vittorio Lanternari describes "another example of a new religion founded as a result of a prophetic dream among people living in precarious conditions [that] has recently occurred in a poor Negro neighborhood in Kingston, Jamaica. It is the Afro-Christian religious movement created by the prophet Kapo. The following dream account was directly recorded by the ethnographic filmproducer A. Pandolfi.... Having had a somewhat superficial Christian education during childhood, Kapo still felt deep down the influence of African religiousness.... Through his dream Kapo knew that he had a mission to accomplish: that of teaching his people a new religion.... This is his story: 'When I was twelve years of age, I was put on to this way of Christianity, and develop afterwards into art. When I was twelve years of age I dreamt one night that I saw a man. He was not a white man, and he was not a very dark man. But he came and he took me from my father's home, down a glade, underneath a white coco tree. Reaching the white coco tree, he asked me the question if I know who he was. I told him "no." He asked me a second time, and then a third time, and I remember that I said to him "If I knew who you were, I would have told you." He said, "My name is the Lord Jesus Christ," and he took a bottle from his pocket, about the length of my hand, and he anointed me from my head down to my foot. And then he said I was to go and tell the Nations, my mother and also

my father, that he, Jesus, was in need of them.'" Kapo went on to preach the gospel among his people for 25 years.[9]

6) Among the Zulu people of South Africa dreams have inspired the creation of many new religious movements that address spiritual needs which are unmet by both Christian missionaries and traditional religious beliefs. According to religion scholar Donald M'Timkulu, "one clear illustration of this kind of development is a separatist group in South Africa called the 'Shembites.'... It began in the early 1930's when people were beginning to feel the effects of the Great Depression, especially in the urban areas.... At this time a man called Shembe who had been working on the farms and in the small town areas of the Free State found himself 'called' to go back to his people in Natal, the home of the Zulus, to give them the teachings which had come to him as part of his dreams. His particular emphasis was to find some salvation for his people during the difficult times. He had one great gift which came to him when he received the dream message from God. This was the gift of healing. Not only Africans but also whites and Indians would come to him and he would 'lay hands' on their sick, breaking through racial differences. Shembe as a nominal Christian was struck by the similarity of his power of healing to that of Jesus. This convinced him even more of the importance of the message he had received in his dream.... The Shembe movement now has a very large membership; estimates of its size vary from 120,000 to 150,000."[10]

7) Dreams have played an important role in converting people to Islam, especially in African cultures. As anthropologist Humphrey Fisher describes it, there is "abundant evidence of their [dreams'] utility in easing the first introduction of Islam, as well as in stimulating changes and developments within Islam.... [T]he progress of Islam in areas such as black Africa is often spread over a broad continuum, beginning with the mildest adhesion and advancing through various stages of deeper understanding and more vigorous reform. The process of conversion is thus a long drawn-out affair and needs recurrent reinforcement. Looking at the history of Muslim black Africa, we find dreams proving the vital activation at various stages. Dreams have encouraged people to embark on missionary journeys.

The celebrated saint of the Somali, Shaykh Ishaq, came from Arabia, sailing across the sea on his prayer mat after God in a dream had summoned him to preach Islam in Somaliland.... Dreams may also prepare the welcome of such missionaries or other distinguished visitors. When, in 1519, a *sharif* from Arabia was about to arrive at Timbuktu, the *qadi* there dreamt of the Prophet [Muhammed], who came on a camel. The camel knelt, the *qadi* kissed the Prophet on the forehead, they chatted of various matters, and the Prophet told of the *sharif* who would arrive the next day, just in time to lead the festival prayer. Then a dog bayed, the camel leapt up, and the Prophet mounted and departed. The *qadi* awoke, did his ablutions, and at dawn went out and traced a circle around the marks left by the Prophet's camel. The *sharif* came as prophesied."[11]

8) In his book *Dojo: Magic and Exorcism in Modern Japan*, Winston Davis describes Sukyo Mahikari, one of the many "new religions" that have proliferated in Japan after World War II. Sukyo Mahikari ("The True-Light Supra-Religious Organization") was founded by a man named Okada Yoshikazu, the descendant of a long line of samuri warriors and military leaders. During and after the war, Okada suffered various illnesses and misfortunes that led him to join the Church of World Messianity. As Davis reports, "on February 22 of [1959] he developed a high fever and became unconscious. Suddenly he found himself transported to the astral world, where he saw an old man with white hair standing in a white cloud and washing clothes in a golden tub. Later, Okada interpreted this vision as a revelation of the Su-god (the Lord God) and of the cleansing mission that was about to be entrusted to him. Five days after the vision, on his birthday, Okada was awakened at five o'clock in the morning by a divine voice saying, 'Get up. Change your name to Kotama (Jewel of Light). Raise your hand. Trials and tribulations are coming!'... As the [Sukyo Mahikari] movement expanded, Okada's messianic consciousness grew deeper.... Throughout this period, revelations continuously came to Okada during the night that he jotted down in 'automatic writing' with incredible speed. These were later collected in a 486-page volume called the *Goseigenshu*, the scriptures of Mahikari."[12]

9) Smohalla was the founder of one of the "dreamer religions" that flourished among many Native American cultures in the early nineteenth century, a time of sharp conflict with white culture (the pejorative "dreamer religions" came from U.S. government officials who saw the movements as anti-Christian and politically subversive). Historians Clifford Trafzer and Margery Ann Beach describe Smohalla's most important religious experience: "Between 1858 and 1860, following the disastrous attempt by the Plateau tribes to stand against the United States Army, Smohalla moved his small band up the Columbia River to a fishing area known as Priest Rapids. There, the Prophet built a small village, living in a large A-framed mat lodge with his ten wives and one daughter. Smohalla had chosen his daughter to succeed him as the keeper of the faith, but even before the girl had gone on her *wyak,* or vision quest, she became ill with disease and died. Neither Smohalla's medicine nor that of the other religious leaders could save the girl and she died. While sitting at his daughter's grave praying, singing, and mourning, Smohalla had his second and most significant religious revelation. He died and once again traveled to the spirit world where God taught him a sacred washat or dance and numerous religious songs. The dance and songs formed the basis of a religious revival of the old Washani faith and a renewed interest among many Indians in traditional spiritual beliefs. When Smohalla awoke from his comatose state, he found himself lying within his own lodge.... Smohalla explained [to his followers] that *Nami Piap* [God] had not permitted him to remain in the land of the dead, because [he] was to return to the earth and teach the people a special *washat,* and over 120 songs to add to the old Washini songs. Smohalla had been told by *Nami Piap* to 'teach the Wanapums and others to be good, do good, and live like Indians. Give them this song and show them this dance.'"[13]

10) An even earlier Native American revitalization movement originating out of a dream vision occurred among the Iroquois in 1799. A man named Handsome Lake had been sick for some time with an undiagnosed malady. As anthropologist Anthony Wallace recounts the story in *The Death and Rebirth of the Seneca,* Handsome Lake's daughter "had been sitting outside the house in the

shed, cleaning beans for the planting. The sick man had
been within, alone. Suddenly through the open door they
heard him exclaim, '*Niio!*'—'So be it!' Then they heard him
rising in his bed, and heard him walking across the floor
toward the door. Then the daughter saw her father, who
was 'but yellow skin and dried bones,' coming out of doors.
He tottered, and she rose quickly and caught him as he fell.
They thought he was dead or dying...." The villagers
gathered around him, waiting for any sign of life from the
motionless body. After two hours, "Handsome Lake's eyes
opened and his lips began to move as if he wanted to speak.
Blacksnake asked, 'My uncle, are you feeling well?' And
Handsome Lake answered, 'Yes, I believe myself well.'
Then, after a pause, he began to describe his vision....
Handsome Lake heard his name called and left the house.
Outside he saw three middle-aged men dressed in fine
ceremonial clothes, with red paint on their faces and
feathers in their bonnets, carrying bows and arrows in one
hand and huckleberry bushes in the other. Handsome Lake
collapsed from weakness, but the angels caught him and let
him down gently. They told him they were sent by the
Creator to visit Handsome Lake, whose constant
thankfulness had earned him the right to help from his
sickness." These angels then instructed Handsome Lake in
the proper performance of certain religious rituals and told
him to preach a message of repentance to all his people.
Wallace says that "the relating of [Handsome Lake's] vision
produced a profound effect on its audience.... This was the
beginning of the new religion."[14]

These reports of dream-prompted spiritual conversions
contain many of the key elements that religion scholars believe
are integral to the conversion experience. In his recent book
Understanding Religious Conversion, theologian Lewis Rambo
describes the primary themes that run through virtually all
conversion experiences. One is that the convert feels a new sense
of relationship with the divine; Rambo says, "God is no longer an
abstract concept but a living reality. Although the details given by
converts may differ, there is a sense of intimacy and connection
that was not there before."[15] A second common consequence is
that the convert gains a strong sense of mission, a belief that he
or she has been called to carry out some special purpose in life.[16]

We find both these themes running through the dream reports above. In each case the dreamer has a personal encounter with a powerful spirit being; from that encounter a relationship develops that guides the dreamer into a new spiritual world-view. The relationship may be warm and caring, as when Jesus personally annoints Kapo from head to foot (13.5) and when Victoria sees an image of God in a clearing filled with her favorite foods (13.4). Or the relationship may be rather demanding and harsh, as when a divine voice sharply orders Okada Yoshikazu to change his name and prepare for future difficulties (13.8) and when God orders that the indecisive Jerome be scourged (13.2). No matter what the emotional valence, the underlying experience in all these cases is an intimate connection between the dreamer and the spirit being. This experience of becoming closer to the sacred is, as we have seen in earlier chapters, a central feature of spiritually significant dreams. The dream reports in this chapter show how that intimacy with the sacred can lead the dreamer change his or her entire spiritual world-view.

The new sense of mission or purpose that Rambo and other religion scholars find in conversion experiences also comes through very clearly in these dream reports. Jerome says that after his dream he read the Bible with more zeal than he had ever given to reading the classics (13.2). The Muslim saint Shaykh Ishaq (13.7) was motivated to begin his missionary work by a revelatory dream. And the religious movements initiated by Pyanjuwa in New Guinea (13.3), Kapo in Jamaica (13.5), Shembe in South Africa (13.6), Okada Yoshikazu in Japan (13.8), and Smohalla (13.9) and Handsome Lake (13.10) in North America were all prompted by powerful, spiritually transformative dreams. These individuals try to bring their religious dream experiences *into* their communities, to share their discoveries, insights, and passions with other people—they try to *give form* to their dream revelations. In this regard, conversion dreams illustrate that same impulse toward expression we have already seen in reports of creative dreams, healing dreams, and prophetic dreams. The dreamers portrayed in this chapter evidently feel the same strong urge to give form to the spiritual power they experience in their dreams, to bring forth that power into their waking worlds.

Many studies of conversion concentrate on the various crises that can precipitate a conversion experience. Most people who convert to a new religious or spiritual world-view do so in the context of some kind of deeply troubling, highly stressful situation in which they feel trapped; the conversion marks a resolution of the crisis, an escape from a situation that had seemed inescapable. In this regard, the prominence of dreams in conversion experiences should not surprise us. One of the primary psychological functions of dreams (as discussed in chapters 3 and 10) is to help us adapt to and overcome crises of various sorts. Many modern research studies have demonstrated that dreams respond, directly and creatively, to deaths, illnesses, accidents, divorces, job losses, school failures, natural disasters— to almost every kind of stressful, anxiety-provoking, traumatizing experience of our lives. Psychologist David Koulack states that "during dreaming, there is a flexibility and fluidity of thought and emotion not generally available during our waking lives," which seems to "help us to deal with stressful or troublesome waking events."[17] Similarly, psychologist Alan Siegel, who has extensively studied the role of dreams in coping with life crises, says that post-traumatic dreams and nightmares "are a vital source of information that can help us focus our recovery on the issues that have wounded us most deeply."[18] Conversion dreams can therefore be regarded as instances in which the crisis-resolving function of dreams reaches an unusual degree of intensity, power, and effectiveness.

Still, skepticism may linger. Conversion dreams may well be reported throughout history; they may possess all the essential features of conversion experiences; and they may display the same crisis-resolving effect that psychologists believe is a basic function of "real" dreams. But still, many reports of conversion dreams just sound fake; they sound too coherent, too structured, too well-crafted to be believed. Jerome's dream, for example, has such an elaborate, polished narrative structure. It is hard not to suspect that he made it up—perhaps by referring to the well-known biblical story of the prophet Isaiah's humbling experience before the throne of the Lord (Is 6).

At this point, the recent work of psychologically-minded anthropologists can be of help. Barbara Tedlock, Waud Kracke, Rosalind Shaw, Gananath Obeyesekere, and many other anthropologists have demonstrated that individual dream experiences and the dreamer's culture exert a mutual influence on one another (as we discussed in chapter 8). On the one hand the customs, languages, social structures, religious beliefs, etc. at work in a given culture directly and profoundly influence people's dreams. On the other hand individual dreams frequently inspire cultural innovations in matters such as healing practices, ritual performances, works of art, and religious and mythological narratives. Obeyesekere, in his book *Medusa's Hair: An Essay on Personal Symbols and Religious Experience*, provides an excellent account of the mutual influence between dreams and myths:

> Knowledge and meaning can be derived from hypnomantic states: dream (vision), trance, ecstasy, concentration. I believe that this mode of knowledge...is one of the most powerful and ancient forms of knowing.... Myth is often generated out of the hypnomantic consciousness.... Insofar as some myths (not all of them) are constructed during hypnomantic states, they must partake of the type of thought characteristic of these states.... Yet, more than ordinary dreams, certain hypnomantic states such as trance and dream vision are also influenced by the culture and by the personal quest of the seeker after truth.... [The myths] in turn feed back into the hypnomantic state, influencing the thought structure of these states and the nature of our unconscious, including our dream life. The chicken and egg are not isolatable things: they belong to a single interlocking, yet causally interdependent, mutually interacting system. In other words, it is possible for a person to dream a myth rather than a dream, though the latter is the model for the former."[19]

Seen in this light, Jerome's conversion dream appears much more credible. Jerome seems to have *dreamed a myth*: his dream draws on religious themes and images that were prominent in his culture, and uses those themes and images to frame, to make sense of, his personal struggle. The result is a deeply meaningful and powerfully transformative experience that converts Jerome to the Christian faith. Jerome himself anticipates the skepticism that people might feel when hearing of his story. Granting that it was not an "ordinary" dream, Jerome still insists that he has accurately reported his experience. The research of anthropologists like Obeyesekere gives strong support to the legitimacy of his claim.

Each of the dreams reported above occurs not just in the context of a *personal* crisis, but in the context of a *cultural* crisis as well. Jerome is caught in the conflict between the Graeco-Roman world and the Judeo-Christian world (13.2); Smohalla's and Handsome Lake's peoples are locked in a bitter, violent conflict with the white settlers pushing westward (13.9 and 13.10); Okada lives in the tumultuous culture of post-war Japan (13.8); Shembe's people are suffering from the global effects of the Great Depression (13.6); and the traditional cultures of Pyanjuwa's New Guinea (13.3), the Aladura church member's Yoruba-land (13.1), Victoria's Nigeria (13.4), Kapo's Jamaica (13.5), and the *qadi's* Timbuktu (13.7) are struggling with the sudden incursions of new, more powerful cultures. In all these reports, the dreamer's cultural world is filled with tension, stress, and suffering, and their dreams respond to that broader waking world situation. "Conversion dreams" do not occur in a cultural vacuum; they emerge out of crises that have both personal and cultural roots. Once we recognize this, we are able to appreciate the most distinctive feature of these dreams: the highly creative integration of these personal and cultural elements within the dream experience.

The Christian Graveyard Cult founded by Pyanjuwa (13.3) offers an excellent illustration of this. Like so many native cultures that have come into contact with western colonial powers, the New Guinea Highlanders are clearly caught between the pull of their traditional spiritual beliefs and the push of the teachings of the Christian missionaries. By means of dream experiences, Pyanjuwa and his followers are able to integrate their traditional spirituality with Christianity—their dreams provide a bridge to connect and synthesize beliefs that had been in conflict at both the personal and the cultural level. The result is a new "cult" that stirs up tremendous energy and religious enthusiasm. As the missionary Osborne uneasily admits, Pyanjuwa has found a way "to make Christianity more meaningful to his people" by encouraging them to listen to their dreams.

The other examples in this chapter also reveal this capacity of dreams to integrate the new and the traditional, the personal and the cultural, the material and the spiritual—dreams have the capacity to bring all these disparate elements together into a creative synthesis that speaks directly to the dreamer's present life. It is this capacity of dreams that has made them so prominent in conversion experiences, revitalization movements, cargo cults, and new religions of various sorts. When people face a crisis (personal and/or cultural) that challenges their spiritual beliefs, powerful dreams often emerge: dreams that respond to the crisis, integrate the painfully conflicting elements in the dreamer's life, and give the dreamer a new, energetic sense of spiritual purpose that he or she carries back into the waking world. Such dream experiences bring the renewing powers of the sacred into the dreamer's present, conflict-ridden life. The sacred is no longer simply a subject of sermons, teachings, and traditions. By means of the dream, the sacred becomes a living, vital force in the individual's world.

Conclusion

*W*oody Allen once said, "There is no question that there is an unseen world. The problem is, how far is it from midtown and how late is it open?"[1] The answer, if the preceding thirteen chapters have demonstrated anything, is that the "unseen world" is as close as our pillows, and it's open twenty-four hours a day.

This book has presented spiritual dreams experienced by a limitless variety of people: by men and women, by the young and the old, by the powerless and the powerful, by the "civilized" and the "primitive," by the "religious" and the "secular." The cross-cultural and historical evidence indicates that dreams offer a universally accessible means of becoming closer to the sacred. Spiritual dream experiences are not restricted to people with special qualities, training, or social status. It seems that every person has at least the potential to experience numinous, existentially-meaningful dreams. The Muslim scholar Ibn Khaldun wrote in his fourteenth-century A.D. work the *Muqaddimah* (*An Introduction to History*) that all humans have an innate faculty or "preparedness" for spiritual perception in dreams; "dream vision...is a particular quality of the human soul common to all mankind."[2] The Mohave people of the American southwest believed that every person could experience a *sumach ahot*, a "power-bestowing dream" that came without preparation or warning; a "sumach ahot was the basis of success in life, and, by reason of its involuntary character, anyone might have one."[3] Solomon Almoli, a Jewish doctor of sixteenth-century Constantinople, wrote in his *Pitron Chalomot* (*The Interpretation of Dreams*) that "Providence brings dreams to the righteous and the wicked alike, just as all living things

156

receive their worldly sustenance from the same source."[4] Tibetan Dzogchen master Namkhai Norbu says that "clarity dreams," i.e. dreams that address the dreamer's spiritual condition and potential, are possible for anyone: "dreams linked with clarity do exist for everyone. Everyone has innate clarity."[5]

The most eloquent assertion of the universal accessibility of spiritual dream experience comes from Synesius of Cyrene, an early fifth-century A.D. Neo-Platonist who converted to Christianity and became famous as bishop of Ptolemais. In his treatise on dreams Synesius writes:

> 1) [T]he dream is visible to the man who is worth five hundred medimni, and equally to the possessor of three hundred, to the teamster no less than to the peasant who tills the boundary land for a livelihood, to the galley slave and the common labourer alike, to the exempted and to the payer of taxes. It makes no difference to the god whether a man is an *eteoboutades* or a newly bought slave. And this accessibility to all makes divination [through dreams] very humane; for its simple and artless character is worthy of a philosopher, and its freedom from violence gives it sanctity.... Of divination by dreams, each one of us is perforce his own instrument, so much so that it is not possible to desert our oracle there even if we so desired. Nay, even if we remain at home, she dewlls with us; if we go abroad she accompanies us; she is with us on the field of battle, she is at our side in the life of the city; she labours with us in the fields and barters with us in the market place. The laws of a malicious government do not forbid her, nor would they have the power to do so, even if they wished it, for they have no proof against those who invoke her.... A tyrant could never enjoin us not to gaze into dreams, at least not unless he actually banished sleep from his kingdom.... To her then we must go, woman and man of us, young and old, poor and rich alike, the private citizen and the ruler, the town dweller and the rustic, the artisan and the orator. She repudiates neither race, nor age, nor condition, nor calling. She is present to every one, everywhere, this zealous prophetess, this wise counsellor, who holdeth her peace."[6]

Dreaming offers a means of relating to the sacred that is readily available to *all* people, regardless of their age, gender,

race, or social status. Dreams are not extremely rare phenomena, like visions, trances, and other ecstatic states. No
special tools, techniques, or preparations are required to
experience a spiritually meaningful dream.[7] Dreaming can
therefore be considered a *natural* means of sacred experience,
natural in the sense of being an inherent capacity of all human
beings.

While all humans may have the potential to experience
spiritually meaningful dreams, the actualization of this potential
is always influenced by the particular circumstances of the
dreamer's personal and cultural context. We have seen numerous instances in which the capacity for spiritual dreaming has
been cultivated, encouraged, and actively promoted. Discussing
spiritual dreams in communal settings, sharing mythic stories
about dreams, expressing dreams in art, incorporating dreams
into rites of initiation, and, of course, practicing dream
incubation rituals—all of these work to *stimulate* the experience
of spiritual dreams. In many cultures, people share their dreams
each morning as a regular part of daily life.[8]

The innate human capacity for spiritual dreaming is not
imperishable, however. Synesius speaks too optimistically when
he says that "a tyrant could never enjoin us not to gaze into
dreams." Unfortunately, dreams can be deeply affected, and
severely disrupted, by antagonistic cultural and social forces.[9]

> 2) Anthropologist W.J. Wallace comments on the destructive
> effects of white culture on the Mohave experience of *sumach
> ahot*: "As Mohave culture gradually deteriorated the power-
> giving dream tended to disappear. The pattern depended
> upon the normal functioning of the culture and, as this
> declined, the *sumach ahot* also diminished in importance.
> Many of the older Mohave have had a great dream, but
> scarcely any of the young people. Some deny that revelations
> occur any more. [Said one Mohave youth] 'I don't think that
> they have dreams like that any more. There are no new songs.
> Sometimes a young fellow says he has had a *sumach ahot* and
> is a doctor, but I don't believe it.'"[10]

> 3) The Ojibwa and Ottawa peoples of North America long
> practiced a ritual of dream fasting at puberty (see 12.1). But
> as happened with the Mohave, the Ojibwa and Ottawa's

dream experiences changed dramatically after contact with white culture: according to anthropologist Paul Radin, "[B]y the beginning of the nineteenth century, with the whole social and economic structure of the culture so irretrievably shattered and broken up, it [the dream fast] had become merely a static and unchanging ritual utterly divorced from reality.... By [the 1920s] fasting had apparently become something to which unpopular grandparents drove their unwilling grandchildren. Ojibwa and Ottawa culture had ceased to function even in a remotely significant manner. The old formulae are beginning to show definite indications of wear and tear and the purely personal content of the dream [now devoid of cultural and spiritual meanings] is everywhere apparent."[11]

4) In his autobiography *Memories, Dreams, Reflections*, Carl Jung describes the following experience from a journey he took to visit the Elgonyis people of eastern Africa: "One time we had a palaver with the *laibon*, the old medicine man. He appeared in a splendid cloak made of the skins of blue monkeys—a valuable article of display. When I asked him about his dreams, he answered with tears in his eyes, 'In old days the *laibon* had dreams, and knew whether there is war or sickness or whether rain comes and where the herds should be driven.' His grandfather, too, had still dreamed. But since the whites were in Africa, he said, no one had dreams any more. Dreams were no longer needed because now the English knew everything!"[12]

Perhaps the most striking, and most poignant, evidence of how tyrants can indeed disrupt our dreams comes in Charlotte Beradt's book *The Third Reich of Dreams*. Beradt secretly gathered and preserved more than three hundred dream reports from people living in Germany from 1933–1939–the years of Adolph Hitler's rise to power. These dreams are deeply moving reflections of the psychological and spiritual violence these people suffered under the National Socialist regime. In many of the dreams a common household object, like a stove, desk, or bedside lamp, "turns traitor" and informs the Nazis of the dreamer's hidden beliefs; one woman dreamed that "simply everything we have ever thought or said among ourselves is known."[13] Another woman dreamt that she was sleep-talking in

Russian, "so I'd not even understand myself and so no one else could understand me in case I said anything about the government, for that, of course, is not permitted and must be reported."[14] The violence of these people's world became so terrible that it threatened their very ability to dream: one young man reported to Beradt that "I dreamt that I no longer dream about anything but rectangles, triangles, and octagons, all of which somehow look like Christmas cookies—you see, it was forbidden to dream."[15]

The capacity to dream, and to become closer to the sacred in our dreams, may be a gift that we all are born with. But if so, it is a gift that may also be stolen away.

The specter of a world in which increasing numbers of people actually cease to dream reminds me of a passage in Lewis Carroll's *Through the Looking-Glass and What Alice Found There*. Alice and her newfound companions Tweedledee and Tweedledum are walking through the forest when they come upon the Red King, asleep and snoring very loudly. When Tweedledee asks Alice what she thinks the King is dreaming about, she replies that no one can tell what another person is dreaming. And where, Tweedledee slyly asks, would Alice be if the King happened to wake up? Startled, Alice says she'd be right where she is now. Tweedledee triumphantly informs Alice that the Red King is in fact dreaming of *her*, and that she is only a "sort of a thing in his dream!" Alice indignantly denies it, but Tweedledum adds, "if that there King was to wake, you'd go out—bang!—just like a candle!" Alice, deeply flustered by this sudden existential dilemma, begins laughing and crying at the same time. Alice's bewilderment stems from the rational, common-sense assumption that what other people dream, or *don't* dream, has no effect on us. The Red King's dreams are his own affairs; if he stops dreaming, it couldn't possibly affect Alice—or could it? Alice isn't sure, and neither am I.

Appendix 1:
Hermeneutics: The Interpretation
of Spiritual Dreams

Dreams have always been a fertile source of spiritual reflection, thought, and speculation. Throughout history dreams have challenged people to expand, deepen, and refine their understandings of the sacred. This appendix will provide an overview of the various ways that people have tried to make sense of their religious dream experiences—how people have tried to analyze, classify, categorize, explain, interpret, and understand dreams in their capacity as spiritual revelations. Such efforts are the province of hermeneutics, the discipline concerned with the rules and principles guiding our interpretations of religious, artistic, and historical texts. The term "hermeneutics" stems from the Greek deity Hermes, god of journeys, passages, and exchanges.[1] One of Hermes' chief tasks was the delivery of messages (often in the form of dreams) from the gods of Mount Olympus to the humans residing below on earth. A hermeneutics of dreams, then, involves the attempt to interpret and understand dreams as possible messages from the gods, as possible revelations of the sacred.

The simplest, and perhaps safest, hermeneutic stance toward the realm of dreaming is this: dreams cannot be trusted as spiritual guides, so for all practical purposes they should be *ignored*.

1) The Old Testament is filled with passages warning that dreams are deceptive, unreliable, and frequently dangerous.

161

One of the best known passages is from Ecclesiastes: "For a dream comes with much business, and a fool's voice with many words.... For when dreams increase, empty words grow many" (Eccl 5:3, 7). But the most vigorous denunciation of dreams comes in the apocryphal book of Sirach: "A man of no understanding has vain and false hopes, and dreams give wings to fools. As one who catches at a shadow and pursues the wind, so is he who gives heed to dreams. The vision of dreams is this against that, the likeness of a face confronting a face. From an unclean thing what will be made clean? And from something false what will be true? Divinations and omens and dreams are folly, and like a woman in travail the mind has fancies. Unless they are sent from the Most High as a visitation, do not give your mind to them. For dreams have deceived many, and those who have put their hope in them have failed. Without such deceptions the law will be fulfilled, and wisdom is made perfect in truthful lips" (Sir 34:1-8).

2) The Roman writer Lucretius (95–55 B.C.) is our best source for the philosophical teachings of the Epicureans, who offered a highly rationalist vision of the universe as consisting solely of atoms moving in a godless void. In his book *On Nature* Lucretius says this about the deceptiveness of dreams: "And when sleep has prostrated the body, for no other reason does the mind's intelligence wake, except because the very same images provoke our minds which provoke them when we are awake, and to such a degree that we seem without a doubt to perceive him whom life has left and death and earth gotten hold of. This nature constrains to come to pass because all the senses of the body are then hampered and at rest throughout the limbs and cannot refute the unreal by real things. Moreover memory is prostrate and relaxed in sleep and protests not that he has long been in the grasp of death and destruction whom the mind believes it sees alive."[2]

3) Wang Ch'ung, a Chinese philospher from the first century A.D., takes a dim view of the supposed "realness" of dreams. Commenting on the well-known story of Shu-sun Mu-tzu's dream of heaven, Wang Ch'ung says, "Shu-sun Mu-tzu dreamed that heaven weighed down upon him. If this had been real, then heaven must have descended and

reached the earth. Upon reaching the earth, it would have met the barrage of mansions and terraces. Hence it could not have touched him. For if it had, then the mansions and terraces would have been crushed. That they remained intact indicates that heaven did not reach earth. If it did not reach the earth, then it did not weigh down upon the man. If it did not weigh down upon him, then what did weigh down upon him was not heaven itself but rather the image of heaven."[3]

4) In the sixth century A.D. leaders of the Eastern Orthodox church began denouncing the heretical threats posed by dreams. As historian Steven Oberhelman notes, church leaders begin to view dreams as satanic torments and seductions. "Resorting to ancient views on physiology and to Christian demonology, Eastern fathers like Evagrius and John Climacus reduced the vast majority of dreams to demon-inspired torments; the few dreams not so reduced were considered nonimportant images of mental illusion or warnings sent by God to sinners to beware of judgement and punishment. Dreams, in other words, fall into complete mistrust. Not even images of Jesus, angels, or saints can be trusted, since Satan and demons can and will disguise themselves as the Lord and heavenly beings, in order to destroy the dreamer's peace of mind. Any dream, therefore, should be considered the devil's deceit."[4]

5) Antiochus Monachus, a seventh-century A.D. Christian monk living in a monastery near Jerusalem, gave a homily on dreams in which he condemned virtually all dream experiences: dreams, Antiochus argues, "are nothing other than things of the imagination and hallucinations of a mind led astray. They are the illusions of evil demons to deceive us and result from their enticements with the attendant purpose of carrying off a man to pleasure.... Now then, if a light or some shape in the form of fire appears to one of those who strive (for a spiritual life), let him in no way whatsoever admit this vision. It is a patent delusion of an inimical and wicked scheme. It is this that the apostle teaches us, saying that he (Satan) is transformed 'into an angel of light.'... Even though, as is likely, a vision may have been sent down to us by divine revelation, let us not pay attention to it lest we accept smoke in lieu of light. In this

way we do not stir up the Lord's anger, but rather He may also approve our guarding, with the help of fear, the treasure (i.e., the divine revelation) entrusted by Him to us."[5]

6) The sixteenth-century Protestant reformer Martin Luther also refused to have anything to do with the seeming revelations of dreams: "I care nothing about visions and dreams. Although they seem to have meaning, yet I despise them and am content with the sure meaning and trustworthiness of Holy Scripture."[6]

7) Thomas Nashe, a sixteenth-century English playwright and novelist, provides one of the most florid denunciations of dreams ever written: "A dream is nothing else but a bubbling scum or froth of the fancy, which the day hath left undigested; or an after-feast made of the fragments of idle imaginations.... No such figure of the first Chaos where the world was extraught, as our dreams in the night. In them all states, all sexes, all places, are confounded and meet together. Our cogitations run on heaps like men to part a fray, where everyone strikes his next fellow. From one place to another without consultation they leap, like rebels bent on a head. Soldiers just up and down they imitate at the sack of a city, which spare neither age nor beauty; the young, the old, trees, steeples, and mountains they confound in one gallimaufry.... There were gates in Rome out of which nothing was carried but dust, and dung, and men to execution; so, many of the gates of our senses serve for nothing but to convey out excremental vapours and affrighting deadly dreams that are worse than executioners unto us. Ah, woe to the solitary man that hath his sins continually about him, that hath no withdrawing place from the devil and his temptations!"[7]

8) In his classic work of political philosophy *Leviathan* (1651), Thomas Hobbes discusses the relationship of dreaming to waking perceptions. He says dreams are "caused by the distemper of some of the inward parts of the body"; however, people rarely recognize the absurdities of their dreams for what they are. Thus, Hobbes says, "from this ignorance of how to distinguish dreams, and other strong fancies, from vision and sense, did arise the greatest part of the religion of the gentiles in time past, that

worshipped satyres, fawnes, nymphs, and the like; and now arises the opinion that rude people have of fayries, ghosts, and goblins; and of the power of witches...." Hobbes believes such ignorance poses a threat to a well-ordered society: "In a common-wealth, a subject that has no certain and assured revelation particularly to himself concerning the will of God, is to obey for such, the command of the common-wealth: for if men were at liberty, to take for God's commandments, their own dreams, and fancies, or the dreams and fancies of private men; scarce two men would agree upon what is God's commandment; and yet in respect of them, every man would despise the commandments of the common-wealth."[8]

A thorough distrust of dreams is certainly the safest hermeneutic attitude one can take from a *political* perspective—rejecting all dreams keeps a person out of trouble with the authorities. The writer of the book of Sirach (A1.1), the Eastern Orthodox fathers (A1.4), the monk Antiochus (A1.5), and Martin Luther (A1.7) all warn that dreams can lead people to stray from religious orthodoxy; and Hobbes (A1.8) is explicit in saying that supposed revelations through dreams pose a threat to a well-ordered society, an argument similar to the one made in Plato's *Republic* about the political dangers of dreams (5.13).[9] As discussed at the end of chapter 11 (in relation to Jewish and Christian criticism of dream incubation rituals), dreams frequently have the effect of challenging the official doctrines of churches, movements, and governments. It is understandable that people who prize social and religious stability would denounce dreams in general as dangerous, heretical, and subversive.[10]

A total distrust of dreams is also the safest hermeneutic stance one can take from a purely *intellectual* perspective. For those who believe that rationality is our greatest faculty, the stubbornly irrational phenomenon of dreaming can only be regarded as a nuisance. Lucretius (A1.2) dismisses dreams as nonsensical fancies that are able to arise only because reason, memory, and the senses lie "prostrate" during sleep. Similarly, Wang Ch'ung (A1.3) ridicules those people who are gullible enough to believe that dreams are *real*, when their contents are so obviously contrary to fact and common sense. And Thomas

Nashe (A1.6) rejects dreams for their absurd irrationality, their "fragmentary," "undigested," "chaotic" nature; how, Nashe asks, can we take seriously a phenomenon that "confounds" all the rational categories of waking life into one great muddled "gallimaufry"?

However, the severe distrust we find in these examples is relatively rare; from a cross-cultural and historical perspective, such absolute skepticism appears very infrequently. By far the most common and widespread hermeneutic attitude toward dreams involves making distinctions— classifying *some* dreams as true, meaningful, and/or spiritually valuable, and classifying *other* dreams as false, meaningless, and/or spiritually insignificant (even in the preceding examples, many of the writers grudgingly admit that some dreams may be significant). What follows are accounts of some of the classification systems people have developed to distinguish various types of dreams:

9) The native people of Hawaii have a number of different dream classes, according to anthropologist E.S. Craighill Handy. Hawaiians distinguish dreaming in deep sleep (*moe uhane*) from the swift vision in half sleep (*hihi'o*). They also differentiate between unpremeditated dreams (*me ka noonoo mua ole*) and premeditated dreams (*i loaa mamuli o ka mana'o*). Handy quotes Kepelino, a native folklorist, as saying "some dreams were true dreams and some not true. In olden days dreams were taught by dream interpreters and their teachings spread everywhere even to this day.... Their meanings were memorized like a catechism learned by memory in childhood.... There were two important kinds of dreams as regards the dreamer, unpremeditated dreams and those which were the result of premeditation on the part of the dreamer. Of all dreams the most significant ones were those which came when one was startled in a very deep sleep or just as the eyelashes closed together when falling into a doze. These were true dreams."[11]

10) We have already noted the Mohave distinction between "the traditional power-bestowing dream (*sumach ahot*, 'dream lucky') and the less significant, everyday sleep experiences (*sumach*, 'dream')." Anthropologist W.J. Wallace goes on to say that for the Mohave, "not all dreams are equally significant. The criterion used in determining

what is important is often difficult to ascertain. The real test sometimes seems to be whether or not the dream comes true. A few dreams are regarded as having no meaning whatsoever. [An informant said] 'Some dreams, like if I dreamt I went to the store, don't mean anything and people forget about them right away.'"[12]

11) A leader of the Jamaa movement, a charismatic movement that flourished in the Congo in the 1950s, described to anthropologist Johannes Fabian this theory of significant and insignificant dreams: "So, there are dreams that come from man alone, and dreams that come from God to teach man, to make him understand how God loves.... And then there are just dreams.... Therefore, the dream we receive from the *mawazo* [spiritual teaching] of God, the dream that comes from God, we may take as *mawazo*, yes. Because God has thought out and given the dream. It's a *mafundisho* [instruction] by God himself. But the dream that comes only from us: this is the second case. We have a dream that comes from us, the dream we have at night. One dream we receive as a holy dream, the one we regard as *mawazo* coming from God; that's how we call it, yes, that sort of dream is *mawazo*. Another dream is just a dream, senseless things that come from man alone, yes."[13]

12) The Mehinaku of central Brazil distinguish between dreams of greater and lesser significance, according to anthropologist Thomas Gregor: "A dream, for the Mehinaku, is an experience well worth remembering. It is, they say, like a shaman's prophecy in that the dreamer can learn much of what is to occur in the future. Upon entering periods of seclusion associated with adolescence, for example, boys have dreams that are regarded as sure indications of their longevity, health, and social status. Other dreams, admittedly rare, can herald the career of new shamans. These so-called true dreams (*jepuni yaja*) are given the closest attention by the initiates and their parents. Ordinary, everyday dreams (*jepuni he te*, literally 'mere dreams') are also important, however. Each morning the villagers recall such dreams and weigh them for their possible significance. The Mehinaku are aware, for example, that dreams are often constructed out of the residue of daily events. A man may explain a dream in

which he went fishing or went hunting monkeys by recalling that he had done these things the previous day. Alternatively, the villagers may occasionally interpret their dreams as expressions of wish fulfillment. One young man told me he dreamed he had received a certain gift because he had wanted it for a long time."[14]

13) In book 19 of Homer's *Odyssey* Penelope describes a dream in which twenty fat geese are slaughtered by a mountain eagle. She tells the dream to a kind beggar, whom she does not recognize as her husband Odysseus; he has disguised himself, and is plotting revenge against the suitors who have plundered his home. Odysseus assures Penelope that the dream's meaning is clear: her husband will return and kill the suitors. Penelope, however, is not so certain, and says, "Friend, many and many a dream is mere confusion, a cobweb of no consequence at all. Two gates for ghostly dreams there are: one gateway of honest horn, and one of ivory. Issuing by the ivory gate are dreams of glimmering illusion, fantasies, but those that come through solid polished horn may be borne out, if mortals only know them. I doubt it came by horn, my fearful dream—too good to be true, that, for my son and me."[15]

14) John Brennan, a scholar of Chinese literature, tells of how dream inerpretation was an official function of the Chinese government as far back as the middle of the second millennium B.C. A text called the *Zhou li*, which describes the governmental structure of the Zhou dynasty (eleventh century to 221 B.C.), includes dream divination among the various bureaucratic positions of the ancient Chinese state and provides a table of organization for officers involved with divinatory practices. The text goes on to outline the duties of the Examiner of Dreams (*zhan meng*). Brennan says, "The Examiner of Dreams is charged with divining the good or ill fortune of the six types of dreams, taking into account the positions of the sun, moon, and stars, distinguishing between the yin and the yang, observing the conjunction of heaven and earth according to the seasons. The six types of dreams are given as: 1) Regular or restful dreams (*zheng meng*); 2) Startling or disturbing dreams (*e meng*); 3) Reflective dreams (*si meng*); 4) Daydreams (*wu meng*); 5) Happy dreams (*xi meng*); 6) Frightening dreams (*ju*

meng). This is the first typology of dreams encountered in Chinese literature. There is no correspondence between the type of dream and whether it is divined as auspicious or inauspicious. Startling or frightening dreams, though unsettling, can be favorable omens and happy or restful dreams may be unlucky.... The lack of linkage between the typology of dreams in the *Zhou li* and the divinatory significance of dreams strongly suggests that the basic meaning and cause of dreams is not to be found in the mental state of the dreamer, but in a broader, impersonal system of signification and causality such as that which underlies the *Book of Changes* [*I Ching*].[16]

15) An ancient Indian medical text attributed to Caraka presents this classification of dreams, as described by Wendy Doniger O'Flaherty in *Dreams, Illusion, and Other Realities*: Caraka's text "divides dreams into several categories: dreams that reflect what has been seen in waking life (*drsta*), dreams that reflect what has been heard in waking life (*sruta*), dreams that reflect what has been experienced (*anubhuta*), dreams that foretell the future (*bhavika*)... dreams that reflect the disturbance of a particular bodily humor (*dosaja*)... dreams that dramatize individual fantasies (i.e. things unseen), though perhaps based on memory data (*kalpita*); and dreams that are wish-fulfillments, gratifying desires that could not be gratified in the waking state (*prarthita*). These seven categories of Caraka thus cover waking experiences, somatic impulses, imagination, and the influence of the supernatural."[17]

16) The Jewish philosopher Philo (born c. 20 B.C.) wrote a three-part work, *On Dreams, That They Are God-Sent*, of which only the last two parts have survived. Philo introduces the final section by saying, "the first kind of dreams we saw to be those in which God originates the movement and invisibly suggests things obscure to us but patent to Himself: while the second kind consisted of dreams in which the [human] understanding moves in concert with the soul of the Universe and becomes filled with a divinely induced madness, which is permitted to foretell many coming events.... [The] third kind of dreams arises whenever the soul in sleep, setting itself in motion and agitation of its own accord, becomes frenzied, and with

the prescient power due to such inspiration foretells the future." Philo says that the first kind of dreams are perfectly clear, "of the nature of plain oracles"; the second kind are enigmatic, but "not in very high degree concealed from the quick-sighted," as in the case of Jacob's dream at Bethel of the heavenly ladder; and the third kind are more "obscure...owing to the deep and impenetrable nature of the riddle involved in them"; these require interpretation by men skilled in this science (e.g. Joseph, Daniel, etc.).[18]

17) In his *Oneirocritica*, Artemidorus begins by making some distinctions among the different types of dream experiences. He says there is a major distinction between *enhypnion* and *oneiros*. *Oneiros* indicates a future state of affairs, while *enhypnion* relates to a present state of affairs. Examples of the latter type, Artemidorus says, would be a lover dreaming of his beloved, a frightened man dreaming of what he fears, a hungry man dreaming of eating. Another major distinction is between allegorical dreams and theorematic dreams. Allegorical dreams signify one thing by means of something else; theorematic dreams are those that present themselves plainly and directly. Artemidorus says he does not speculate about whether dreams are sent by the gods or not; he uses the term "godsent dreams" in the customary sense by which we speak of anything that is unforeseen.[19]

18) In his *Treatise on the Soul*, the Christian theologian Tertullian categorizes dreams in this way: "We declare, then, that dreams are inflicted on us mainly by demons, although they sometimes turn out true and favorable to us. When, however, with the deliberate aim after evil, of which we have just spoken, they assume a flattering and captivating style, they show themselves proportionately vain, and deceitful, and obscure, and wanton, and impure. And no wonder that the images partake of the character of the realities. But from God...must all those visions be regarded as emanating, which may be compared to the actual grace of God, as being honest, holy, prophetic, inspired, instructive, inviting to virtue, the bountiful nature of which causes them to overflow even to the profane.... The third class of dreams will consist of those which the soul apparently creates for itself from an intense application

to special circumstances.... Those [dreams], moreover, which evidently proceed neither from God, nor from diabolical inspiration, nor from the soul, being beyond the reach as well of ordinary expectation, usual interpretation, or the possibility of being intelligibly related, will have to be ascribed in a separate category to what is purely and simply the ecstatic state and its peculiar conditions."[20]

19) *The Commentary on the Dream of Scipio*, by the fourth-century A.D. Roman writer Macrobius, presents a classification of dreams that has had a huge influence on western thinking about dreams. "Scipio's Dream" was originally the concluding section of Cicero's *Republic*, a work of political philosophy arguing that the Roman Republic represents the ideal state. The "dream" involves Scipio being led by his long-dead grandfather on a tour of the cosmos; by discovering the rewards and punishments given to departed souls, Scipio gains new motivation to lead an upright, law-abiding life. In his commentary on the dream, Macrobius begins by describing the various types of dreams recorded in classic literature. He says that dreams may be classified into five different categories: enigmatic dreams, prophetic visions, oracular dreams, nightmares, and apparitions. Macrobius says, "the last two, the nightmare and the apparition, are not worth interpreting since they have no prophetic significance. Nightmares may be caused by mental or physical distress, or anxiety about the future: the patient experiences in dreams vexations similar to those that disturb him during the day.... The apparition comes upon one in the moment between wakefulness and slumber, in the so-called 'first clouds of sleep.'... To this class belongs the incubus, which, according to popular belief, rushes upon people in sleep and presses them with a weight which they can feel.... We call a dream oracular in which a parent, or a pious or revered man, or a priest, or even a god clearly reveals what will or will not transpire, and what action to take or avoid. We call a dream a prophetic vision if it actually comes true.... By an enigmatic dream we mean one that conceals with strange shapes and veils with ambiguity the true meaning of the information being offered, and requires an interpretation for its understanding.... The dream which Scipio reports that he saw embraces the three reliable types mentioned above.... [T]he purpose of the dream is to teach

us that the souls of those who serve the state well are returned to the heavens after death and there enjoy everlasting blessedness."[21]

20) Alex Wayman's "Significance of Dreams in India and Tibet" describes several dream classification systems found in these cultures: "In the sixty-eighth *parisista* of the *Athara-Veda* [a sixth-century A.D. Hindu religious text] men are said to have the temperaments bilious (fiery), phlegmatic (watery), and sanguine (windy). Different dreams are attributed to such persons respectively: for the bilious, dreams, for example, of arid land and of burning objects; for the phlegmatic, dreams, for example, of nature in splendor and burgeoning life; for the sanguine, dreams, for example, of racing clouds and of forest creatures running in terror. In the *Questions of King Milinda* [a famous Buddhist text from the second century A.D.], there are said to be six men who dream: the foregoing three, 4) those under influence of a deity, 5) those who dream under influence of their experiences, and 6) those with prophetic dreams.... The Buddhist Mahayana text '*Meeting of the Father and Son*' (*Pitrputrasamagama*) gives dreams based on all six senses, the usual five plus the mind as the sixth sense; but here again the basic classification is threefold by the three 'poisons', lust (=attraction), hatred (=repulsion), and delusion (=incapacity), because the text gives a sample dream for each of the three in terms of each of the senses [making 18 different categories in all]."[22]

21) The Muslim philosopher Ibn Arabi (1164–1240 A.D.), who created a grand metaphysical system merging Islamic theology with Greek philosophy, argued that there are three basic types of dreams. As described by historian Rom Landau, "Ibn Arabi regards dreams as *khayal*, or mental images (imaginings) which represent something between the real and the phenomenal worlds.... It is during dreams that imagination is at its most active, producing ordinary dreams. According to Ibn Arabi, it is then that imagination gets hold of experiences of daily life, and presents them to the 'inward eye' (of the heart). In the inward eye, they are magnified as though in a mirror, and it is the subsequently distorted image of those experiences that fill our dreams. Usually these images become the foci or symbols of our

desires. There also exists a second type of dream, which Ibn Arabi regards as of far greater significance, the material for which comes not from our ordinary daytime experiences, but direct from the Universal Soul or, as Ibn Arabi sometimes calls it, the 'Guarded Table'. In such a dream man's (rational) soul perceives the archetypal ideas contained in the Universal Soul. But even in such dreams imagination gains possession of the received ideas, and distorts them. As a result, man's 'inward eye', while in direct contact with the Universal Soul, nevertheless does not act as a perfect mirror but as a 'running, yet undefiled, stream wherein are reflected illuminated objects of all descriptions'.... In consequence, these dreams, being symbolical, have to be interpreted.... There is, however, one type of dream that is not symbolical but a direct revelation of Reality. Imagination does not enter into it, and the 'inward eye' reproduces the exact reflection of the impression received.... They are the direct vision of Reality, of Universal Truth."[23]

22) *The Sefer Hasidim*, the work of thirteenth-century German Jewish pietists, distinguishes between different types of dreams: "In the prophetic dream the prophets' personal thoughts were not intermingled, nor were the words of the demon. In the dreams of ordinary people, however, the words of the demon are intermingled." The text goes on to say that if a man goes to sleep thinking about a woman, he will dream of "intimacies with a woman," and that if a man needs to "evacuate" he will dream of being weary. "All such dreams are not dreams told by the angel but come from one's thoughts, and in these one sees their symbol.... But a dream that comes through an angel, even though one did not imagine things or speak, before rising the angel comes to tell him; for his thoughts and sinful fancies had already ceased.... The angel turns the thoughts into thinking about those things that God decrees. It is certainly so when one sleeps and reason does not direct the mind: For it is said 'I will bless the Lord, who hath given me counsel; Yea, in the night seasons my reins instruct me [Ps. 16:7].'"[24]

23) In his fourteenth-century A.D. work *Muqaddimah* ("An Introduction to History") the Muslim scholar Ibn Khaldun

explained the different types of dreams in this way: "Real dream vision is an awareness on the part of the ratonal soul in its spiritual essence, of glimpses of the forms of events.... This happens to the soul [in the form of] glimpses through the agency of sleep, whereby it gains the knowledge of future events that it desires and regains the perceptions that belong to it. When this process is weak and indistinct, the soul applies to it allegory and imaginary pictures, in order to gain [the desired knowledge]. Such allegory, then, necessitates interpretation. When, on the other hand, this process is strong, it can dispense with allegory. Then, no interpretation is necessary, because the process is free from imaginary pictures.... One of the greatest hindrances [to this process] is the external senses. God, therefore, created man in such a way that the veil of the senses could be lifted through sleep, which is a natural function of man. When that veil is lifted, the soul is ready to learn the things it desires to know in the world of Truth. At times, it catches a glimpse of what it seeks.... Clear dream visions are from God. Allegorical dream visions, which call for interpretation, are from the angels. And 'confused dreams' are from Satan, because they are altogether futile, as Satan is the source of futility."[25]

24) In his book *Pitron Chalomot*, the sixteenth-century Jewish scholar Solomon Almoli reminds his readers that most dreams involve representations of the ordinary dreamer's thoughts and daily concerns. The interpreter of dreams has the responsibility of recognizing that "this type of dream is insignificant, as its source is not the Master of Dreams [the archangel Gabriel]; it is simply the product of one's imagination." Almoli says that the best way of distinguishing true from ·ıntrue dreams is "by the degree of excitement experienced by the dreamer. If one dreams of powerful fantasy images that cause him to be excited or to feel anger during the dream itself, this is a true dream; but if the images are insipid and arouse no strong feelings, the dream is not true. The reliability of any dream is thus in proportion to its level of excitement."[26]

25) The Islamic theologian Abdalghani an-Nabulusi (1641–1731) wrote an encyclopedic work on dream interpretation in which he provides an elaborate classification system.

Dreams can be divided into three basic categories: glad tidings from God (e.g. dreams cited in religious texts); dreams of warning from the devil; and dreams that originate from the dreamer's own self. Nabulusi says that dreams from the devil are false and require no interpretation. Examples of dreams that originate in the self are the person dreaming of being with a loved one, seeing something he is afraid of, or eating when he is hungry. Nabulusi goes on to divide false dreams into seven types: 1) dreams originating in desire and ambition; 2) sexual dreams, which require the dreamer to purify himself upon awakening; 3) warnings from the devil; 4) dreams shown by sorcerers; 5) dreams shown by Satan; 6) dreams that result from disturbances in the humors; and 7) "reversion" dreams, in which the dreamer sees himself as he was many years in the past. True dreams, Nabulusi says, are of five different types: 1) the trustworthy dream, which is a form of prophecy; 2) glad tidings from God; 3) dreams shown by the angel of dreams; 4) symbolic dreams, from spirits; and 5) the dream "that is valid for the viewer and exerts an overpowering influence upon him."[27]

If nothing else, this group of dream classification systems should put to rest forever the notion that people in non-western, pre-modern cultures are fundamentally *ignorant* about dreams— i.e. they cannot distinguish between "dreams" and "reality," they gullibly believe that all dreams come from the gods, and they do not understand how dreams are rooted in the mundane experiences of a person's daily life.[28] The historical and cross-cultural fact is that people have *always* distinguished between dreams that are more spiritually significant and dreams that are less spiritually significant. People from many, many different cultures have found a clear-eyed skepticism toward some dreams to be entirely compatible with a reverential appreciation of the deep religious value of other dreams.

Looking more carefully at the examples above, we find in a number of them a clear recognition of the rootedness of dreams in the dreamer's personal life. For instance, the Mohave acknowledge that some dreams "don't mean anything" (A1.9). Macrobius says that in most nightmares "the patient experiences in dreams vexations similar to those that disturb him during the day" (A1.19). Caraka's Indian medical text speaks of dreams stemming from what has been seen, heard, and experienced in waking life (A1.15) Nabulusi describes dreams that "originate in the aspirations of the self," as when a hungry man dreams of eating (A1.25). These examples, with their matter-of-fact awareness of the connection between dreams and recent waking life experiences, give us a new perspective on the twentieth-century dream theories of Sigmund Freud and Calvin Hall. Freud claims that every dream can be related to some incident or experience from the dreamer's recent past, and Hall's "continuity hypothesis" proposes that there is a close correspondence between people's dreams and their acts and thoughts in waking life.[29] In this regard, then, Freud's and Hall's theories simply reformulate a point that has been made countless times through history. The difference is that the non-western, pre-modern classification systems assert that while some dreams seem to be rooted in the experiences of our ordinary waking lives, other dreams seem to be rooted in powers and realities that *transcend* our personal existence. This is a notion that Freud, Hall, and many other modern dream researchers have difficulty accepting (although Freud does say, in one of the most cryptic footnotes in *The Interpretation of Dreams*, that "There is at least one spot in every dream at which it is unplumbable—a navel, as it were, that is its point of contact with the unknown"[30]).

We also find in many of these examples an awareness that dreams differ in terms of their clarity: some dreams are relatively straightforward in their images and meanings, while other dreams are more enigmatic. Artemidorus distinguishes between "theorematic" (or direct) and "allegorical" dreams (A1.17), although he does not explain why a dream takes one form or the other. Both Ibn Arabi (A1.21) and Philo (A1.16) account for the difference between clear and symbolic dreams by referring to the distorting effects of the human imagination: symbolic dreams occur because our limited human faculties can only imperfectly perceive the sacred, while clear dreams are revelations received directly and immediately from God. Ibn Khaldun (A1.23) claims that "confused dreams" are caused by the deceptive influences of Satan, and the *Sefer Hasidim* likewise accounts for murky, unintelligible dreams by referring to the malevolent activities of demons (A1.22).

Occasionally a false, deceptive dream is attributed not to evil spirits, but to the gods. The Islamic prophet Muhammed was sent a false dream by Allah so that he would lead his troops into a difficult but ultimately successful battle. Muhammed writes in the *Koran*, speaking of himself:

> 26) You were encamped on this side of the valley and the unbelievers on the farther side, with the caravan below. Had they offered battle, you would have surely declined; but Allah sought to accomplish what He had ordained, so that, by a miracle, he that was destined to perish might die, and he that was destined to live might survive. Allah hears all and knows all. Allah made them appear to you in a dream as a small band. Had He showed them to you as a great army, your courage would have failed you and discord would have triumphed in your ranks. But this Allah spared you. He knows your inmost thoughts.[31]

But not everyone is as fortunate as Muhammed, whose deceptive dream actually helped him. The second book of Homer's *Iliad* presents a dream sent by the almighty Zeus to Agammemnon specifically in order to trick the Greek warrior into a deadly trap on the battlefield:

> 27) Zeus "cried out to the dream and addressed him in winged words: 'Go forth, evil Dream, beside the swift ships of the Achaians [Greeks]. Make your way to the shelter of Atreus' son Agamemnon; speak to him in words exactly as I command you. Bid him arm the flowing-haired Achaians for battle in all haste; since now he might take the wide-wayed city of the Trojans....' So he spoke, and Dream listened to his word and descended...." After finding Agamemnon, who was sleeping in his tent with the other Greek troops, "Dream stood then beside his head in the likeness of Nestor, Neleus' son, whom Agamemnon honoured beyond all elders beside. In Nestor's likeness the divine Dream spoke to him: 'Son of wise Atreus breaker of horses, are you sleeping?... Listen quickly to what I say, since I am a messenger of Zeus, who far away cares much for you and is pitiful. Zeus bids you arm the flowing-haired Achaians for battle in all haste; since now you might take the wide-wayed city of the Trojans....' So he spoke and went away, and left Agamemnon there, believing things in his

heart that were not to be accomplished." When Agamemnon awakened, he reported the god-sent dream to his comrades; they believed it to be a favorable omen, and roused themselves to arms. But the ensuing battle brought not the victory Agamemnon thought his dream promised, but the bloody death of countless Greek warriors.[32]

Agamemnon's "evil dream" illustrates the dangers posed by all dreams: how to tell what exactly they mean. Throughout history, people have feared the consequences of misinterpreting their dreams. These fears have been widely expressed in myths, stories, and legends from around the world.[33] For example, when Gilgamesh has three horrible nightmares at Cedar Mountain, his friend Enkidu misinterprets them as omens of success in battle.[34] King Nebuchadnezzar, as we have already seen, completely misses the warning in his dream of the great human statue, misinterpreting it as a sign that he should *build* such a statue (4.11). Euripides' tragedy *Iphigenia in Tauris* opens with the heroine recounting a nightmare, which she mistakenly believes is an announcement of her brother Orestes' death.[35] An especially moving account of the anxiety people have felt over misinterpreting dreams comes in the Indian epic *The Ramayana*. The princess Sita is a captive in the castle of demon king Ravana; but when the monkey Hanuman, an ally of her husband prince Rama, sneaks into the castle and tells Sita that help is on the way, she is afraid to believe it. Sita says:

> 28) Today I have seen a grotesque dream, the dream of a monkey.... But this cannot be a dream, for I am so tortured by sorrow and misery that I cannot sleep.... I have been thinking constantly about nothing but Rama all day today, obsessed by the mental image of him alone, and that is why I have seen and heard these things. This is just wishful thinking—but nevertheless, I wonder about it, for this monkey speaks to me and has a clearly visible form.... What if you are a form of Ravana himself, the master of illusion, once more engaging in magic illusion to make me suffer?... I have been held captive for so long that I find great happiness in a dream. If I saw Rama and Laksmana [Rama's brother] even in a dream, I would not despair; even a dream can be exhilarating. But I don't think this can be a dream, for if you see a monkey in a dream it is an omen of nothing

good, but something good has happened to me. This could
be a delusion in my mind, or some disturbance caused by
indigestion, or madness, or a mental distortion, or a
mirage. But it is not madness or delusion, for I am in my
right mind, and I see both myself and this monkey.[36]

It would require another entire book to make an adequate
survey of the various strategies people in different cultures have
used to interpret the meanings of symbols in dreams. We can
note, however, that many of these strategies correspond closely
to the basic methods of dream interpretation used by contemporary psychotherapists—for example, relating the dream to the
dreamer's personal life context; looking for evidence of puns
and wordplay in the dream; trying "a contrario" interpretations
(i.e. interpreting a dream of death as meaning "new life");
connecting the dream to religious, philosophical, and/or
psychological beliefs in the dreamer's culture; viewing recurrent
dreams as bearers of especially important meanings; and
discussing dreams in group settings.

Looking at these different classification systems, we can
draw some very general conclusions regarding what humans
dream about. People dream about their daily experiences, their
bodies, their relations with other people, their fears and wishes,
their futures, and their relations with the sacred. We can also
conclude, again in a very general sense, that people have
historically distinguished between "ordinary" dreams and
"extraordinary" dreams—the former referring to the dreamer's
waking life experiences, and the latter bringing the dreamer into
contact with sacred powers and realities.

But I would be hesitant to draw conclusions about human
dreaming experience that are any more specific than this, at
least given the present state of our historical and cross-cultural
knowledge. In particular, I would caution against efforts to try
to reconcile the various dream classification systems we have
discussed, to try to devise a "system of dream systems." The
primary obstacle to such a tempting goal is that the different
dream classifications presented above answer to extremely
different questions, concerns, and interests. For example, some
of them distinguish dreams according to their meanings (e.g.
true vs. false, happy vs. fearful, clear vs. confused), some of

them distinguish dreams according to their causes (e.g. the gods, the soul, the body, demons, angels), and some of them distinguish dreams according to both meanings and causes. I find it hard to imagine how such different conceptual systems could be intelligibly, let alone usefully, reconciled.

Perhaps the best example of these difficulties regards one of the classification systems that seems clearest and most straightforward to us—the gate of horn vs. gate of ivory distinction that Penelope makes in book 19 of Homer's *Odyssey* (17.13). Most western readers have assumed that Penelope's distinction is merely a poetic way of saying that some dreams are true and others false. Horn is a relatively clear and transparent substance, while ivory is opaque; thus, true dreams can be said to pass through a "gate of horn" and false dreams through a "gate of ivory." But classicist Anne Amory argues that a closer reading of the passage reveals this common reading of the text to be mistaken. The distinction, Amory says, is not between true and false dreams, because the first lines of the passage ("Friend, many and many a dream is mere confusion, a cobweb of no consequence at all") indicate that virtually *all* dreams are confused and perplexing; Amory says: "Penelope means that dreams are bewildering things and hard to understand; confronted with them, the dreamer tends to feel helpless.... [A]t this point she is speaking of dreams in general, not just those which come through the gates of ivory."[37] So there is not a sharp contrast here between qualitatively different types of dreams; rather, there is a contrast between the different *effects* that dreams can have in waking life. According to Amory,

> Penelope is saying that the dreams which come through the gate of horn have power, or are effective, in reality. The previous contrasted phrase for the dreams which come through the ivory gate...will then mean that these dreams bring mere words, without any consequences in actuality.... In sum, Penelope's speech does not seem, upon careful examination, to lend any support to a thesis...that there are two radically different kinds of dreams. The impression given is rather that she is expressing metaphorically the common belief that some dreams predict the future and come true, while others merely seem to predict, but do not

come true in reality, although both kinds of dreams are hard to interpret.[38]

If it is this easy to misunderstand a dream classification system that appears so simple and familiar to us, we should be very cautious in trying to make broader generalizations about how people have distinguished different types of dreams through history.

Penelope (like Sita, another captive woman) knew that dreams often bear valuable and important revelations, but she also knew that they are terribly difficult to understand. It can be dangerous to ignore dreams, and yet dangerous to interpret them incorrectly. Penelope's fearful uncertainty illustrates what I believe is the deepest and most widespread feeling people have about dreams: *ambivalence*. A profound ambivalence lies at the heart of human experience with dreams. Some dreams bring us closer to the gods, to the divine, to the realm of the spirit; other dreams are trivial, insignificant, and/or false; still other dreams seem to mix potent revelations with vain self-deceptions. And no matter what, it is extremely difficult to interpret the true meaning of any one particular dream. This ambivalence cannot be relieved by sternly rejecting all dreams as worthless, nor by gullibly embracing all dreams as divine inspirations.

In this regard, it is worth remembering that Hermes is not only the messenger of the gods—he is also the great *trickster*; Hermes is a wily thief, a cunning liar, a sly seducer.[39] A true "hermeneutics of dreams," then, recognizes that dreams *reveal* as well as *deceive*. Our fate as mortals, it seems, is to struggle over the difference.

Appendix 2:
Dreams and Conceptions of the Soul, Reality, and Reason

*T*his appendix provides a survey of the many ways in which dreams have influenced human thinking about three different but related metaphysical concepts: the soul, reality, and reason.

The connection between dreams and beliefs about the soul has long been recognized by western scholars. But many researchers, following the work of anthropologist E.B. Tylor, have done little more with this connection than conclude that the dreaming experiences of primitive people were the *origins* of their notion of the soul. Primitives, in this view, explained their activities in dreams by devising the idea of a "soul" or "spirit double" that is able, when the physical body sleeps, to travel and interact other spiritual beings.[1] Tylor's theory may or may not be valid; it is notoriously difficult to justify claims about the "origins" of *any* phenomenon, let alone one as complex as the idea of the soul. But either way, we should not let the debate over Tylor's theory distract us from looking more closely at the rich and diverse *interplay* between people's dream experiences and their speculations about the soul.

> 1) The Mehinaku people of central Brazil begin narrations of their dreams with the phrase, "Far, far away my soul wandered last night," according to anthropologist Thomas Gregor. The Mehinaku theory of dreams depends on their particular concept of souls. The Mehinaku believe that each person has several souls, including the shadow soul, the sweat soul, and most importantly of all, the eye soul. This

182

soul can be seen in the reflection of the iris of the eye, and it serves two key functions. One is to travel to the village in the sky (*enu taku*, "sky place") when the person dies, and the other is to roam about while the person sleeps, in a dream. Gregor says that the Mehinaku have no explanation as to why the soul leaves the body, other than to say "'it has always been that way.'... Having no particular motives for leaving its host's body, [the soul] nonetheless takes to wandering about at night. Although the villagers are unclear as to the precise connection between the soul and the sleeping individual, somehow the soul's nightly expeditions are experienced as dreams. As the Mehinaku put it, dreams just 'come up' into a dreamer's awareness, 'like corn comes from the ground.'"[2]

2) In *Fortune Tellers and Philosophers*, historian Richard Smith tells of how people in Chinese culture have regarded the relationship between dreams and the soul: "A Chinese proverb states: 'Dreams come when the connection between body and soul (*xingshen*; lit. shape and spirit) is broken.' In Qing times [1644–1912 A.D.] virtually all Chinese believed that the human soul consisted of two parts: a *yang* component, identified with wood and known as hun; and a *yin* component, identified with metal and known as *po*. Dreams arose from the activity of one or both of these souls. Most people assumed that the *po* component could temporarily leave the body during periods of sleep or unconsciousness." Smith cites a text by Chen Shiyuan called *Mengzhan yizhi* (*An Easy Guide to Dream Divination*), in which dreams are said to reflect the wandering spirit's capacity to perceive the future and the stable spirit's ability to remember things. Chen Shiyuan says, "'The *hun* soul can know the future; the *po* soul is able to treasure experience. In the daytime a person's *hun* is connected with the eye, and at night the *po* lodges in the liver. Because of the *hun's* connection with the eye, sight is possible; and because the *po* resides in the liver, dreams are possible.'"[3]

3) The Mae Enga people of the Western Highlands of New Guinea account for dreams by saying that at birth each human being receives an individual spirit-double or breath from its ancestors. When the individual dies this spirit, which the Mae Enga differentiate from the person's passive

shade-double, is released and merges again with its ancestors. According to anthropologist M.J. Meggitt, "because the spirit is clean and the flesh is not, the link between these two elements which make up the individual is inherently unstable. They are always liable to a separation that may expose their owner to injury or death.... [The Mae Enga] believe also that a person's spirit may absent itself temporarily while he sleeps and his body is quiescent, and that at such times it may range abroad, visiting distant localities and meeting the spirits of the living and of the dead. In this way the people account for the occurrence of dreams.... [T]he Mae Enga do not regard the dream simply as a kind of 'thinking' or as a process going on 'inside' the individual, his heart, or his spirit. Rather the individual (or more accurately his spirit) is thought to be 'inside' the dream, behaving *in* a situation just as he does in waking life. That is to say, the dream is taken to be essentially a context of action, not simply its cognitive accompaniment or content. Nevertheless, people have no doubt that dream events also differ qualitatively from waking events."[4]

4) Anthropologist Barbara Tedlock compares the dream beliefs of the Quiche people of Guatemala and the Zuni people of New Mexico. She says that the Quiche have two major theories regarding the experience of dreaming. In one, the dreamer's luck or destiny (*uwach uk'ij* or *nawal*), what Tedlock labels the "free-soul," departs from the dreamer's body and travels about in the world, meeting the free-souls of other people and animals. In the other theory, the dreamer's body is visited by the gods or ancestors, who awaken the lightning-soul (*copoya*), which then compels the visitors to give the dreamer a message (*ubixic*). Tedlock says the Zuni theory holds that in dreaming a part of the dreamer's self journeys outside the body to various times and places. However, Zunis differ on what part of the dreamer they believe makes these journeys. Some Zunis say that the dreamer's mind or emotions leave the body and wander (*an tse'makwi allu'a*, "his or her thought/emotions are wandering") outside into the night. Other Zunis believe that the dreamer's breath wanders (*an pinanne allu'a*, "his or her wind or breath is wandering") out through the world. Tedlock says that "for a knowledgable Zuni, who has but one soul or essence known as the breath (*pinanne*), dreaming is a

more dangerous activity than for a Quiche, whose body always has its breath-soul (*uxlab*) present during the dream wanderings of the free-soul (*nawal* and *uwach uk'ij*)." Tedlock notes that underlying this contrast are linguistic differences—in the Quiche language the verb "to dream" (*wachic'aj*) is transitive, meaning that the individual while dreaming is believed to act upon or toward something, while in the Zuni language the verb "to dream" (*halowa*) is intransitive, suggesting that the experience of dreaming is a state of being.[5]

The experience of going to sleep, dreaming, and waking up is one of the few truly universal phenomena in human life, and it has throughout history raised provocative existential questions regarding personal identity, agency, and potential. *What happens when we dream?* What part of us is involved in our dream experiences? Where do dreams occur? What is the relationship between our "dreaming" selves and our "sleeping" selves? What is the nature of the beings we encounter in our dreams?

Just in the few examples above, we find a wide variety of different answers to these questions. This variety of answers should make us wary of translating non-western concepts with the Christian term "soul."[6] But, if we proceed cautiously, we may still make some interpretive comments regarding the views of dreams and the soul portrayed above. In each of the examples above, dreaming is conceived in a general sense as a *detachment* from the sleeping body of a non-physical aspect of the dreamer's self—the Chinese proverb about dreams coming when the connection between the body and soul is broken seems to express views held in all these cultures.[7] That non-physical aspect, which becomes detached from the body during sleep, seems to bear an essential quality of the dreamer's identity, one of the most important, powerful and enduring qualities of the dreamer's self. The different cultures may conceptualize this non-physical aspect in separate ways, but they all value it equally highly, as that which constitutes the spiritual or religious essence of human beings. And in each of the above examples, dreaming is considered to be the *wandering* of that non-physical aspect of the self; liberated from the body, it is free to roam, to range through time and space. We find no explanations in these examples of why the dreamer's "soul" journeys about like this, with no particular goals or purposes.[8] This is simply what happens when we dream: *our souls wander.*

So does this mean that dreaming is indeed the "origin" of the idea of the soul? It certainly appears that people's dream experiences have profoundly shaped and influenced their particular religious conceptions about the non-physical aspects of the self. Throughout history dreaming has provided *prima facie* evidence for the existence of the "soul"—people know from their own direct experiences that at night, while their physical bodies rest, some non-physical parts of themselves become active, sometimes *very* active, occasionally traveling to wonder-ous other-worldly realms and meeting powerful spiritual beings. To this extent, dreams have undoubtedly been a primary experiential source of the various conceptions of the "soul" that we find in cultures all over the world.

However, it is also clear that a person's dreaming experi-ences are shaped and influenced by his or her cultural context—including the given culture's views of the "soul." Tedlock's research provides an excellent window onto this process, for she demonstrates that Quiche and Zuni dream theories are "nested" within the religious, philosophical, and psychological systems of the two cultures.[9] Once again, we reach a point where dichotomous, reductionistic, cause-and-effect models fail to do justice to the diversity and complexity of human dream experience. Religious conceptions of the soul influence dream experiences *at the same time as* dream experiences shape those religious conceptions. There seems to be a lively interplay between experiences and conceptions, an interplay that cannot be dissected into causes and effects.

In addition to studying relations between dreams and ideas of the soul, western scholars have also devoted considerable attention to the reality of dreams. When the body sleeps and those non-physical aspects of the self wander about, does the dreamer have real experiences? Dreams certainly *feel* real. When we dream of being chased by a tiger, we wake up with our hearts pounding, even though the tiger isn't "really" there; when we dream of making love, we may experience an orgasm, even though our lover isn't "really" there. How do the seemingly real experiences of our dreams relate to reality of our waking lives?

Modern scholarship has concentrated almost exclusively on

using a culture's view of the reality of dreams as a measure of that culture's intellectual development: believing in the reality of dreams is a characteristic of primitive cultures, while realizing that dreams are in fact unreal is a hallmark of civilized cultures (like our own). But if we look more carefully at the ideas that various cultures have developed about the reality of dreaming, we will realize the great difficulty of trying to make such distinctions.

5) According to anthropologist William Merrill, "The Raramuri Indians of northern Mexico consider dreams to be the activities of a person's principal soul during sleep. They value dreams highly, for it is primarily through dreams that they communicate with their deities, diagnose illness, and acquire information about the future.... For the Raramuri, dreams are real events." Merrill says that people frequently described to him amazing personal experiences, neglecting to mention that the experiences took place in dreams until he asked them. However, the Raramuri do distinguish between waking and dreaming events: the main difference, Merrill says, is that the Raramuri believe that while dreaming people's souls move freely from their bodies, while in waking the soul and the body operate together. Dreaming is not, therefore, considered a loss of control or a failure of perception; rather, dreaming involves the free and independent activity of the person's principal soul.[10]

6) The benandanti were members of an agrarian cult that flourished among the peasantry of sixteenth and seventeenth century Europe. Historian Carlo Ginzburg describes in *The Night Battles* the persecutions that the Benandanti suffered at the hands of the Inquisitors, who suspected that these people were engaging in witchcraft and devil-worship (see 6.3). Ginzburg recounts the interrogation of a benandanti named Paolo Gasparutto. Gasparutto says he was called to join the benandanti in his sleep, and the Inquisitor asks how he could have answered, if he was asleep; Gasparutto explained, "'My spirit replied to him...and if by chance while we are out someone should come with a light and look for a long time at the body, the spirit would never re-enter it until there was no one left around to see it that night; and if the body, seeming to be dead, should be buried, the spirit would have to wander

around the world until the hour fixed for that body to die.'"
Ginzburg comments, "this departure of the spirit from the
body, which was left lifeless, was understood as an actual
separation, an event fraught with perils, almost like death....
The soul which left the body to go to the witches'
conventicles or to the jousts of the benandanti was
considered in both cases as something very real and
tangible, usually an animal.... Should the nocturnal
gatherings and the battles which [the benandanti]
described be understood as dreams and fantasies, or as real
events? There were no doubts on this score, as we have
seen, among the benandanti themselves: conventicles and
battles were very real, even if only their spirits
participated."[11]

7) The Jesuits began their missionary work with the Iroquois
people of North America in the seventeenth century, and
quickly discovered how "real" the Iroquois believe dreams to
be. A Jesuit named Father Fremin wrote, "the Iroquois have,
properly speaking, only a single Divinity—the dream. To it
they render their submission, and follow all its orders with
the utmost exactness. The Tsonnontouens [Seneca] are
more attached to this superstition than any of the others;
their Religion in this respect becomes even a matter of
scruple; whatever it be that they think they have done in
their dreams, they believe themselves absolutely obliged to
execute at the earliest moment.... [T]his people...would think
itself guilty of a great crime if it failed in its observance of a
single dream. The people think only of that, they talk about
nothing else, and all their cabins are filled with their
dreams. They spare no pains, no industry, to show their
attachment thereto, and their folly in this particular goes to
such an excess as would be hard to imagine. He who has
dreamed during the night that he was bathing, runs
immediately, as soon as he rises, all naked, to several cabins,
in each of which he has a kettleful of water thrown over his
body, however cold the weather may be. Another who has
dreamed that he was taken prisoner and burned alive, has
found himself bound and burned like a captive on the next
day, being persuaded that by thus satisfying his dream, this
fidelity will avert from him the pain and infamy of captivity
and death—which, according to what he has learned from his
Divinity, he is otherwise bound to suffer among his enemies.

Some have been known to go as far as Quebec, travelling a hundred and fifty leagues, for the sake of getting a dog, that they had dreamed of buying there...." Father Fremin went on to express his deep fear that the Iroquois might actually murder the Jesuits if one of the natives simply happened to dream of it.[12]

8) The collection of Hindu religious and philosophical texts known as the *Upanishads*, dating from the sixth century B.C., present a number of reflections on the relationship between reality and dreams. The texts describe four states of being: waking, dreaming, dreamless sleep, and the transcendent state of identity with Godhead. The Brihad-Aranyaka Upanishad contains this passage, specifically on the nature of dreams: "When one goes to sleep, he takes along the material (*matra*) of this all-containing world, himself tears it apart, himself builds it up, and dreams by his own brightness, by his own light. Then this person becomes self-illuminated. There are no chariots there, no spans, no roads. But he projects from himself chariots, spans, roads. There are no blisses there, no pleasures, no delights. But he projects from himself blisses, pleasures, delights.... For he is a creator. On this point there are the following verses: 'Striking down in sleep what is bodily, sleepless he looks down upon the sleeping [senses].... In the state of sleep going aloft and alow, a god, he makes many forms for himself—now, as it were, enjoying pleasures with women, now, as it were, laughing, and even beholding fearful sights." An earlier section in the Brihad-Aranyaka Upanishad describes sleep and dreaming in these terms: "As a spider might come out with his thread, as small sparks come forth from the fire, even so from this Soul come forth all vital energies (*prana*), all worlds, all gods, all beings. The mystic meaning (*upanishad*) thereof is 'the Real of the real (*satyasya satya*). Vital energies, verily, are the real. He is their Real."[13]

9) At the end of his article "The Visionary Dream in Islamic Spirituality," scholar of Islam Henri Corbin explains the "reality" of dream visions described by Muslim mystics like Ibn Arabi and Shamsoddin Lahiji. He says that these mystics developed the notion of a third world midway between the realm of our ordinary sense perceptions and

the realm of the rational intellect. They called this third world '*alam al-mithal*, a place of autonomous forms and images existing in a spiritual state. The physical senses and the intellect are incapable of apprehending '*alam al-mithal*; it can only be grasped by a kind of imaginative consciousness.[14]

10) The Makiritare people living in the Guyana highlands of Venezuela believe there is an invisible world that mirrors the tangible forms of the visible world. Anthropologist David Guss says the Makiritare view is that the primary means of passing between the two worlds is dreaming. Dreaming for the Makiritare is *adekato*, or "the voyage of the double." Each person is endowed at birth with an *akato*, or spirit double (from the word *aka*, "two") which is conceived in heaven. "When a person sleeps, his double, or *akato*, enjoys going out traveling. When the *akato* returns to the person, it reveals all the details of its adventures while outside. It is this revelation or retelling that is called *adekato* and forms the content of the dream.... The Makiritare conceive of the dream as an actual event experienced by their double or *akato*. This event is considered significant because of its occurrence in the invisible world of the spirits. Because of its importance, the Makiritare have incorporated it into their daily lives, subjecting their dreams to collective analysis and interpretation. The dreams therefore give the Makiritare a sense of power and defense in their everyday dealings with the world. The validation of the dreams and their importance also serves as an important spiritual reaffirmation of their belief system: to recognize the reality of the dream is to daily recognize the reality of the individual who stands in a temporal, vulnerable relation to the eternal powers of the invisible universe. To be aware of the dream is quite simply and literally to be aware of one's soul."[15]

11) The Fijian people living on the small island of Fuluga have the misfortune of believing both that dreams are *real* (based on the teachings of the native culture) and that dreams are *demonic* (thanks to the influences of Christian missionaries). As anthropologist Barbara Herr reports, the "Fijians believe in soul departure during dreams and hence believe that what they think and feel and do in dreams are

'real' experiences of the soul (*yalo*), encountering as it does in its nocturnal wanderings both the souls of other living persons (*yalo bula*), good and evil, and numerous other spirit entities *tevoro*). As ardent Methodists, however, they have also been taught and have attempted to embrace the notion that there is only one god (*kalou*), that all the ancestors and spirits they believed in before...are and were 'devils' (*tevoro*).... If one considers that the major means of combating fear aroused by nightmares in our [Western] society is, in lay terms, the reassurance that they are not *real*...the potential impact of such experiences in a context where they in fact *are* believed to be real experiences becomes more understandable. Fulagans tend to view their having dreams at all as succumbing to the enticement of the devil."[16]

These examples bring forth a number of interesting points about the relationship between dreams and reality. The Raramuri (A2.5) and the benandanti (A2.6) both believe that their dreaming experiences involve only their "souls" or "spirits," and not their bodies; both admit that their experiences do not occur in the ordinary physical world. Nevertheless both the Raramuri and the benandanti insist that their dreams *are real*—in other words, they do not define reality strictly in terms of our physical existence. Like many of the other people and cultures we have studied, the Raramuri and the benandanti understand perfectly well the significant differences between waking and dreaming experiences. They simply choose to conceptualize *both* kinds of experience as having qualities of "realness."

In the case of the Iroquois (A2.7), dreaming is taken as a legitimate source of motivation for waking life activities. The nervous Jesuit missionaries clearly believe that the Iroquois take their dreams far, far too seriously—the natives know no bounds in their obsessive efforts to re-enact their dreaming experiences in the waking world. This alleged worship of the "Dream Divinity" by the Iroquois is one of the most oft-cited examples in discussions of how non-western peoples fail to distinguish adequately between the fantasies of dreams and the reality of daily life. But as even the Jesuit missionaries recognized, the Iroquois were in fact remarkably competent in their dealings with the waking world, competent enough to feed, clothe, and defend themselves quite effectively. The Iroquois certainly did know how to distinguish an enemy warrior in a dream from an enemy warrior in waking life. But rather than radically separating the two phenomena and labeling the one "fantasy" and the other "real," the Iroquois perceived a strong and potentially positive relationship between their dreaming and their waking lives. To cultivate, enhance, and celebrate this relationship was evidently the goal of the Iroquois dream "worship."

The passages from the *Upanishads* give us yet another perspective on the multiple connections between dreams and reality. The Brihad-Aranyanka Upanishad portrays dreaming as a special realm of creativity, a realm in which the dreamer wields the same primal forces used by the gods to form the Cosmos. These are the "vital energies" that "*are* the *real*," that generate the ultimate reality of all life. As Wendy Doniger O'Flaherty notes, the same verb (*srj*) is used in this text and throughout Indian literature to describe dreaming, speaking, imagining, emitting a web (like a spider), emitting semen (like a man), and creating the universe (like a god).[17] Dreaming is real because in dreams we *create*, and the power to create is itself the ultimate basis of all reality.

The Muslim notion of '*alam al-mithal* (A2.10) differs from the *Upanishads'* teachings in that this intermediary realm is conceived as existing autonomously of the dreamer. The difference could be due to the fact that the Muslims are discussing visionary dreams, while the *Upanishads* are describing dreams in general; the difference might also reflect a difference between polytheistic and monotheistic religions. In either case, what is interesting from our perspective is the insistence that a true understanding of the "third world" of '*alam al-mithal* cannot be gained by the intellect or the physical senses alone; Muslim mystics argue that a kind of imaginative consciousness (as is found in certain visionary dreams) is required to perceive the reality of this spiritual realm. In this line of reasoning, the skeptical statement "dreams are unreal" could be translated as "our ordinary senses and faculties are unable to *perceive* the reality of dreams." The same essential argument was used by Albert Einstein to explain our difficulties in grasping the reality of the fourth dimension: Einstein asked people to imagine a *two*-dimensional realm, in which two-dimensional beings lived in an infinite plane; the ordinary faculties of such beings would simply be incapable of perceiving the reality of a *three-*dimensional world.[18]

The Makiritare (A2.10) and the Fijian people of Fuluga (A2.11) illustrate, in contrasting fashion, the effects of a culture's conception of the reality of dreams on individual members of the culture. The Makiritare people attach a remarkably high value to dreams, to dream-sharing, and to all efforts at expressing dreams in the waking world of the community. Dreams thereby serve to reaffirm the individual's identity and to strengthen his or her sense of belonging in the cosmos. As Guss comments, by validating the reality of *dreams* the Makiritare validate the reality of the *dreamer*. The Fijians of the island of Fuluga, on the other hand, live in a culture that has uneasily merged native and Christian views of dreams: the people believe that dreams are *real*, yet *demonic*. Not surprisingly, these people experience their dreams as deeply frightening events that are rarely discussed or expressed in any form. Caught in the midst of a struggle between native and colonial ideologies, the Fijians are left to curse, silently, the tormenting reality of their dreams.

By now it should be clear that 1) no culture or group of people has ever *failed utterly* to distinguish dreaming life from waking life and 2) we cannot divide "primitive" from "civilized" cultures based on their different understandings of the reality or unreality of dreams. The evidence is that most cultures have examined the characteristics of dreaming experience very carefully and have devoted serious, reasoned reflection to the question of how dreams relate to reality. We should not dismiss the conclusion of many cultures and traditions that dreams are real as the product of ignorance, superstition, or primitive thinking.

Underlying the modern debate over primitive and civilized beliefs about dreams are questions about the nature of reason, its development, and its value for human life and society. In western civilization, reason has long been regarded by philosophers as our most important faculty, that which distinguishes humans from animals and that which enables us to grasp the cosmos. To strive toward the further development of reason thus becomes a primary goal of life: to grow in rationality, to promote and expand our powers of logical thought, is a fundamental good in both individual and social existence. Many western philosophers have looked closely at the relationship between reason and dreams, and particularly at the relevance of dreaming to the cause of promoting human rationality. In the following four examples we see dreams characterized both as a threat to this cause and as an aid to it.

12) In Plato's *Republic*, Socrates and his pupils discuss the concept of justice, and analyze various forms of government according to how just or unjust they are.[19] In book nine Socrates describes the powerful desires hidden within every human soul, the desires "that are active during sleep." These "bestial and savage" desires run riot through our dreams, aggressively seeking satisfaction without regard to morality (see 5.13). Socrates says that a "well-governed soul" is one that "neither starves nor surfeits" these desires. The dreams of a well-governed soul can thus be genuine revelations of truth, because before going to sleep such a person soothes the desiring and spirited elements of the soul and rouses the reasoning element, the soul's best part: "In such a case you know that he [the well-governed soul] comes nearer to grasping the truth than at any other time, and the visions of his dreams are never unlawful." By contrast, a "tyrannical soul" is completely ruled by those violent desires: Socrates says, "let us sum up the worst of men.... He is surely the man who expresses in waking reality the character we attributed to a man in his dreams."[20]

13) Aristotle's short treatise *On Dreams* examines the causes of our dreaming experiences. Aristotle starts with the observation that when we sleep our faculties of sense-perception cease their normal operations; likewise, our intellectual faculties suspend their ordinary functions during sleep. So dreams do not arise from sense-perceptions or the intellect, what Aristotle believes are the only faculties by which we acquire knowledge. He claims that dreams are caused by echoes of emotionally-charged sense-perceptions from our daily lives: after the external objects we perceive have left the range of our senses, there are still impressions from that object within us, and those impressions themselves become new objects of perception.

· The problems begin, Aristotle says, when we fail to distinguish those internal impressions from the external objects—as occurs in dreams. Indeed, dreams are especially liable to mislead us because of the role played in them by the emotions: "we are easily deceived respecting the operations of sense-perception when we are excited by emotions, and different persons according to their different emotions; for example, the coward when excited by fear, the amorous person by amorous desire; so that, with but little resemblance to go upon, the former thinks he sees his foes approaching, the latter, that he sees the object of his desire; and the more deeply one is under the influence of the emotion, the less similarity is required to give rise to these illusory impressions...." Aristotle says these deceptive, emotionally-charged sense-perceptions make an even greater impact on us when we are asleep. This can be proven, he argues, if a person "attends to and tries to remember the affections we experience when sinking into slumber or when being awakened. He will sometimes, in the moment of awakening, surprise the images which present themselves to him in sleep, and find that they are really but movements lurking in the organs of sense. And indeed some very young persons, if it is dark, though looking with wide open eyes, see multitudes of phantom figures moving before them, so that they often cover up their heads in terror."[21]

14) *The Meditations Concerning First Philosophy* (1641) is René Descartes' most thorough presentation and defense of his philosophy. The goal of these meditations, Descartes says, is to "destroy" all his previous opinions and beliefs and to "start again from the very beginning," building his knowledge upon only those premises that are absolutely certain. In the first meditation he states that the deepest challenge to his project is the possibility that everything may be just a *dream*: "I must remember that I am a man, and that consequently I am accustomed to sleep and in my dreams to imagine the same things that lunatics imagine when awake, or sometimes things which are even less plausible. How many times has it occurred that the quiet of the night made me dream of my usual habits: that I was here, clothed in a dressing gown, and sitting by the fire, although I was in fact lying undressed in bed!... When I

consider these matters carefully, I realize so clearly that there are no conclusive indications by which waking life can be distinguished from sleep that I am quite astonished, and my bewilderment is such that it is almost able to convince me that I am sleeping...." Descartes decides that if he is to succeed in his quest for absolutely certain knowledge, he must somehow defeat the skeptical assumption that "a certain evil spirit...has bent all his efforts to deceiving me," and that all the seemingly real objects of the world "are nothing but illusions and dreams that he has used to trick my credulity." Descartes ultimately concludes that because God necessarily exists, and because God necessarily is not a deceiver, "everything which I conceive clearly and distinctly is necessarily true," whether or not he is dreaming—"even if I were asleep, all that appears evident to my mind is absolutely true." Thus, in the sixth and final meditation Descartes says he may now "reject all the doubts of these last few days as exaggerated and ridiculous, particularly that very general uncertainty about sleep, which I could not distinguish from waking life. For now I find in them a very notable difference, in that our memory can never bind and join our dreams together with the course of our lives, as it habitually joins together what happens to us when we are awake.... [W]hen I perceive objects in such a way that I distinctly recognize both the place from which they come and the place where they are, as well as the time when they appear to me; and when, without any hiatus, I can relate my perception of them with all the rest of my life, I am certain that I perceive them wakefully and not in sleep.... For, from the fact that God is not a deceiver, it necessarily follows that in this matter that I am not deceived."[22]

15) Friedrich Nietzsche's first book, *The Birth of Tragedy* (1872), is a study of tragedy, of Greek civilization, and of the relation of art to science. The basic theme of the book is the contrast in Greek culture between the Apollonian art of sculpture and the Dionysian art of music, and their "mystical union" in the art of tragedy. Nietzsche introduces these two powers in the first chapter by comparing them to "the separate art worlds of *dreams* and *intoxication*": he says we experience the "Apollonian" in contemplating the beautiful illusions of our dreams, and we experience the "Dionysian" in ecstatically losing ourselves in intoxicated revelries. Then,

some pages later, Nietzsche says this "dream analogy" reveals something important about art, and about philosophy: "Let us imagine the dreamer: in the midst of the illusion of the dream world and without disturbing it, he calls out to himself: 'It is a dream, I will dream on.' What must we infer? That he experiences a deep inner joy in dream contemplation; on the other hand, to be at all able to dream with this inner joy in contemplation, he must have completely lost sight of the waking reality and its ominous obtrusiveness.... Though it is certain that the two halves of our existence, the waking and the dreaming states, the former appeals to us as infinitely preferable, more important, excellent, and worthy of being lived, indeed, as that which alone is lived—yet in relation to that mysterious ground of our being of which we are the phenomena, I should, paradoxical as it may seem, maintain the very opposite estimate of the value of dreams. For the more clearly I perceive in nature those omnipotent art impulses, and in them an ardent longing for illusion, for redemption through illusion, the more I feel myself impelled to the metaphysical assumption that the truly existent primal unity, eternally suffering and contradictory, also needs the rapturous vision, the pleasurable illusion, for its continuous redemption.... If, for the moment, we do not consider the question of our own 'reality,' if we conceive of our empirical existence, and of that of the world in general, as a continuously manifested representation of the primal unity, we shall then have to look upon the dreams as a *mere appearance of mere appearance*, hence as a still higher appeasement of the primordial desire for mere appearance."[23]

These four philosophers are saying something much more interesting than "dreams are unreal."

Socrates' description of the terrible desires that run riot through our dreams reflects a view of dreams that differs sharply from the beliefs held in the cultures and traditions we discussed earlier. For Socrates, dreams do not involve the "wandering" of the soul through otherworldly realms; rather, dreaming occurs *within* the soul of the dreamer. In this, Socrates agrees with the earlier Greek philosopher Heraclitus (540–475 B.C.), who asserted that in dreams each individual retreats into a private world of his or her own creation. But for Socrates, the idea that dreams occur inside of the individual implies that dreams are capable of revealing elements of the soul that remain hidden during ordinary waking life. So in place of the "detachable soul" wandering through the cosmos, Socrates presents a vision of the "*deep* soul," a soul in which dark, anarchic desires lurk about, waiting impatiently for the opportunity sleep provides to rise up and seize control of the individual's dreaming experiences. For Socrates, dreams do involve the dreamer's soul and are real, but in this way: they demonstrate the reality of the most horrible urges and desires living within each of us. From this perspective, the Iroquois (18.8) could be considered the "worst people" in history, if we believe the Jesuit accounts of how the Iroquois zealously insisted on acting out their dreams in waking life.[24]

Dreams pose a threat to reason, in this passage from the *Republic*, in that they bring forth our most aggressive, violent, horrible desires—desires that have the power to overthrow reason entirely. Socrates says we have the examples of the "tyrannical man" and the "tyrannical state" to teach us the genuine danger we face from these desires. The "reasoning part" of ourselves must beware of allowing the bestial character that governs our dreams to control our behavior in waking life. But this is exactly why dreams may also be considered a valuable aid to reason: dreams teach us about our depths, our darkness, our soul's "worst" elements. In this regard, Socrates truly does anticipate Freud's claim that dreams are "the royal road to a knowledge of the unconscious."[25] To learn about our hidden depths strengthens us, opening the way to an integration of all our soul's elements, an integration which Socrates says characterizes the truly "just," "well-governed" soul. And Socrates claims that for the people who manage to approach that ideal condition of the soul, their reason-guided dreams enable them to "come nearer to grasping the truth than at any other time." Socrates evidently believes that dreams have the potential to reveal the good as well as the evil in human life, to enrich human reason as well as to menace it.

Aristotle's analysis in *On Dreams* focuses on the rootedness of dreams in human physiology—he concludes that dreams are caused by the mind's fanciful interpretation of residual sense-perceptions from the previous day's activities. Just as we imagine we see distinct shapes and figures in the passing clouds, so we imagine we meet people and travel to magical realms while leftover sense-perceptions pass through our sleeping minds. And, Aristotle says, the more our minds are clouded by strong emotions (e.g., fear, anger, "amorous desire"), the more likely we are to transform these residual sense-perceptions into fantastic, outlandish dream images. According to Aristotle's analysis, then, dreams are real in that they stem from real physiological processes; but they are definitely not real in the way believed by those "very young persons" cowering under their blankets, hiding from the phantoms of their nightmares. Just as Socrates seems to have prefigured Freudian dream theory, so Aristotle anticipates the basic thrust of modern sleep laboratory research. Dreams are fundamentally grounded in human physiology, they do not come from the gods, and they do not transmit symbolically encoded messages. The only difference is that Aristotle speaks of the "sense-perceptions" lingering from our external experiences, while sleep laboratory researchers speak of the "random neuronal firings" generated from within the brain.

So for Aristotle, dreams pose less of a *moral* threat than a *cognitive* threat: dreaming provides clear evidence of how emotions can confuse, mislead, and betray our reason. In dreams we see how a mind agitated by emotion becomes unable to grasp the true nature of that which is before it. Because dreams are so overflowing with emotions, Aristotle is quite skeptical about efforts to divine the possible meanings in dreams. But, recalling his examination of prophetic dreams (see chapter 10), Aristotle does not dismiss dreams as entirely worthless. His analysis indicates that if the dreamer's mind is able to recognize and account for the distorting influence of his or her emotions, then the dreamer may gain genuine and quite valuable knowledge—for while dreaming we sometimes discover in those residual sense-perceptions important features of the world, features that we had overlooked in the busy activity of our waking life. Aristotle compares dreams to forms reflected in a pool water. When the water is calm, the reflected forms can easily be perceived; but when the water is troubled (i.e. when the mind is agitated by the emotions), the reflection becomes distorted and unintelligible.[26] According to Aristotle, the trick to becoming a "skilful interpreter" is learning how to "rapidly discern, and at a glance comprehend, the scattered and distorted fragments of such forms, so as to perceive that one of them represents a man, or a horse, or anything whatever."[27] If we can develop this skill, which Aristotle defines as "the faculty of observing resemblances," we may truly enhance the power and scope of our rational minds.

For Descartes, the whole project of promoting the greater development of human reason must halt before this devilish gauntlet: What is the difference between our daily experiences of conscious rationality and our nightly experiences of unconscious irrationality? How can we tell them apart? Descartes' anxious concern is that we cannot trust any element of our knowledge if we cannot determine with certainty when we are awake and not dreaming. In the opening pages of the *Meditations*, dreaming is identified with deception and illusion; thus, whatever we believe we know while in a dream is the absolute antithesis of real, genuine knowledge. The "astonishing," "bewildering" experiences of our dreams stand directly in the way of reason's great quest for true knowledge.

Descartes' basic argument is that only that which we conceive with *clarity* and *distinctness* can be considered true and certain knowledge.[28] But once he lays out this argument, he admits that "clear and distinct" conceptions can be formed not only in waking life, but also *while we are dreaming*—"even if I were asleep, all that appears evident to my mind is absolutely true." So whether we are awake or dreaming, our knowledge is certain if our conceptions are "clear and distinct." Descartes insists that we rarely form such clear and distinct conceptions while we dream, a fact which enables us to determine with confidence when we are awake and when asleep. However, Descartes must confess that "because the exigencies of action frequently do not allow us the leisure to examine these things with sufficient care," most of us operate in our *waking* lives on the basis of conceptions that are neither clear nor distinct.[29] Thus, Descartes' original contrast between waking and dreaming collapses entirely: we may form true conceptions in our waking *and* our dreaming lives, and we may succumb to false conceptions while awake *and* while asleep.

Descartes wrote of his anxieties about distinguishing dreams from waking life at roughly the same time (the seventeenth century) as the inquisitors were suspiciously interrogating the benandanti about their "night battles" and as the Jesuit missionaries were worrying about the possibly murderous dreams of their Iroquois hosts. In all three cases, dreams are seen as posing a *threat*—to reason, to religious authority, to life itself. But in the *Meditations*, Descartes finally allows that it is possible, in rare circumstances, for dreams to provide us with genuine knowledge and may thus contribute to the further development of human reason. *Spiritual Dreaming* could, in this light, be considered a study of that possibility: many of the dream experiences described in this book have struck the dreamers with just the qualities that Descartes describes. These dreams have been felt to be intensely "clear and distinct" experiences, as clear and distinct as anything the dreamer has experienced in waking life. In fact, these dreams have compelled people to ask if there might be *other* levels, realms, and dimensions of reality beyond what human reason is able to perceive and conceptualize in ordinary waking life. Dreaming would thus be less of an anxiety-provoking threat to reason than a vision-expanding aid to reason.

While Descartes accepts such a possibility only grudgingly, Nietzsche celebrates it. Nietzsche has played the role in western philosophy of the great adversary of reason—ridiculing the vain pretensions of human rationality and praising the infinitely more powerful *irrational* forces that pulse through life. It comes as no surprise that Nietzsche would, in relation to philosophers like Socrates, Aristotle, and Descartes, "maintain the very opposite estimate of the value of dreams." But at least as I read him, Nietzsche does not reject reason; rather, he strives to deflate reason's overbearing pride in itself, to chastise it for its arrogant demand that all of life must submit to its control, and thereby to train it for its proper, limited role in the further development of the human spirit.

Nietzsche's particular interest in dreams stems from this broader philosophical project of humbling human reason. In dreams, he says, we combine *contemplation* with *self-forgetfulness*. At one level we stand before our dreaming experience at a distance, as an artist stands before his or her creation; but at another level we abandon our ordinary self-identity and become absorbed in the rich, sensual dreaming world. This oneiric integration mirrors the artistic integration Nietzsche admires so deeply, that between the Apollonian and the Dionysian in Greek tragedy. For Nietzsche, both art and dreams offer means not to a grasp of truth, but rather to an expression of "the truly existent primal unity," to "that mysterious ground of our being of which we are the phenomena."

From here the discussion could easily branch out in a dozen different directions, but hopefully the basic point has been made: that dream experience has provided a rich source of philosophical and theological reflection in almost all the world's religions, cultures, and traditions.

Appendix 3:
Methodological Issues

Any attempt to study spiritual dream experiences in various cultures and historical eras faces a number of serious methodological difficulties. What follows are my thoughts on how best to address and to overcome these difficulties.

Are These "Real" Dreams? The first methodological question is: How do we know when we are looking at a "real" dream? When we encounter a dream in a sacred text, in a myth, in a work of literature, in a biography, in an historical or ethnographic report, how do we know it is a "real" dream and not a fiction, not a deliberate creation of the dreamer's and/or the author's conscious mind?

The only honest answer is that we can't ever be sure. But we can, if we take some time to examine the matter closely, make some good guesses. We can draw upon psychological research on the regular, universal characteristics of human dream experience, and we can refer to historical, anthropological, and literary critical studies of the features that regularly characterize "fictional" dreams. With this material to guide us, we can offer some well-reasoned guesses about the "realness" of these dreams.[1]

But honesty is not the only policy we should follow here. We also need to ask a different question: What exactly *is* a "real" dream anyway? Is it *ever* possible, even in the best of circumstances, to get access to "real" dreams? Modern dream research is leading us toward the frustrating conclusion that it may *not* be possible. Written dream reports certainly do not give us access to the "real" dream, even when the reports are written by the

203

dreamer immediately upon awakening, because such reports are inevitably distorted by the structures of language and grammar and by people's variable abilities to communicate their experiences. Even the dreamer's own private memory of the dream does not give a reliable access to the "real" dream, because such memories are always distorted by time, by psychological resistances, and by the cognitive structures that govern memory.

It would seem, then, that the only thing that can count as the "real" dream is the immediate intrapsychic experience of the dreamer within sleep, the dream as it is being dreamed. But even *this* is not so clear. Freud notes in *The Interpretation of Dreams* that secondary revision, the dream-work mechanism by which dreams are subtly modified to fit more readily into the dreamer's pre-existing mental structures, occurs *within* the dreaming process itself.[2] In other words, it seems that even when we are in the very midst of dreaming our mind is actively shaping, altering, and influencing the experience.

We can add a final Alice-in-Wonderland twist to this issue. Many anthropologists have shown that the linguistic, sociological, and epistemological structures of the dreamer's culture are directly involved in the creation of the dream experience.[3] At times, cultural narratives and fictions about dreams are woven directly into people's dream experiences—so what is a "fictional" dream can in certain cases *become* a "real" dream (see chapter 8 for additional comments on this methodological issue).

I believe that the only reasonable conclusion to draw is this: there is no simple, clear-cut distinction between "real" and "fictional" dreams. It is more accurate and more helpful to posit a *continuum* between an individual's private, intrapsychic experiences during sleep ("real" dreams) and publicly reported, culturally elaborated accounts of such experiences ("fictional" dreams). *Spiritual Dreaming* includes reports of dreams from all across this continuum. I have tried not to ignore the many important differences between the various kinds of dream reports, but neither have I drawn arbitrary lines between what is "real" and what is "fictional." Even patently fabricated dreams, even those dreams that were obviously created by a writer to serve a literary function, have been included in this book—for again, "fictional" dreams can have powerful influences on "real" dreams. In this sense, it is important not only to learn *what* people have dreamed, but what they have *believed* that people have dreamed.

What Is a "Spiritual" Dream? Another methodological question that immediately presents itself is: What is going to count as a "spiritual" dream? As outlined in the first few pages of the introduction, I take a broad view of what constitutes a "spiritual" dream: spiritual dreams are those dreams that bring people experientially closer to the powers of the sacred and that speak meaningfully to people's ultimate existential concerns. What I have proposed is clearly a broad-ranging, widely-inclusive approach to the definition of spirituality. Critics may view this as a poorly disguised effort to avoid the important question of what is and is not a spiritual dream. My primary defense against this charge is provided by the dream reports gathered in the thirteen chapters and two appendices that precede this discussion of methodology. These dream reports are so remarkably diverse that I could devise no better theoretical model to use in organizing them than the one I have offered.

What Is the Difference Between a Dream and a Vision? As we look at this material, another important question emerges. How do we distinguish dreams from visions, trances, possessions, meditational states, out-of-body-experiences, hallucinations, and various other "altered states of consciousness"? If an experience is not explicitly categorized in the given text, how can we tell whether or not it is a dream?

As with the question of "real" vs. "fictional" dreams, the only honest answer is that in such cases we can't tell. Unfortunately for us, many non-western cultures are not very interested in sharply distinguishing dreams from visions and other kinds of extraordinary experience. And even when they *are* interested in making such distinctions, they may draw the lines in very different places from where we draw them. One culture might set a particular experience in their "vision" category, while we might define it as a dream, a psychotic episode, or a bad trip.[4]

Again, I have taken a very broad, very inclusive approach to the material. When a text explicitly states that an experience is a dream, I have accepted it as such. When a text is unclear about whether or not an experience is a dream, I have looked for other distinctive features of dreaming. One key characteristic is, of course, a night setting: to the extent that humans usually sleep, and dream, at night, extraordinary visionary experiences that occur at night stand a good chance of being dreams. Another distinctive characteristic is the person's physical position: if the person is lying down, in bed, or in some dark, enclosed place like a cave, and has an extraordinary visionary experience, there's a strong chance that it is a dream. Similarly, there are temporal characteristics that indicate an experience is likely a dream: e.g. if we are told that, right after the experience, morning came or the person woke up.

An inclusive approach seems to me to be essential if we are to learn anything *new* from the material. It is, I admit, a genuine danger that I have included in *Spiritual Dreaming* experiences that are not dreams. But I believe it would have been far worse if I had used criteria that were so cautious and condition-laden that I inadvertently excluded experiences that really *were* dreams. If we use excessively restrictive criteria, we risk missing precisely those dreams that are most unusual, that deviate the most from our conventional understandings, and that can therefore teach us something truly new about the varieties of spiritual dream experiences. It is much better, I believe, to cast a wide net and sort through our catch once we've hauled it on board, instead of using a smaller net that keeps out unwanted flotsam but that also prevents us from ever catching some of the most interesting fish.

How Can We Translate Dreams? It would seem that in a book like this, where we are looking at dreams from a wide variety of different cultures, we would face a major problem with the question of what gets *lost* when dreams are translated from one language to another. Many of the distinctive qualities of every language—the images, the metaphors, the multiple connotations, the subtle ambiguities, the intricate webs of reference—are irretrievably lost in any translation. Psychoanalyst Sandor Ferenczi has gone so far as to say that every tongue has its own dream language.[5] Erik Erikson demonstrated the considerable truth of this claim by showing how the first English translations of Freud's "specimen dream" failed to convey crucial meanings that were embedded in the original German version of the dream.[6]

But as with so many of the methodological problems that

face the study of dreams, this one can be (and often has been) greatly exaggerated. Yes, tremendous difficulties arise when we try to translate a dream from one language to another. But if we reflect carefully upon these difficulties, we realize that they are not restricted to this particular instance; we realize that in an important sense *every* dream poses these same difficulties of translation.

Take the case of an English-speaker trying to understand the dreams of another English-speaker—say that the dreamer is a teenage surfer from California, and the would-be interpreter is a classically-trained psychoanalyst from New York City. Here there is no formal translation from one language to another, as when we try to translate Freud's "Irma" dream from German into English. But does that mean that our analyst is free from the difficulties that plague formal translations? Hardly. The California surfer and the New York analyst will use a huge number of words, concepts, and grammatical structures in radically different ways (such as the word "radical"). The simple fact that they both speak the English language by no means guarantees that the analyst will have direct, trouble-free linguistic access to the surfer kid's dreams.

The problems do not end with the issue of language, however. Dreams are a complex synthesis of emotional, visual, auditory, and kinesthetic experience. Many contemporary psychotherapists argue that dreams are primarily *bodily* experiences, and that we utterly fail to understand dreams if we ignore these sensory-spatial aspects and focus only on the linguistic and cognitive aspects.[7] When we acknowledge that dreams regularly involve feeling tones, bodily sensations, and ineffable kinesthetic experiences which defy direct verbal expression, we realize that the translation problem goes far beyond mere language differences. We realize that every person's dreams are, in a sense, untranslatable; from this perspective, it is impossible *ever* to grasp someone else's dream, whether that person speaks our language or not.

With methodological problems such as this one, I believe it is helpful to push them and push them until they reach their absolute, logical, ridiculous extreme. That way we are forced to reflect on how we have framed the problem—have we posed it in such a way that a workable solution is impossible? I believe that in this case we have. Most discussions about the translation of dreams assume that the ultimate goal is to transfer the dream from one language to another and to restate it objectively, without any alterations in its original meaning. That goal, I would argue, is impossible to achieve—ever—in any case, no matter how perfect the conditions or how methodolgically rigorous the efforts. We need to admit, right at the outset, that our ability to understand the dreams of other people is *limited*. It may be more limited with the dreams of people from distant cultures, and less limited with the dreams of our neighbors, but it is always limited. We will always fail to grasp some meanings of another person's dreams, and we will always change, transform, and distort other meanings.

When we make this humbling admission, the problem suddenly looks much less imposing. Now we can concentrate our efforts on understanding as much of other persons' dreams as is possible, and as is helpful. We can do our best to learn about their language, their culture, and their distinctive means of expression. We can reflect continuously on our own subjective biases—at times our biases may limit our perceptions, and at other times they may actually improve our sensitivities. We should not delude ourselves into thinking that we have ever "objectively" grasped the "original" dream, but neither should we chastise ourselves excessively for failing to achieve that goal. In sum, we should measure our success by how much we are *able* to understand, instead of by how much we *fail* to understand.[8]

Other "Histories of Dreams." There have been seven major twentieth-century efforts at writing a "history of dreams": the first chapter of Freud's *The Interpretation of Dreams* (1900), J.S. Lincoln's *The Dream and Primitive Culture* (1935), Geza Roheim's *The Gates of the Dream* (1952), Norman MacKenzie's *Dreams and Dreaming* (1965), Morton Kelsey's *God, Dreams, and Revelation* (1978), Parts I and II of J. Allan Hobson's *The Dreaming Brain* (1988), and Robert Van de Castle's *The Dreaming Mind* (1994). Each of these works provides an interesting perspective on the great diversity of human dream experience and offers a thought-provoking interpretation of the various ways that people have tried to understand their dreams. I have found valuable material in all seven of these works. However, each of them has certain limitations and theoretical biases that render their approach to spiritual dreams unsatisfactory. If we look at how these works have treated, and mistreated, the subject of spiritual dreams we will gain some further insights on the methodological difficulties in this particular field of study.

Freud, of course, hated religion. He believed that religion was the product of an unfortunate fixation at, or regression to, an infantile stage of psychological development. Freud's study of dreams was part of his larger psychoanalytic project of promoting the kind of psychological maturity, characterized by rationality, independence, and a freedom from all "illusions," that would render religion unnecessary. His historical review in Chapter 1 of *The Interpretation of Dreams* gives an excellent survey of western efforts (particularly by nineteenth-century scientific researchers) to understand the causes and meanings of dreams. But Freud's work has obvious limitations in its capacity to promote our understanding of spiritual dreams.

The works of both Lincoln and Roheim come from those heady days of the mid-twentieth century when the combination of psychoanalysis and anthropology seemed to offer the key to all knowledge and understanding. Lincoln's and Roheim's books are unabashed attempts to demonstrate that the historical and anthropological material on dreams serves to prove the validity of psychoanalytic theory. Even worse than in Freud's work, Lincoln and Roheim invariably view reports of spiritually meaningful dreams as the infantile, neurotic delusions of pre-rational savages.

Mackenzie's friendly, polemics-free book is certainly a change from the plodding psychoanalytic reductionism of Lincoln and Roheim, but it is not much of an improvement in terms of giving us a better understanding of spiritual dreams. *Dreams and Dreaming* is written for a popular audience, and the dream material it presents is framed by the simplistic but extremely widespread popular belief that western history has, in its essence, been a process of the "progress" of modern science and the "decline" of religious superstition. As a result, MacKenzie's treatment of spiritually meaningful dreams through history is pleasant but condescending, polite but dismissive.

Morton Kelsey's *God, Dreams, and Revelation* is far and away the best single work on spiritual dreams through western history. Kelsey has done painstaking work in tracking down material on the role of dreams in early Christianity, and he has made a number of obscure ancient texts available to modern readers. But for all that, Kelsey's book suffers from two major limitations. The first is that he talks *only* about Christianity; there is a little information on dreams in Judaism and in Greek culture, and virtually nothing on dreams in any other religious tradition. The second is that Kelsey is frequently guilty of a kind of Jungian reductionism, which leads him into the same problems that plague Lincoln and Roheim. Just as they invariably claim that historical and anthropological dream reports validate Freudian theory, Kelsey invariably claims that the dream reports of Christian history validate Jungian theory. Kelsey is not openly hostile toward religion the way that Freud, Lincoln, and Roheim are; but his historical review is at times flawed by similar reductionistic tendencies.

The anti-religion polemics return with Hobson's *The Dreaming Brain*, although with a surprising and ironic twist. Hobson not only denounces the foolishness that has led people in the past to believe that dreams are religiously meaningful—he also attacks *Freud* for proposing an essentially "religious" theory of dreams! In Hobson's view, ancient priests and modern psychoanalysts both teach that dreams come from mysterious sources (gods, the unconscious), have strange, cryptic meanings (prophecies, symbols), and require experts to interpret them (priests, psychoanalysts). So at a stroke, Hobson sweeps away all religious views of dreams and all psychoanalytic views of dreams. In his view, neither of these approaches has anything significant to tell us about dreams. Hobson devotes the bulk of his historical review to surveying the discoveries of western scientific dream researchers in the nineteenth and twentieth centuries. As interesting and important as this review is, it offers little help to the study of spiritual dreams.

Of all these books, Van de Castle's *The Dreaming Mind* comes the closest to integrating successfully the historical material on dreams with the findings of modern dream psychology. But from our perspective, *The Dreaming Mind's* treatment of spiritual dreams lacks both cross-cultural breadth and theoretical sophistication. The material is simply dropped in the reader's lap, with little analysis or evaluation. Van de

Castle does offer good summaries of modern research on pre-cognitive dreams and on lucid dreams, and he presents a number of compelling anecdotes regarding the power of dreams to transform people's lives; but unless one shares his general assumption that dreams do have a spiritual dimension, the book is likely to generate only more skepticism.

A look at these seven works reveals that none of them offers a satisfactory review of specifically spiritual dreams in different cultures and historical eras. In fact, these books reveal additional methodological challenges facing any study of spiritual dreams. First, almost all of these books assume that spiritual dreams are not "really" spiritual but are "really" something else. The challenge, then, is to explore these types of dream experiences using languages and theoretical models that respect rather than explain away their spiritual dimensions. I have tried to meet this challenge by relying on the works of religion scholars Mircea Eliade and Rudolph Otto. Second, these books are seriously limited in the range of cross-cultural and historical material they cover. Here, the challenge is to draw upon the leading research from the fields of psychology, anthropology, history, philosophy, literary criticism, and religious studies. *Spiritual Dreaming* does draw upon research from many different disciplines, although I expect that as soon as the manuscript leaves my hands I will find new material that I wish I could have included in the book.

And third, these seven books tend to exaggerate either the *continuities* or the *discontinuities* in the historical material they review. Freud concludes at the end of Chapter 1 of *The Interpretation of Dreams* that virtually all previous dream theories are worthless; in the rest of his book Freud insists that he is presenting a radically new theory of dream interpretation, one that is essentially discontinuous with all such theories in the past. Lincoln agrees with Freud, and draws sharp contrasts between the pre-rational dream theories of "primitive" cultures and the enlightened dream theory of modern psychoanalysis. Similarly, MacKenzie and Hobson see a dramatic discontinuity between the "religious" dream theories of the past and the "scientific" dream theories of the present. Roheim, Kelsey, and Van de Castle, however, strongly emphasize the continuities in the kinds of dream experiences that people have had in the past and in the present. Roheim argues that the dreams of humans in every historical era are essentially the same; the manifest imagery may be different, but the latent wishes and conflicts are identical, whether the person is an Australian aborigine or a modern westerner. Kelsey also claims that there is a fundamental continuity between the dreams of people in past historical eras and the dreams of modern westerners, but he believes that the basis for this continuity is Jung's collective unconscious, not (as Roheim argues) Freud's Oedipus complex. Van de Castle's discussion of the "twilight zone" of dreams speaks of general dream capacities without addressing the cultural and historical factors that always influence people's spiritual dream experiences. The methodological challenge is to do justice to both the continuities and the discontinuities, to strike a fair balance between unique, particular elements and universal, cross-cultural themes. On this point all I can say is: I've tried.

These points of criticism are not meant to take away from the considerable value of these seven works. Rather, they are meant to clarify more sharply the methodological orientation of *Spiritual Dreaming*.

Notes

INTRODUCTION

1.Dawood 1973, pp. 328-329. This story is used, in a Jewish version ("The Rabbi from Cracow"), in Wendy Doniger O'Flaherty's *Other People's Myths* (1988, pp. 137-138). The story is also presented in a fifteenth-century English context in Robert Van de Castle's *The Dreaming Mind* (1994, pp. 21-22).

2. Otto 1958, p. 26.

3. Quoted in Lakoff 1987, p. 92.

1. THE DEAD

1. Quoted in Roheim 1952, pp. 73-74.

2. Degarrod 1990, p. 112.

3. Quoted in Harris 1963, p. 75.

4. Pauw 1975, pp. 157-158.

5. Meggitt 1962, pp. 222-223.

6. Quoted in Lai 1982, p. 31.

7. Daneel 1971, p. 99.

8. Homer 1951, Book 23, vv. 65-76, 94-104.

9. Malinowski 1987, p. 327.

10. Quoted in Lincoln 1935, p. 25.

11. Josephus 1987, p. 529.

12. Strathern 1989, pp. 304-305.

13. See also Shaw 1992, pp. 40-41, Watson and Watson-Franke 1977, p. 393, and Tuzin 1975, p. 565.

14. Ong 1985, pp. 18, 29.

15. Best 1898, p. 125.

16. Kilborne 1981b, p. 306.

17. Strathern 1989, p. 304.

18. See Freud 1965a.

19. Freud 1965a, pp. 547-548: "The preliminaries to this model dream were as follows. A father had been watching beside his child's sick-bed for days and nights on end. After the child had died, he went into the next room to lie down, but left the door open so that he could see from his bedroom into the room in which his child's body was laid out, with tall candles standing round it. An old man had been engaged to keep watch over it, and sat beside the body murmuring prayers. After a few hours' sleep, the father had a dream that *his child was standing beside his bed, caught him by the arm and whispered to him reproachfully, 'Father, don't you see I'm burning?'* He woke up, noticed a bright glare of light from the next room, hurried into it and found that the old watchman had dropped off to sleep and that the wrappings and one of the arms of his beloved child's dead body had been burned by a lighted candle that had fallen on them." Freud says that this dream fulfilled the father's wish that his child was still alive.

20. Freud 1965a, pp. 281-301.

21. See Jones 1951, Lincoln 1935, Roheim 1952, Devereux 1957 and 1969, Freeman 1967, LaBarre 1970, Crapanzano 1975, Kilborne 1981a and 1981b, Kracke 1979 and 1981.

22. Ong 1985, pp. 93-94.

23. Nashe 1965, pp. 146, 148.

2. SNAKES

1. Van de Castle 1994, pp. 304-310.

2. Park 1934, p. 101.

3. Padwick 1939, pp. 208-209.

4. King 1942, p. 232.

5. Oppenheim 1956, p. 251.

6. Dronke 1984, p. 2.

7. Eggan 1955, pp. 450-451.

8. Aeschylus, 1989, pp. 113-114.

9. Shaw 1992, p. 45.

10. Hosain 1932, p. 581.

11. Holy 1992, pp. 93-94.

12. Foster 1973, p. 111.

13. Driberg 1927, p. 142.

14. Artemidorus 1975, pp. 97, 213.

15. Achmet 1991, p. 237.

16. See Mundkur 1983 for a detailed examination of snake worship around the world.

17. See Eliade 1958, pp. 164-171.

18. Genesis 3:5.

19. Quoted in Mundkur 1983, pp. 263-264.

20. Except, of course, in order to reduce people's experiences of the sacred to psychoanalytic categories like "wish-fulfillment," "illusion," and the "cosmic narcissism."

21. Otto 1958, p. 31.

3. GODS

1. I once received a letter from neuroscientist J. Allan Hobson, author of *The Dreaming Brain* (1988), about an article I'd written suggesting that his scientific research actually supports the idea that dreams are spiritually meaningful (Bulkeley 1991). Hobson said he found my basic

argument "quite reasonable," but he could not help asking me this question: "Do you, sir, now think or believe that dreams are caused by angels?" For Hobson, and for many other people, an appreciation for the spiritual powers of dreaming seems to require a belief in gods, angels, and other supernatural beings.

2. Morris 1971, p. 107.

3. Quoted in Festugiere 1954, pp. 95-96.

4. Dentan and McClusky 1993, p. 505.

5. Severus 1949, pp. 106-107.

6. Gibbons 1984, pp. 40-41.

7. Bland 1856, p. 149.

8. Oppenheim 1956, p. 251.

9. Russell 1991, pp. 6-7.

10. Swedenborg 1986, p. 160.

11. Tanabe 1992, p. 174.

12. See Daneel 1974, p. 142, on how the "high" gods do not appear in the dreams of members of Shona Independent Churches.

13. See Eliade 1957 and 1958.

14. See the works of Sigmund Freud, Calvin Hall, and J. Allan Hobson, and my discussion in *The Wilderness of Dreams* (1994) of their views regarding the religious or spiritual dimensions of dreams.

15. See Moffitt, Kramer, and Hoffmann, 1993.

16. Kramer 1982, pp. 96-97.

17. Cartwright 1992, pp. 114-136.

18. French and Fromm 1964, p. 178.

19. Levin 1990, p. 38.

20. For a critique of the idea that dreams have a problem-solving function, see Blagrove 1992.

21. Genesis 15:7-15.

22. Genesis 28:10-17.

23. It is worth noting that these dreams portray Yahweh, who is much closer to the human realm than the later Elohim, who accelerates the movement toward the status of *Deus Otiosus*, in Eliade's terms.

24. Ultimately, we can't ever know that any dream report represents a "real" dream experience—in studying dreams we are *always* operating with a degree of uncertainty as to the "realness" of any given dream report. This is just as true with dreams from the Old Testament as with dreams from the sleep laboratory. The only way to minimize this uncertainty is do what I've just done, namely to compare particular dream reports with our general knowledge about dreams. In this regard, one of the primary goals of *Spiritual Dreaming* is to expand that knowledge, and thus to broaden our understanding of the range and diversity of human dreaming experience. Abram's and Jacob's dreams seem "unreal" when compared to dream reports gathered in sleep labs; but their dreams suddenly appear much more understandable, much more "real," when compared with cross-cultural and historical accounts of spiritual dreams. For further discussion of this issue, see Appendix 3.

25. See David Tracy's discussion of "classic" texts in *The Analogical Imagination* (1981).

4. NIGHTMARES

1. Morgan 1931, p. 390.

2. Job 1:1, 2:7, 7:11-15, 33:12-18.

3. Reay 1962, pp. 460-461.

4. Gardner and Maier 1984, pp. 67, 81-82.

5. Padwick 1939, p. 208.

6. Josephus 1987, p. 315.

7. Schneider and Sharp 1969, p. 105.

8. Eusebius 1953, pp. 344-345.

9. Degarrod 1990, p. 114.

10. Shastri 1985, Ayodhya Kanda, chap. 69.

11. Daniel 4.

12. Crapanzano 1975, p. 148.

13. Freeman 1967, p. 318.

14. Jedrej 1992, pp. 114, 112.

15. Job 42:5.

16. Hartmann 1984, pp. 5, 10.

17. The third possible type of distinct nightmare Hartmann mentions is the post-traumatic nightmare, which is a graphic repetition of a traumatic event suffered by the dreamer. See Hartmann 1984, chapters 8 and 9.

18. Kracke 1979, p. 133.

19. Hufford 1976, p. 74.

20. Foster 1973, p. 109.

21. Another relevant account comes from anthropologist Robert Brain's study (1970) of child-witches among the Bangwa people of Camaroon.

22. Jung 1964, p. 34.

23. Mack 1970, pp. 234-235, 233.

24. See Jane White Lewis, in press.

25. 1 Samuel 28:6, 15.

26. Gardner and Maier 1984, p. 196.

5. SEXUALITY

1. Freud 1965a, p. 215.

2. Freud 1965a, p. 194.

3. See Hall and Van de Castle 1966, Garfield 1988, Delaney 1994.

4. Some contemporary writers have found that sexual dreams may offer wonderfully positive experiences of spiritual change and growth. Jeremy Taylor writes in *Dream Work* that "dreams with pleasant, enjoyable, and rapturous sexual images are often associated with solving spiritual and moral problems" (1983, p. 151). Patricia Garfield's book *Pathway to Ecstasy* (1979) tells in great detail of her experiences of spiritual discovery through sexual dreams. The potentially positive spiritual impact of sexual dreams has certainly been borne out in my own dream experiences. But in my historical and cross-cultural research I have found few dream reports that correspond to what these contemporary writers describe.

5. Lorand 1957, p. 95.

6. Freeman 1967, p. 318.

7. O'Flaherty 1981, p. 292.

8. Jedrej 1992, pp. 46-47.

9. Zwemer 1916, pp. 366-367.

10. Eliade 1958, p. 208.

11. Reay 1962, p. 462.

12. Artemidorus 1975, p. 65.

13. Eliade 1964, p. 72.

14. Herr 1981, p. 343.

15. Crapanzano 1975, p. 147.

16. Freeman 1967, p. 336.

17. Augustine 1961, pp. 233-234. Augustine goes on to assert in *City of God* that "a Christian mind trusts in its God, places its hope in him, and relies on his help. It is true that insubordinate desires are still to be found in our mortal bodies, acting as it were by laws of their own without reference to the law of our will. Such disobedience of the body is not to be blamed when one is asleep, still less when there is no consent" (1971, p. 36). Sexual dreams have long been a concern in the Judeo-Christian religious tradition. More specifically, sexual dreams have been seen by this tradition as a danger, a threat to piety of the faithful. Priests, monks, and ascetics are thought to be in special

danger from such dreams. Flavius Josephus, a Jewish historian from the first century A.D., describes the dream of the high priest Matthias, in which he has intercourse with a woman; this dream deeply troubled Matthias, and rendered him impure for ritual activities. (Quoted in Josephus 1989.) The fifth-century A.D. Christian theologian John Cassian wrote a brief text on dreams and nocturnal emissions. Because nocturnal emissions were considered polluting, Cassian asked whether the sexual dreams that accompanied them would render a monk unfit to participate in the eucharist. Cassian concluded that if a person's life was blameless and righteous, then these polluting dreams must be sent by Satan and therefore do not reflect any moral stains in the dreamer (see Kelsey 1975, p. 141). Lest it be thought that these concerns only reflect pre-modern anxieties about sexuality, consider this passage from the chapter on dreams in the *Theological Dictionary of the New Testament*, published in 1967: in the dreams recorded in the New Testament there is "a complete exclusion of everything scabrous, vulgar, base, disgusting, sexual, unnatural or egocentric. The things which dominate the ordinary dream world of antiquity, the riotous superstition, curiosity, perversion...are all completely obliterated, swallowed up in the peace of God. God is at the centre." After noting that Christians continued to take interest in sexual dreams, the chapter concludes with this sentence: "Thus the muddy waters of antiquity, not without a misuse of holy things, nor without the guilt of the Church, debouch into the sink of new superstition" (pp. 236, 238).

18. Plato 1957, p. 336.

19. See Foucault 1980.

20. Eliade 1960, p. 144.

21. Bilu 1979.

22. Eliade 1960, p. 74.

23. Otto 1958, p. 19.

24. The example of "the venerable Liou" says nothing about her fertility or children, but it is significant that we hear the story from the perspective of her husband; his discovery of "a scaly dragon on top of his wife" emphasizes the social breach caused by Liou's dream.

25. See Cuddy and Belicki, in press.

26. Kramer and Sprenger, 1971, p. 134.

6. FLYING

1. Corbin 1966, pp. 396-397.

2. Roheim 1952, p. 143. Roheim comments, "This dream is his initiation dream as a medicine man.... It is quite evident that we have here the typical erection and flying dream with castration anxiety and the formation of a series of doubles." In *The Gates of the Dream* Roheim expands on Freud's claim that flying dreams are essentially sexual in nature. It is clear that flying dreams do have a sexual dimension to them, as many of the examples in this chapter indicate. But to repeat the argument I have been making throughout this book, there is no reason to assume that the sexual meanings of flying dreams or any other dreams are the "true" meanings. As we saw in the previous chapter, sexuality itself has a strong spiritual quality and can be a powerful means of relating to the sacred.

3. Ginzburg 1992, pp. 102-103.

4. Artemidorus 1975, p. 238.

5. Swedenborg 1986, pp. 126-127.

6. Strathern 1989, pp. 309-310. Strathern notes that "further dreams she has had reveal intertwining themes of religion and sexuality."

7. Ong 1985, p. 78.

8. Hallowell 1966, pp. 284-285.

9. Kroeber 1957, p. 207.

10. Tonkinson 1970, pp. 280-281.

11. I thank Pedro Sanchez for sharing this insight with me.

12. There is some evidence that the sensation of flying during dreams has roots in the physiology of REM sleep (and in particular in the phasic activation of the vestibular nuclei during REM sleep). In other words, the physiology of REM sleep appears to predispose us toward dreams that include the sensations of flying, floating, and rolling. However, this still tells us nothing about what such dreams mean. Just because we know, say, that the physiology of our vocal chords "predisposes" us to make certain sounds, that gives us no real insight into the meaning of a song, a poem, a speech, or a moan.

13. This may also help us understand a curious fact of cross-cultural dream research: the first "modern" image to appear in the dreams of non-western native peoples is the image of the airplane—something that flies but that is not entirely understood. See Lincoln 1935, Wallace 1947, Tonkinson 1970, and Schneider and Sharp 1969.

14. See Tylor 1889, Spencer 1882, Hallpike 1979.

15. Kaplan and Werner 1956, p. 867.

16. Eliade 1960, p. 122.

17. Duerr 1985, pp. 86-87. See also Hartmann 1984 on "boundaries" of the mind as an explanatory concept in nightmare research.

18. Mpier 1992, p. 105.

7. LUCIDITY

1. See Barrett 1991 on the relationship between flying dreams and lucid dreams.

2. See LaBerge 1985, Gackenbach 1989, Gackenbach and LaBerge 1988.

3. See Gillespie 1988, Kelzer 1987, Garfield 1974, Green 1968.

4. Gackenbach 1991, p. 123.

5. Guss 1980, p. 306.

6. Quoted in Rupprecht 1990, p. 121.

7. Ong 1985, pp. 62-63.

8. Quoted in Lincoln 1935, p. 304,

9. Lhalungpa 1985, p. 129.

10. Quoted in Coles 1992, pp. 35-37.

11. Castaneda 1993, pp. 19, 23-25.

12. Stewart 1969, pp. 162-163.

13. Augustine 1870, pp. 272-276.

14. See Gackenbach 1991 for a "typology" of lucidity.

15. Hobson and Lavie 1986, p. 232.

16. Domhoff 1985.

17. Doniger, in press.

18. The most infamous case of this kind of "popularizer vs. debunker" debate involves Margaret Mead's popular books on the people of Samoa and Derek Freeman's vigorous critique of Mead's anthropological methods and findings.

19. Norbu 1992, pp. 28-29.

20. This is a similar concluding note to the one struck by LaBerge in *Lucid Dreaming*. However, LaBerge and I seem to have very different understandings of what it means to be "more aware in our waking world" (see Bulkeley 1988, 1989, in press).

8. CREATIVITY

1. Geijbels 1978, p. 177.

2. Laufer 1931, pp. 212-213.

3. Oppenheim 1956, pp. 250, 202-203.

4. Graham 1991, p. 12.

5. Flannery and Chambers 1985, pp. 3, 6, 17.

6. Plato 1961, pp. 43-44.

7. Jedrej 1992, pp. 120, 121.

8. Harris 1963, pp. 51-52.

9. Stephen 1979, pp. 8-9.

10. Freud 1965a, pp. 384-5; see also p. 454.

11. Devereux 1957, pp. 1044.

12. Eggan 1955, p. 453; Graham 1991; Urban and Kent 1991, p. 21. In Eggan's article, "The Personal Use of Myth in Dreams," she looks at the relations between a Hopi man's dreams and the primary myths of

his culture. She argues that in her research "an interaction between mythology and dreams becomes apparent, for the dreamer not only uses myths modified by his own psychology in his dreams, but to the extent that he relates his dreams convincingly [to the others in his community], he introduces new emphases and directions into Hopi lore. In [this man's] village, for instance, we have noted a gradually increasing interest in the possibility of a more active personal guide than the rather vague [spirit guide] whom they discussed with us a decade ago. The name remains the same, but in this village the spirit has become somewhat more real" (p. 453).

13. For similar arguments see Lanternari 1975, Charsley 1973 and 1987, Bourgignon 1954, Wallace 1958.

14. I draw this notion in part from Winnicott's discussion (1971) of transitional space.

15. Tonkinson 1970, pp. 283-284.

16. Dilley 1992, pp. 77, 78, 80.

17. Blau 1963, pp. 233, 236-237, 239, 242, 245. Blau notes with some amazement that the Dream Guessing Rite has been practiced in the same basic form for more than three hundred and fifty years, indicating the great value it seems to have among the people performing it.

18. These three examples demonstrate the folly of trying to draw sharp, absolute distinctions between what comes from the individual dreamer and what comes from the dreamer's culture. The dreams of the people of Jigalong, the Mabube weavers, and the Iroquois are all thoroughly shaped by their cultural settings; and yet their dreams also include distinctive, idiosyncratic, "creative" features. Anthropologists like Roy D'Andrade (1961, 298) and J.S. Lincoln (1935, 76) have worried over the difficulty of proving whether a particular creative expression really came from a dream, or whether the creative expression was only "confirmed" by the dream. This is the dream studies field's rendition of the chicken and egg routine.

19. This raises some interesting questions regarding the place of dreams in modern western culture. The best evidence available from dream researchers indicates that dreams are inevitably influenced by the dreamer's culture—by the language, customs, religious beliefs, educational programs, family structures, etc. The evidence we have considered in this chapter suggests that such cultural influences may,

in the right circumstances, have relatively positive effects on the dreamer and on the community. The questions, then, are these: 1) What are the specific influences wielded by modern western culture on the dreams of its members? 2) Could we characterize these influences as relatively positive or negative? 3) Are there any reforms we could institute—say, in the realm of early child education—to enhance the positive influences?

9. HEALING

1. Jung 1966, pp. 142-143.

2. Kakar 1982, pp. 47, 46, 50, 43.

3. Centlivres, Centlivres, and Slobin 1971, pp. 161, 164.

4. Reynolds 1992, pp. 22, 25, 31.

5. Young 1983, pp. 213-214.

6. Norbu 1992, p. 38.

7. Harrington 1908, pp. 326, 335.

8. Ong 1985, p. 50.

9. Handy 1936, pp. 121-122.

10. Daneel 1974, p. 147.

11. Aristides 1981, pp. 306, 307, 311, 305.

12. Frank 1973, p. 66.

13. Another excellent source for information on spiritual healing methods, and on the prominent role of dreams in such methods, is Ari Kiev's *Magic, Faith, and Healing* (1964).

10. PROPHECY

1. In current dream research, the technical term used to refer to this phenomenon is "precognitive dreaming."

2. Konje 1985.

3. Evans-Pritchard 1937, pp. 174-175, 230.

4. Smith 1991, p. 246.

5. Kracke 1987, p. 33; 1979, p. 130.

6. Sperling and Simon 1949, Gen., Vayashev 183b. This passage may qualify the argument I make in the conclusion that social and cultural forces in the twentieth-century west may be diminishing people's capacities to experience spiritual dreams. The passage here suggests that a view of the past as a time of spiritually richer dreaming (also related, perhaps, to the Australian Aboriginal notion of "dreamtime") may express a nostalgia for the mythically pristine past—Eliade's *in illo tempore* (1957, 1958, 1960). See also O'Flaherty 1988.

7. Reid 1986, p. 7.

8. Quoted in Sharma and Siegel 1980, pp. 6-7. Sharma and Siegel describe how the mothers of Jainist religious leaders are believed to have fourteen specific symbolic dreams before the birth of their sons.

9. Cicero 1876, p. 168.

10. Matthew 1:18-22, 24-25. See Gnuse 1990.

11. Augustine 1961, pp. 68-69.

12. Quoted in Lincoln 1935, p. 86.

13. 2 Macc. 15:11-18.

14. Ong 1985, pp. 15-16.

15. Firth 1934, p. 68.

16. Miller 1994, p. 236.

17. Plato 1956, p. 52.

18. There has been a great deal of modern research done on the subject of dreams and pregnancy, indicating that pregnant women, and expectant fathers, experience unusually vivid dreams. See Maybruck 1989, Garfield 1988, and Siegel 1990.

19. One of the biographers of General George Patton, the military leader of Allied forces in World War II, gives extensive accounts of Patton's reliance on intuitions gleaned from his sleep for plotting battle strategies. See Kelsey 1974, pp. 119-120.

20. Williams 1936.

21. Williams 1936, p. 33. The passage goes on: "The habit of regarding dreams as prophetic is so widespread throughout the world, and so ancient, that it would be ridiculous to guess any time, place or manner for its origin. Incidentally I think it would be equally ridiculous to assume that the habit had a single origin. I suggest, on the contrary, that it may be born and reborn, again and again, wherever and whenever a striking dream is followed by some striking event which serves to recall it. The habit is based on the fallacy of post hoc ergo propter hoc, and this fallacy is universal, prior to, and independent of all dissemination of culture."

22. Herr 1981 makes similar argument, p. 334.

23. Jung 1974, p. 41; the passage goes on: "Its symbolic content sometimes outlines the solution of a conflict, excellent examples of this being given in Maeder. The occurrence of prospective dreams cannot be denied. It would be wrong to call them prophetic, because at bottom they are no more prophetic than a medical diagnosis or a weather forecast. They are merely an anticipatory combination of probabilities which may coincide with the actual behavior of things but need not necessarily agree in every detail. Only in the latter case can we speak of 'prophecy.' That the prospective function of dreams is sometimes greatly superior to the combinations we can consciously foresee is not surprising, since a dream results from the fusion of subliminal elements and is thus a combination of all the perceptions, thoughts, and feelings which consciousness has not registered because of their feeble accentuation. In addition, dreams can rely on subliminal memory traces that are no longer able to influence consciousness effectively. With regard to prognosis, therefore, dreams are often in a much more favorable position than consciousness."

24. French and Fromm 1964.

25. Cartwright and Lamberg 1992, p. 269.

26. Dickens 1980.

27. Aristotle 1941b.

28. Aristotle explains these terms as follows: "I use the word 'cause' in the sense in which the moon is [the cause] of an eclipse of the sun, or in which fatigue is [a cause] of fever; 'token' [in the sense in which] the entrance of a star [into the shadow] is a token of the eclipse, or [in

which] roughness of the tongue [is a token] of fever; while by 'coincidence' I mean, for example, the occurrence of an eclipse of the sun while some one is taking a walk; for the walking is neither a token nor a cause of the eclipse, nor the eclipse [a cause or token] of the walking. For this reason no coincidence takes place according to a universal or general rule" (p. 626).

29. Aristotle 1941b, p. 626.

30. Cartwright and Lamberg 1992 give extensive research data on the occurrence of such dreams, 156-179.

31. Aristotle 1941b, p. 627; he goes on to give a more detailed account of how in dreams we are able to perceive these "movements" and "beginnings" in ways that exceed our conscious, waking abilities. In this his views anticipate those of Jung, outlined earlier in this chapter.

32. Aristotle 1941b, p. 627.

33. Aristotle 1941b, p. 626.

34. Aristotle does grant that friends are especially likely to dream "prophetically" of each other, because they are so familiar with the other person's appearance and movements.

11. RITUALS

1. See Delaney 1979 and 1991, Taylor 1983 and 1992, Garfield 1974, Faraday 1972 and 1974, Reed 1985, Siegel 1990. There are also a number of excellent academic studies of dream incubation practices from historical and psychological perspectives: see Edelstein and Edelstein 1975, Jayne 1925, Meier 1967, Oppenheim 1956, Dodds 1951.

2. Meier 1992, pp. 106-107.

3. Herodotus 1990, p. 79.

4. Briggs and Briggs 1991, p. 13.

5. Trimingham 1959, p. 123.

6. Laufer 1931, pp. 211-212.

7. Ong 1985, pp. 42-43.

8. Brown 1987, pp. 163, 159.

9. Covitz 1990, pp. 135, 139.

10. Meier 1967, pp. 314-315.

11. Achmet 1991, pp. 52-53.

12. Park 1934, pp. 102-103.

13. Trompf 1990, p. 111. Trompf goes on to say, "perhaps here we have the nearest thing to the Senoi 'clinic,' the onus being on all those involved to contribute to a consensus interpretation."

14. Artemidorus 1975, p. 188.

15. Isaiah 65:4.

16. Quoted in Kelsey 1974, p. 137.

17. Quoted in Kelsey 1974, p. 264.

18. In the light of these theological and political concerns, we gain some new insights into the "unintentional" dream incubations we find in the Old Testament. The great dream theophanies experienced by Abram (3.12) and Jacob (3.13) have many elements of incubated dreams. Both of them are deeply troubled by anxieties about the future safety of themselves and their people; Abram performs a sacrifice before a "deep sleep" falls upon him, and Jacob sleeps in the wilderness, far from his family; both of them receive dreams from God in which their prosperous futures are revealed to them. However, in both cases the initiative for the dream revelation clearly lies with God; Abram and Jacob do not expect God to appear in their dreams. The dream experience of Samuel is even more explicit in emphasizing how "unintentional" and unexpected the dream was: "Now the boy Samuel was ministering to the Lord under Eli. And the word of the Lord was rare in those days; there was no frequent vision. At that time Eli, whose eyesight had begun to grow dim, so that he could not see, was lying down in his own place; the lamp of God had not yet gone out, and Samuel was lying down within the temple of the Lord, where the ark of God was. Then the Lord called, 'Samuel! Samuel!' and he said, 'Here I am!' and ran to Eli, and said, 'Here I am, for you called me.' But he said, 'I did not call; lie down again.' So he went and lay down.... [After this happened two more times] Eli perceived that the Lord was calling the boy. Therefore Eli said to Samuel, 'Go, lie down; and if he

calls you, you shall say, "Speak, Lord, for thy servant hears."' So Samuel went and lay down in his place. And the Lord came and stood forth, calling as at other times, 'Samuel! Samuel!' And Samuel said, 'Speak, for thy servant hears.' Then the Lord said to Samuel, 'Behold, I am about to do a thing in Israel, at which the two ears of every one that hears it will tingle....' Samuel lay until morning; then he opened the doors of the house of the Lord." Samuel is sleeping in the temple of the Lord, right next to the ark of the covenant, the most sacred object of the Hebrew people. It is hard to believe anyone living in the ancient Near East, where dream incubation practices flourished, would not expect that a revelatory dream might come in such a setting. But even after Samuel is called by name three different times, he still must be informed by Eli that the Lord is beckoning him. The theological and political message is clear: good, righteous Jews do not, and should not, practice dream incubation.

12. INITIATION

1. Van Gennep 1960. It is important to note that Van Gennep's, while the most influential theoretical model for understanding rites of initiation, is not the only such model Bruce Lincoln, in *Emerging from the Chrysalis*, has studied various female initiation rituals, and argues that there is a different underlying structure to them—instead of Van Gennep's three stages of separation, transition, and incorporation, Lincoln sees in the initiations of women the three stages of *enclosure*, *metamorphosis* or *magnification*, and *emergence*. Although space constraints prevent me from doing more than noting Lincoln's work, I believe that his model could help to illuminate many interesting features of these dreams that Van Gennep's model obscures or overlooks.

2. Radin 1936, pp. 239-240.

3. Herdt 1977, pp. 155-156.

4. Corbin 1966, pp. 402-403.

5. Apuleius 1960, pp. 238-239.

6. Shaw 1992, p. 48.

7. Pobee 1986, pp. 124-125.

8. Toffelmier and Luomala 1936, pp. 214-217.

9. Kelsey 1974, p. 126.

10. Eliade 1964, pp. 13-14, 33, 36, 38, 103.

11. Ewing 1989, pp. 59, 62.

12. Often, people want to avoid initiatory dreams, precisely because the experience can be so frightening and horrible (as is frequently the case with any encounter with the sacred). See Urban 1991, p. 4; Park 1934, p. 99; Ginzberg 1992, pp. 39, 70; Ray 1992, p. 69; Reynolds 1992, pp. 25-28.

13. The seventeenth-century philosopher Benedict de Spinoza seems to have experienced a kind of "anti-initiatory" dream, a dream that related to his being excommunicated by the Jewish community of Amsterdam for his heretical philosophical views. This is the dream, which he described in a letter to a friend: "When I awoke one morning, when the sky was already growing light, from a very heavy dream, the images which had come to me in my dream remained as vividly before my eyes as if they had been real things, especially the image of a certain black and scabby Brazilian whom I had never seen before. This image for the most part disappeared when, in order to divert myself with something else, I fixed my eyes on a book or some other object: but as soon as I again turned my eyes away from such an object and fixed them on something inattentively, the image of the same Ethiopian again appeared with the same vividness, and that again and again until it gradually disappeared from my presence." Lewis Feuer, in an article on this dream and its relation to Spinoza's life and philosophy (1957), argues that the "black and scabby Brazilian" was "Henrique Diaz, negro commander of the slave insurrectionists" who had revolted against the Dutch colonists, inflicting particular violence upon the Brazilian Jewish community.

14. The same basic point is made, but from a very different theoretical perspective, by Robin Fox in his article "The Passionate Mind: Brain, Dreams, Memory, and Social Categories" (1986). Fox draws on neuroscientific studies of the role of REM sleep in the creation of long-term memory to argue that the social function of initiation rites, i.e. the education of initiates in a society's basic cognitive categories, is strongly aided by the emotionally-charged nature of our dreams. Fox says, "very often societies use a particular process we commonly call 'initiation' to 'educate' young people in the more explicit social categories of the group. While initiations serve many functions, this educative element with its often graphic and traumatic teaching mechanisms is obviously important; and it may represent one way in which the social wisdom is transmitted by evoking dramatic images and

instilling them by repetition and often quite frightening rituals. The dreams and nightmares thus produced, often over a period of years, will do their work of lodging the social categories pretty well... [Social] categories are 'good to think' because they are 'good to remember,' and they are good to remember because the emotional brain has been able to represent them in REM sleep—to dream them into memory" (40-41). Fox's argument points in the same direction that mine does: toward a recognition of the power of dream experiences to transform a person's way of looking at and being in the world.

15. See Bulkeley 1994c.

13. CONVERSION

1. See Lincoln 1935, Osborne 1970, and Lanternari 1975.

2. Kelsey 1974, pp. 116-117.

3. Rambo 1993, p. 3.

4. Kelsey 1974, p. 117.

5. Peel 1968, p. 207.

6. Kelsey 1974, pp. 136-137.

7. Osborne 1970, pp. 11, 12, 14.

8. Curley 1983, pp. 27-28.

9. Lanternari 1975, pp. 226-227.

10. M'Timkulu 1977, pp. 24, 25, 28.

11. Fisher 1979, pp. 232, 233-234.

12. Davis 1980, pp. 3-5.

13. Trafzer and Beach 1985, p. 312.

14. Wallace 1969, pp. 240-242.

15. Rambo 1993, p. 160.

16. These examples, taken as a group, seem to conflict with another of Rambo's main themes, that conversion experiences are much more gradual than is commonly thought. The dream examples in this

chapter appear to be evidence for the more popular image of conversions as relatively sudden, unexpected experiences (with Saul's experience on the road to Damascus being the prototypical example). But my understanding of Rambo's argument is that conversions involve many stages of transformation and that converts move through these stages at different speeds. Thus, the dreamers presented in this chapter may be people who are moving through certain stages of the conversion process at a relatively rapid rate.

17. Koulack 1991, p. 190.

18. Siegel 1990, p. 185.

19. Obeyesekere 1981, pp. 180-182.

CONCLUSION

1. Allen 1989, p. 7.

2. Ibn Khaldun 1967, p. 83.

3. Wallace 1947, p. 254.

4. Covitz 1990, p. 32.

5. Norbu 1992, pp. 92-93.

6. Fitzgerald 1930, pp. 341-342.

7. Although physical ordeals, special techniques, etc. can add new qualities to spiritual dream experiences.

8. See Kracke 1981, Guss 1980, Degarrod 1990, Reid 1986, Gregor 1981a, Whitten 1978, Wallace 1947, Strathern 1989, Herdt 1977, Mpier 1992, Merrill 1987.

9. To the extent that culture wields such a strong influence on dreaming experience, the limitations inherent in modern western theories of what constitutes "normal" dreaming should not be forgotten. Our dreams do not necessarily represent the full range of possible dream experience. On the contrary, what pass for "ordinary" dreams in modern western culture may reflect only a small, narrow band on the broader spectrum of humankind's potential for dreaming. This is one aspect of Nietzsche's comment in the early pages of *The*

Birth of Tragedy that the dreams of the ancient Greeks were richer than the dreams of people in modern western culture (1967, pp. 38-39).

10. Wallace 1947, p. 254.

11. Radin 1936, pp. 233-234. Smohalla resisted this very process, claiming that "those who work can't dream" (Trafzer and Beach 1985, p. 320).

12. Jung 1965, p. 265.

13. Beradt 1966, pp. 45-46.

14. Beradt 1966, p. 52.

15. Beradt 1966, p. 53. For a further discussion of Beradt's book, and of the power of dreams to promote healing, creativity, and renewal even in oppressive social conditions, see Bulkeley 1994b.

APPENDIX 1

1. Bonnefoy 1991, vol. 1, pp. 485-489.

2. Lucretius 1977, pp. 99-106.

3. Ong 1985, p. 69.

4. Achmet 1991, pp. 53-54.

5. Mayerson 1984, pp. 51-52.

6. Luther 1945, vol. 7, p. 120.

7. Nashe 1965, pp. 153-155. I hear some echoes of Nashe's view in the article of Francis Crick and Graeme Mitchison, who propose that dream sleep performs the function of ridding the brain of undesirable elements: "We propose a new explanation for the function of REM sleep. The basis of our theory is the assumption that in viviparous mammals the cortical system...can be regarded as a network of interconnected cells which can support a great variety of modes of mutual excitation. Such a system is likely to be subject to unwanted or parasitic modes of behavior, which arise as it is disturbed either by the growth of the brain or by the modifications produced by experience. We propose that such modes are detected and suppressed by a special mechanism which operates during REM sleep and has the character of an active process which is, loosely speaking, the opposite of learning.

We call this 'reverse learning' or 'unlearning.'... In this model, attempting to remember one's dreams should perhaps not be encouraged, because such remembering may help to retain patterns of thought which are better forgotten. These are the very patterns the organism was attempting to damp down" (1983, pp. 111, 114).

8. Hobbes 1968, pp. 91, 92, 333.

9. See also Kiernan 1985 and Tedlock 1987b.

10. This corresponds to Peter Homans' thesis in *The Ability to Mourn* (1989) that authoritarian political regimes are hostile toward psychological theories and practices.

11. Handy 1936, p. 119.

12. Wallace 1947, pp. 252, 257.

13. Fabian 1966, pp. 551-552.

14. Gregor 1981a, p. 712.

15. Homer 1961, p. 371; see also Virgil 1971, p. 162.

16. Brennan 1993, pp. 74-77.

17. O'Flaherty 1984, p. 24.

18. Philo 1934, vol. 5, pp. 443-445.

19. Artemidorus 1975, pp. 14, 15, 20-21.

20. Tertullian 1870, 517-518.

21. Macrobius 1952, pp. 87-88, 89, 90, 92.

22. Wayman 1967, pp. 4-5.

23. Landau 1957, pp. 60-61.

24. Harris 1963, pp. 58-60.

25. Khaldun 1967, pp. 80-81, 83.

26. Covitz 1990, pp. 25, 26, 28.

27. Von Grunebaum 1966, pp. 7-8.

28. Spencer 1882 and Tylor 1889 give classic nineteenth-century statements on this point, and Hall and Van de Castle 1966 and Hobson 1988 present more recent formulations.

29. See Freud 1965a and Hall and Nordby 1972.

30. Freud 1965a, p. 143.

31. Dawood 1956, p. 317.

32. Homer 1951, pp. 76-77.

33. Although there are also many accounts of "real" misinterpretations of dreams. For example, anthropologist E.W. Gifford recounts this story of how a series of dreams were interpreted, and misinterpreted, by Yuma and Mohave warriors in a campaign against the Maricopa in 1858. A Mohave man told this dream to the Yuma: "I dreamed that I had all kinds of animals and birds around me on the mountain. I laid hold of all these things and killed them. I call upon you to ask you the meaning of this dream." The Yuma interpreted the dream as meaning that the dreamer would be a good warrior and kill many people. The Mohave and Yuma people thus prepared themselves to attack their enemies the Maricopa. But when the Yuma chief heard the Mohave man's dream, he said, "That dream is nothing. I can tell you what your dream means in a minute. It means that you are going to die, and that all kinds of birds and animals are going to come and eat you. That is what the dream means. I do not want you to take my people. You can take your own people." Still, a group of Yuma and Mohave warriors set off into the desert, toward the Maricopa villages. In the ensuing battle, the Maricopa focused on fighting the Yuma; all but seven of the Yuma warriors were killed. Also among the slain was the Mohave man whose dream was responsible for the expedition (Gifford 1926, pp. 64-66).

34. Gardner and Maier 1984.

35. Euripides 1956, pp. 42-62.

36. Quoted in O'Flaherty 1984, pp. 29-30. It is worth noting that right before Hanuman appears to Sita, she has listened to Trijata, one of the demonesses guarding her, recount a dream in which Sita's rescue by Rama is foretold.

37. Amory 1966, p. 17.

38. Amory 1966, pp. 28, 32.

39. Bonnefoy 1991, vol. 1, pp. 485-489.

APPENDIX 2

1. Tylor 1898. For an early critique of Tylor's theory, see Durkheim 1915, pp. 66-77.

2. Gregor 1983, p. 9; 1981a, pp. 710-711.

3. Smith 1991, pp. 248-249.

4. Meggitt 1962, pp. 217-218. The Mae Enga view strikes me as remarkably close to that presented by Medard Boss and other existential psychologists.

5. Tedlock 1987b, pp. 115, 113, 112.

6. See Basso 1987, p. 95.

7. The only exception is the second Quiche theory, according to which the "lightning soul" (*coyopa*) does not seem to go away from the sleeping body, but is visited by another spirit being. This recalls the ancient Greek view of dreams, that the dreamer, while lying asleep in bed, is visited by a deity or spirit being; the Greek view will be discussed later in the Appendix.

8. Seen in this light, the elusive quest for "the function" of dreams conducted by modern western researchers appears rather misguided.

9. Tedlock 1987b, p. 112.

10. Merrill 1987, pp. 194, 200.

11. Ginzburg 1992, pp. 8, 19, 21.

12. Wallace 1958, p. 235.

13. Hume 1931, pp. 95, 134-135.

14. Corbin 1966, pp. 406-407.

15. Guss 1980, pp. 300-301, 304.

16. Herr 1981, pp. 333-334.

17. O'Flaherty 1984, p. 16.

18. See Coulianu 1991, pp. 12-32.

19. Socrates argues that these forms of governing cities can best be understood by examining the corresponding forms of governing individual souls. The specific types of humans and specific types of constitutions must be equal in number, he says, because the constitutions grow organically from the characters of the people who are preponderant in the given cities.

20. Plato 1957, pp. 335-336, 342.

21. Aristotle 1941a, pp. 619, 621, 622, 624-625.

22. Descartes 1960, pp. 75, 76-77, 80, 125, 143.

23. Nietzsche 1967, pp. 33-35, 44-45.

24. The very "worst of men" is, according to Socrates, the man who behaves in waking life the way he does in his dreams. This view finds a powerful artistic expression in Shakespeare's tragedy *Macbeth*, one of western culture's greatest portraits of a man who surrenders to the "worst" desires of the human soul. As Macbeth wonders if he is really capable of committing the bloody deeds that would bring him to the throne, his wife tries to spur him on: "Art thou afeard to be the same in thine own act and valor as thou art in desire?" [I.vii.43-45] Macbeth's horrible fate—to be driven mad by visions and nightmares, and finally slain on the battlefield—can be seen as an illustration of Socrates' warning about obeying the violent desires that arise in our dreams.

25. Freud 1965a. p. 647. Socrates' observations about the soul's hidden desires for "incestual intercourse...with a mother, or with any man or god or beast" seem to anticipate Freud's views of the id, "the dark, inaccessible part of our personality...a chaos, a cauldron full of seething excitations" (1964, p. 65). Freud says of the id, "what little we know of it we have learnt from our study of the dream-work and of the construction of neurotic symptoms, and most of that is of a negative character and can be described only as a contrast to the ego" (1964, p. 65).

26. Aristotle 1941b, p. 630.

27. Aristotle 1941b, p. 630.

28. Descartes 1960, p. 125.

29. Descartes 1960, p. 143.

APPENDIX 3

1. In "The Evil Dreams of Gilgamesh: An Interdisciplinary Approach to Dreams in Mythological Texts" I try to make such a well-reasoned guess (Bulkeley 1993a). I look at the "fictionalized" qualities of the dreams reported in the Gilgamesh epic, and I identify the many ways in which these dreams serve as highly effective literary devices. But at the same time, I show the many ways in which these dreams have all the psychological qualities that we find in "real" dreams.

2. Freud 1965a, pp. 526-546.

3. See Tedlock 1987a.

4. See Tore Nielsen's research (1991) on the difficulties that informants have in properly identifying their own dream experiences.

5. Freud himself says, "It is impossible as a rule to translate a dream into a foreign language" (1965a, p. 132). However, Freud himself frequently compares dream interpretation to the process of translating a text from one language into another, the comparison serving to support Freud's claim that dream interpretation can be an exact, precise matter (Frieden 1990, pp. 109, 111, 114).

6. Erikson 1954.

7. Bosnak 1988, 1989; Mindell 1982; Gendlin 1986. See also Kracke 1987.

8. I have discussed the philosophical questions surrounding the interpretation of dreams at far greater length in part III of *The Wilderness of Dreams* (1994).

Bibliography

Achemet. 1991. *Oneirocriticon* (trans. Steven M. Oberhelman) (Lubbock, TX: Texas Tech University Press).

Aeschylus. 1989. *The Orestia* (trans. David Grene and Wendy Doniger O'Flaherty) (Chicago: University of Chicago Press).

Allen, Woody. 1989. *Without Feathers, Getting Even, Side Effects* (New York, NY: Quality Paperbacks Book Club).

Amory, Anne. 1966. The Gates of Horn and Ivory. *Yale Classical Studies* (vol. 20), 1-57.

Apuleius. 1960. *The Golden Ass* (trans. Jack Lindsay) (Bloomington, IN: Indiana University Press).

Aristides, P. Aelius. 1981. *The Complete Works* (trans. Charles A. Behr) (Leiden: E.J. Brill).

Aristotle. 1941a. *On Dreams*. In Richard McKeon (ed.), *The Collected Works of Aristotle* (New York, NY: Random House).

————. 1941b. *On Prophesying by Dreams*. In Richard McKeon (ed.), *The Collected Works of Aristotie* (New York, NY: Random House).

Artemidorus. 1975. *The Interpretation of Dreams* (trans. Robert J. White) (Park Ridge, NJ: Noyes Press).

Augustine. 1870. *The Works of Aurelius Augustine, Vol. XIII: The Letters of Saint Augustine* (trans. J.G. Cunningham) (Edinburgh: T. & T. Clark).

————. 1961. *Confessions* (trans. R.S. Pine-Coffin) (London: Penguin Books).

_____. 1971. *City of God* (trans. Henry Bettenson) (London: Penguin Books).

Barrett, Deirdre. 1991. Flying Dreams and Lucidity: An Empirical Study of their Relationship. *Dreaming* (vol. 1, no. 2), 129-134.

_____. 1992. Just How Lucid are Lucid Dreams? *Dreaming* (vol. 2, no. 4), 221-228

Basso, Ellen B. 1987. The Implications of a Progressive Theory of Dreaming. In Barbara Tedlock (ed.), *Dreaming: Anthropological and Psychological Interpretations* (New York, NY: Cambridge University Press).

Benedict, Ruth. 1922. The Vision in Plains Culture. *American Anthropologist* (vol. 24, no. 1), 1-23.

Beradt, Charlotte. 1966. *The Third Reich of Dreams* (trans. Adriane Gottwald) (Chicago, IL: Quadrangle Books).

Best, Elsdon. 1898. Omens and Superstitious Beliefs of the Maori. *The Journal of the Polynesian Society* (vol. 7), 119-136.

Beverly, Elizabeth. 1990. Meditation on Suokula: Memory and the Mandinko. *Soundings* (vol. 73, no. 2), 361-381.

Bhattacharyya, Pandit Ramesh Chandra (ed.). 1970. *Interpretation of Dreams According to the Brahmavaivarta Purana* (Calcutta: P.B. Roy, Pratartak Printing and Halftone).

Bible. Revised Standard Version.

Bilu, Yoram. 1979. Sigmund Freud and Rabbi Yehudah: on a Jewish Mystical Tradition of "Psychoanalytic" Dream Interpretation. *Journal of Psychological Anthropology* (vol. 2), 443-463.

Blagrove, Mark. 1992. Dreams as the Reflection of our Waking Concerns and Abilities: A Critique of the Problem-Solving Paradigm in Dream Research. *Dreaming* (vol. 2, no. 4), 205-220.

Bland, Nathaniel. 1856. On the Muhammedan Science of Tabir, or Interpretation of Dreams. *Journal of the Royal Asiatic Society of Great Britain and Ireland* (vol. 16), 118-171.

Blau, Harold. 1963. Dream-Guessing: A Comparative Analysis. *Ethnohistory* (vol. 10, no. 3), 233-249.

Bonnefoy, Yves. 1991. *Mythologies, 2 vols.* (ed. Wendy Doniger) (Chicago, IL: University of Chicago Press).

Bonuzzi, Luciano. 1975. About the Origins of the Scientific Study of Sleep and Dreaming. In Gabrielle C. Lairy and Piero Salzarulo (eds.), *The Experimental Study of Human Sleep: Methodological Problems* (Amsterdam: Elsevier Scientific Publishing Co.).

Bosnak, Robert. 1988. *A Little Course on Dreams* (Boston, MA: Shambhala).

_____. 1989. *Dreaming with an AIDS Patient* (Boston, MA: Shambhala).

Bourguignon, Erika E. 1954. Dreams and Dream Interpretation in Haiti. *American Anthropologist* (vol. 56, no. 2), 262-268.

Brain, Robert. 1970. Child-Witches. In Mary Douglas (ed.), *Witchcraft: Confessions and Accusations* (London: Tavistock Publications).

Brennan, John. 1993. Dreams, Divination, and Statecraft in Chinese Poetry and Prose Commentary. In Carol S. Rupprecht (ed.), *The Dream and the Text: Essays on Language and Literature* (Albany, NY: State University of New York Press).

Breughman, Lucy. 1982. *The Rediscovery of Inner Experience* (Chicago: Nelson-Hall).

Briggs, John P. and Briggs, John. 1991. Unholy Desires, Inordinate Affections: A Psychodynamic Inquiry into John Wesley's Relationship with Women. *Connecticut Review* (vol. 13, no. 1), 1-18.

Brod, Carol. 1991. The Girl Who Was Afraid to Dream: A Case Presentation. Unpublished manuscript.

Brown, Michael F. 1985. Individual Experience, Dreams, and the Identification of Magical Stones in an Amazonian Society. In Janet W.D. Dougherty (ed.), *Directions in Cognitive Anthropology* (Urbana, IL: University of Illinois Press).

_____. 1987. Ropes of Sand: Order and Imagery in Aguaruna Dreams. In Barbara Tedlock (ed.), *Dreaming: Anthropological and Psychological Interpretations* (New York, NY: Cambridge University Press).

Bulkeley, Kelly. 1988. Lucid Dreaming and Ethical Reflection. *Lucidity Letter* (vol. 7, no. 2), 13-16.

————. 1989 Some Further Thoughts on Lucid Dreaming and Ethical Reflection. *Lucidity Letter* (vol. 8, no. 2), 41-43.

————. 1991. Interdisciplinary Dreaming: Hobson's Successes and Failures. *Dreaming* (vol. 1, no. 3), 225-234.

————. 1992. Dreams, Spirituality, and Root Metaphors. *Journal of Religion and Health* (vol. 31, no. 3), 197-206.

————. 1993a. The Evil Dreams of Gilgamesh: An Interdisciplinary Approach to Dreams in Mythological Texts. In Carol Schreier Rupprecht (ed.), *The Dream and the Text: Essays on Language and Literature* (Albany, NY: State University of New York Press).

————. 1993b. Dreaming is Play. *Psychoanalytic Psychology* (vol. 10, no. 4), 501-514.

————. 1993c. Gods and REMS: The Implications of Recent Dream Research for the Psychology of Religion. *Pastoral Psychology* (vol. 41, no. 6), 349-358.

————. 1994a. *The Wilderness of Dreams: Exploring the Religious Meanings of Dreams in Modern Western Culture* (Albany, NY: State University of New York Press).

————. 1994b. Dreaming in a Totalitarian State: A Reading of Charlotte Beradt's The Third Reich of Dreams. *Dreaming* (vol. 4, no. 2), 115-126.

————. 1994c. Dream Sharing as a Means of Revitalizing Communities. Unpublished manuscript.

————. (ed.). In press. *Among All These Dreamers: Essays on Dreaming, Modern Society, and the Future of Dream Studies* (Albany, NY: State University of New York Press).

Bulkeley, Kelly and Doniger, Wendy. 1993. Why Study Dreams? A Religious Studies Perspective. *Dreaming* (vol. 3, no. 1), 69-73.

Cartwright, Rosalind and Lamberg, Lynne. 1992. *Crisis Dreaming* (New York: Harper Collins).

Castaneda, Carlos. 1993. *The Art of Dreaming* (New York, NY: Harper Collins).

Centlivres, Micheline, Centlivres, Pierre, and Slobin, Mark. 1971. A Muslim Shaman of Agfhan. *Ethnology* (vol. 10), 160-173.

Charsley, Simon. 1973. Dreams in an Independent African Church. *Africa: Journal of the International African Institute* (vol. 43, no. 3), 244-257.

————. 1987. Dreams and Purposes: An Analysis of Dream Narratives in an Independent African Church. *Africa: Journal of the International African Institute* (vol. 57, no. 3), 281-296.

Cicero. 1876. *On Divination*. In C.D. Yonge (ed.), *Treatises of Cicero* (London: George Bell and Sons).

Cole, John R. 1992. *The Olympian Dreams and Youthful Rebellion of René Descartes* (Urbana, IL: University of Illinois Press).

Corbin, Henri. 1966. The Visionary Dream in Islamic Spirituality. In G.E. von Grunebaum and Roger Callois (eds.), *The Dream and Human Societies* (Berkeley, CA: University of California Press).

Couliano, I.P. 1991. *Out of this World* (Boston, MA: Shambhala).

Covitz, Joel. 1990. *Visions of the Night: A Study of Jewish Dream Interpretation* (Boston, MA: Shambhala).

Crapanzano, Victor. 1975. Saints, Jnun, and Demons: An Essay in Moroccan Ethnopsychology. *Psychiatry* (vol. 38), 145-159.

Crick, Francis and Mitchison, Graeme. 1983. The Function of Dream Sleep. *Nature* (vol. 304, no. 14), 111-114.

Cuddy, Marion and Belicki, Kathryn. In press. The 55-Year Old Secret: Using Nightmares to Facilitate Psychotherapy in a Case of Childhood Sexual Abuse. In Kelly Bulkeley (ed.), *Among All These Dreamers: Essays on Dreaming, Modern Society, and the Future of Dream Studies* (Albany, NY: State University of New York Press).

Curley, Richard T. 1983. Dreams of Power: Social Process in a West African Religious Movement. *Africa: Journal of the International African Institute* (vol. 53, no. 3), 20-37.

D'Andrade, Roy G. 1961. Anthropological Studies of Dreams. In

Francis L.K. Hsu (ed.), *Psychological Anthropology* (Homewood, IL: The Dorsey Press).

Daneel, M.L. 1971. *Old and New in Southern Shona Independent Churches, Volume I: Background and Rise of the Major Movements* (Paris: Mouton).

————. 1974. *Old and New in Southern Shona Independent Churches, Volume II: Church Growth–Causative Factors and Recruitment Techniques* (Paris: Mouton).

Davis, Winston. 1980. *Dojo: Magic and Exorcism in Modern Japan* (Stanford, CA: Stanford University Press).

Dawood, N.J. (trans.). 1956. *The Koran* (London: Penguin Books).

————. (trans.). 1973. *Tales from the Thousand and One Nights* (London: Penguin Books).

Degarrod, L. Nakashima. 1990. Coping with Stress: Dream Interpretation in the Mapuche Family. *Psychiatric Journal of the University of Ottawa* (vol. 15, no. 2), 111-116.

Delaney, Gayle. 1979. *Living Your Dreams* (New York, NY: Harper and Row).

————. 1991. *Breakthrough Dreaming* (New York, NY: Bantam).

————. 1994. *Sexual Dreams* (New York, NY: Bantam).

Dentan, Robert Knox and McClusky, Laura J. 1993. "Pity the Bones by Wandering River which Still in Lovers' Dreams Appear as Men." In Alan Moffitt, Milton Kramer, and Robert Hoffmann (eds.), *The Functions of Dreaming* (Albany: State University of New York Press).

Descartes, René. 1960. *Discourse on Method and Meditations* (trans. Laurence J. Lafleur) (Indianapolis, IN: Bobbs-Merrill).

Devereux, George. 1957. Dream Learning and Individual Ritual Differences in Mohave Shamanism. *American Anthropologist* (vol. 59, no. 4), 1036-1045.

————. 1969. *Reality and Dream: Psychotherapy of a Plains Indian* (New York: Doubleday Anchor).

Dickens, Charles. 1980. *A Christmas Carol* (New York: New American Library).

Dilley, Roy. 1992. Dreams, Inspiration and Craftwork among Tukolor Weavers. In M.C. Jedrej and Rosalind Shaw (eds.), *Dreaming, Religion and Society in Africa* (Leiden: E.J. Brill).

Dodds, E.R. 1951. *The Greeks and the Irrational* (Berkeley: University of California Press).

Domhoff, G. William. 1985. *The Mystique of Dreams: A Search for Utopia Through Senoi Dream Theory* (Berkeley: University of California Press).

Driberg, J.H. 1927. Notes on Dreams among the Lango and the Didanga of South-Eastern Sudan. *Man* (no. 94), 141-143.

Dronke, Peter. 1984. *Woman Writers of the Middle Ages* (Cambridge: Cambridge University Press).

Ducey, Charles P. 1979. The Shaman's Dream Journey: Psychoanalytic and Structural Complementarity in Myth Interpretation. *Psychoanalytic Study of Society* (vol. 8), 71-118.

Duerr, Hans Peter. 1985. *Dreamtime: Concerning the Boundary between Wilderness and Civilization* (trans. Felicitas Goodman) (New York: Basil Blackwell).

Durkheim, Emile. 1915. *The Elementary Forms of the Religious Life* (trans. Joseph Swain) (New York: The Free Press).

Edelstein, Emma and Edelstein, Ludwig (eds.). 1975. *Asclepius: A Collection and Interpretation of the Testimonies* (New York, NY: Arno Press).

Eggan, Dorothy. 1952. The Manifest Content of Dreams: A Challenge to Social Science. *American Anthropologist* (vol. 54, no. 4), 469-485.

_____. 1955. The Personal Use of Myth in Dreams. *Journal of American Folklore* (vol. 68), 445-453.

_____. 1961. Dream Analysis. In Bert Kaplan (ed.), *Studying Personality Cross-Culturally* (Evanston, IL: Row, Peterson, and Co.).

Eliade, Mircea. 1957. *The Sacred and the Profane* (trans. Willard R. Trask) (New York, NY: Harcourt Brace Jovanovich).

_____. 1958. *Patterns in Comparative Religion* (trans. Rosemary Sheed) (New York: Meridian Books).

_____. 1960. *Myths, Dreams, and Mysteries: The Encounter between Contemporary Faiths and Archaic Realities* (trans. Willard R. Trask) (New York, NY: Harper and Row).

_____. 1964. *Shamanism: Archaic Techniques of Ecstasy* (trans. Willard R. Trask) (Princeton, NJ: Princeton University Press).

_____. 1966. Initiation Dreams and Visions Among the Siberian Shamans. In G.E. von Grunebaum and Roger Callois (eds.), *The Dream and Human Societies* (Berkeley, CA: University of California Press).

Erikson, Erik. 1954. The Dream Specimen of Psychoanalysis. *Journal of the American Psychoanalytical Association* (vol. 2), 5-56.

Euripides. 1956. *Iphigenia in Tauris* (trans. Witter Bynner). In David Grene and Richmond Lattimore (eds.), *Greek Tragedies*, Vol. 2 (Chicago, IL: University of Chicago Press).

Eusebius, Pamphili. 1953. *Ecclesiastical History 1–5* (trans. Roy J. Deferrari). In Roy J. Deferrari (ed.), *The Fathers of the Church* (New York, NY: The Fathers of the Church).

Evans-Pritchard, E.E. 1937. *Witchcraft, Oracles, and Magic among the Azande* (Oxford: Clarendon Press).

Ewing, Katherine P. 1989. The Dream of Spiritual Initiation and the Organization of Self Representations among Pakistani Sufis. *American Ethnologist* (vol. 16), 56-74.

Fabian, Johannes. 1966. Dream and Charisma. "Theories of Dreams" in the Jamaa-Movement (Congo). *Anthropos* (vol. 61), 544-560.

Faraday, Ann. 1972. *Dream Power* (New York: Berkeley Books).

_____. 1974. *The Dream Game* (New York: Harper and Row).

Fernandez, James. 1982. *Bwiti: An Ethnography of the Religious Imagination in Africa* (Princeton, NJ: Princeton University Press).

Festugiere, Andre-Jean. 1954. *Personal Religion Among the Greeks* (Westport, CT: Greenwood Press).

Feuer, Lewis S. 1957. The Dream of Benedict de Spinoza. *The American Imago* (vol. 14), 225-242.

Finkel, Asher. 1963. The Pesher of Dreams and Scriptures. *Revue de Qumran* (vol. 4), 357-370.

Firestone, Melvin. 1985. The "Old Hag": Sleep Paralysis in Newfoundland. *Journal of Psychoanalytic Anthropology* (vol. 8, no. 1), 47-66.

Firth, Raymond. 1934. The Meaning of Dreams in Tikopia. In E.E. Evans-Pritchard, et. al (eds.), *Essays Presented to C.G. Seligman* (London: Kegan Paul, Trench, Trubner, and Co.).

Fisher, Humphrey J. 1979. Dreams and Conversion in Black Africa. In Nehemia Levtzion (ed.), *Conversion to Islam* (New York, NY: Holmes and Meier).

Fitzgerald, Augustine (trans.). 1930. *The Essays and Hymns of Synesius of Cyrene* (London: Oxford University Press).

Flannery, Regina and Chambers, Mary Elizabeth. 1985. Each Man has his Own Friends: The Role of Dream Visitors in Traditional East Cree Belief and Practice. *Arctic Anthropology* (vol. 22, no. 1), 1-22.

Foster, George M. 1973. Dreams, Character, and Cognitive Orientation in Tzintzuntzan. *Ethos* (vol. 1, no. 1), 106-121.

Foucault, Michel. 1980. *The History of Sexuality, Volume I: An Introduction* (trans. Robert Hurley) (New York: Vintage Books).

Fox, Robin. 1986. The Passionate Mind: Brain, Dreams, Memory, and Social Categories. *Zygon* (vol. 21, no. 1), 31-46.

Frank, Jerome. 1973. *Persuasion and Healing* (New York, NY: Shocken Books).

Freeman, Derek. 1967. Shaman and Incubus. *The Psychoanalytic Study of Society* (vol. 4), 315-343.

French, Thomas and Fromm, Erika. 1964. *Dream Interpretation: A New Approach* (New York: Basic Books).

Freud, Sigmund. 1963a. Remarks upon the Theory and Practice of Dream Interpretation. In Philip Rieff (ed.), *Therapy and Technique* (New York, NY: Collier Books).

_____. 1963b. Some Additional Notes on Dream Interpretation as a Whole. In Philip Rieff (ed.), *Therapy and Technique* (New York, NY: Collier Books).

_____. 1965a. *The Interpretation of Dreams* (trans. James Strachey) (New York, NY: Avon Books).

_____. 1965b. *New Introductory Lectures on Psychoanalysis* (trans. James Strachey) (New York, NY: W.W. Norton).

Frieden, Ken. 1990. *Freud's Dream of Interpretation* (Albany, New York: State University of New York Press).

Gackenbach, Jayne. 1989. *Control Your Dreams* (New York, NY: Harper and Row).

_____. 1991. Frameworks for Understanding Lucid Dreaming: A Review. *Dreaming* (vol. 1, no. 2), 109-128.

Gackenbach, Jayne and LaBerge, Stephen (eds.). 1988. *Conscious Mind, Sleeping Brain* (New York, NY: Plenum Press).

Gardner, John and Maier, John (trans.). 1984. *Gilgamesh* (New York, NY: Vintage Books).

Garfield, Patricia. 1974. *Creative Dreaming* (New York, NY: Ballantine).

_____. 1979. *Pathway to Ecstasy* (New York, NY: Prentice-Hall).

_____. 1988. *Women's Bodies, Women's Dreams* (New York, NY: Ballantine).

Geijbels, M. 1978. Aspects of the Veneration of Saints in Islam, with Special Reference to Pakistan. *The Muslim World* (vol. 63), 176-186.

Gendlin, Eugene. 1986. *Let Your Body Interpret Your Dreams* (Wilmette, IL: Chiron Publications).

Gibbons, Francis. 1984. *Joseph F. Smith: Patriarch and Preacher, Prophet of God* (Salt Lake City, UT: Deseret Books).

Gifford, Edward. 1926. Yuma Dreams and Omens. *Journal of American Folklore* (vol. 39), 58-69.

Gillespie, George. 1988. When Does Lucid Dreaming Become Transpersonal Experience? *Psychiatric Journal of the University of Ottawa* (vol. 13, no. 2), 107-110.

Ginzburg, Carlo. 1992. *The Night Battles: Witchcraft and Agrarian Cults in the Sixteenth and Seventeenth Centuries* (trans. John and Anne Tedeschi) (Baltimore, MD: Johns Hopkins University Press).

Gnuse, Robert. 1989. Dream Reports in the Writings of Flavius Josephus. *Revue Biblique* (vol. 16), 358-390.

———. 1990. Dream Genre in the Matthean Infancy Narratives. *Novum Testamentum* (vol. 32, no. 2), 97-120.

Graham, Laura. 1991. Dialogic Dreams. Unpublished manuscript.

Green, Celia E. 1968. *Lucid Dreams* (Oxford: Institute of Psychophysical Research).

Gregor, Thomas. 1981a. "Far, Far Away My Shadow Wandered...": The Dream Symbolism and Dream Theories of the Mehinaku Indians of Brazil. *American Ethnologist* (vol. 8, no. 4), 709-720.

———. 1981b. A Content Analysis of Mehinaku Dreams. *Ethos* (vol. 9, no. 4), 353-390.

———. 1983. Dark Dreams About the White Man. *Natural History* (vol. 92, no. 1), 8-15.

Guss, David. 1980. Steering for Dream: Dream Concepts of the Makiritare. *Journal of Latin American Lore* (vol. 6, no. 2), 297-312.

Hall, Calvin. 1966. *The Meaning of Dreams* (New York: McGraw-Hill).

Hall, Calvin and Nordby, Vernon. 1972. *The Individual and His Dreams* (New York: Signet Books).

Hall, Calvin and Van de Castle, Robert. 1966. *The Content Analysis of Dreams* (New York: Appleton-Century-Crofts).

Hallowell, A. Irving. 1966. The Role of Dreams in Ojibwa Culture. In G.E. von Grunebaum and Roger Callois (eds.), *The Dream and Human Societies* (Berkeley, CA: University of California Press).

Hallpike, C.R. 1979. *The Foundations of Primitive Thought* (Oxford: Oxford University Press).

Hamilton, Mary. 1906. *Incubation; or, the Cure of Disease in Pagan Temples and Christian Churches* (London: Marshall, Hamilton, Kent).

Handy, E.S. Craighill. 1936. Dreaming in Relation to Spirit Kindred and Sickness in Hawaii. In *Essays in Anthropology Presented to A.L. Kroeber* (Freeport, NY: Books for Libraries Press).

Harrington, John P. 1908. A Yuma Account of Origins. *Journal of American Folklore* (vol. 21), 324-348.

Harris, Monford. 1963. Dreams in Sefer Hasidim. *American Academy for Jewish Research Proceedings* (vol. 31), 51-80.

Hartmann, Ernest. 1984. *The Nightmare: The Psychology and Biology of Terrifying Dreams* (New York, NY: Basic Books).

Herdt, Gibert. 1977. The Shaman's "Calling" Among the Sambia of New Guinea. *Journal de la Societe des Oceanistes* (vol. 33), 153-167.

Herodotus. 1990. *The History of Herodotus* (trans. George Rawlinson). In Mortimer J. Adler (ed.), *Great Books of the Western World, vol. 5* (Chicago, IL: Encyclopedia Britannica).

Herr, Barbara. 1981. The Expressive Character of Fijian Dream and Nightmare Experiences. *Ethos* (vol. 9, no. 4), 331-352.

Hobbes, Thomas. 1968. *Leviathan* (London: Penguin Books).

Hobson, J. Allan. 1988. *The Dreaming Brain: How the Brain Creates Both the Sense and the Nonsense of Dreams* (New York: Basic Books).

Hobson, J. Allan and Lavie, Peretz. 1986. Origin of Dreams: Anticipation of Modern Theories in the Philosophy and Physiology of the Eighteenth and Nineteenth Centuries. *Psychological Bulletin* (vol. 100, no. 2), 229-240.

Hodgson, A.G.O. 1926. Dreams in Central Africa. *Man* (vol. 26), 66-68.

Holy, Ladislav. 1992. Berti Dream Interpretation. In M.C. Jedrej and Rosalind Shaw (eds.), *Dreaming, Religion and Society in Africa* (Leiden: E.J. Brill).

Homans, Peter. 1989. *The Ability to Mourn: Disillusionment and the Social Origins of Psychoanalysis* (Chicago, IL: University of Chicago Press).

Homer. 1951. *The Iliad* (trans. Richmond Lattimore) (Chicago, IL: University of Chicago Press).

————. 1961. *The Odyssey* (trans. Robert Fitzgerald) (New York: Anchor Books).

Hosain, M. Hidayet. 1932. A Treatise on the Interpretation of Dreams. *Islamic Culture* (vol. 6, no. 4), 568-585.

Hufford, David J. 1976. A New Approach to the "Old Hag": The Nightmare Tradition Reexamined. In Wayland D. Hand (ed.), *American Folk Medicine: A Symposium* (Berkeley, CA: University of California Press).

Hume, Robert Ernest (trans.). 1931. *The Thirteen Principal Upanishads* (Delhi: Oxford University Press).

James, William. 1958. *The Varieties of Religious Experience* (New York: Mentor Books).

Jayne, Walter. 1925. *The Healing Gods of Ancient Civilizations* (New Haven, CT: Yale University Press).

Jedrej, M.C. 1992. Ingessana Dreaming. In M.C. Jedrej and Rosalind Shaw (eds.), *Dreaming, Religion and Society in Africa* (Leiden: E.J. Brill).

Jedrej, M.C. and Shaw, Rosalind (eds.). 1992. *Dreaming, Religion, and Society in Africa* (Leiden: E.J. Brill).

Johnson, Kenneth E. 1978. Modernity and Dream Content: A Ugandan Example. *Ethos* (vol. 6, no. 4), 212-220.

Jones, Ernest. 1951. *On the Nightmare* (New York, NY: Liveright).

Jones, Russell. 1979. Ten Conversion Myths from Indonesia. In Nehemia Levtzion (ed.), *Conversion to Islam* (New York, NY: Holmes and Meier, Publishers).

Josephus. 1987. *The Works of Josephus* (trans. William Whiston) (Peabody, MA: Hendrickson Publishers).

Jung, C.G. 1965. *Memories, Dreams, Reflections* (trans. Richard and Clara Winston) (New York, NY: Vintage Books).

————. 1966. *The Practice of Psychotherapy* (trans. R.F.C. Hull) (Princeton, NJ: Princeton University Press).

————. 1974. *Dreams* (trans. R.F.C. Hull) (Princeton, NJ: Princeton University Press).

Kakar, Sudhir. 1982. *Shamans, Mystics, and Doctors* (Boston, MA: Beacon Press).

Kant, Immanuel. 1966. *Dreams of a Spirit Seer* (trans. John Manolesco) (New York, NY: Vantage Press).

Kaplan, Bernard and Werner, Heinz. 1956. The Developmental Approach to Cognition. *American Anthropologist* (vol. 58), 866-880.

Keable, Robert. 1921. A People of Dreams. *The Hibbert Journal* (vol. 19), 522-531.

Kelsey, Morton. 1974. *God, Dreams, and Revelation: A Christian Interpretation of Dreams* (Minneapolis, MN: Augsburg Publishing House).

Kelzer, Ken. 1987. *The Sun and the Shadow*. New York, NY: A.R.E. Press.

Kennedy, John G. and Fahim, Hussein. 1974. Nubian Dhikr Rituals and Cultural Change. *The Muslim World* (vol. 64), 205-219.

Kessels, A.H.M. 1969. Ancient Systems of Dream-Classification. *Mnemosyne* (vol. 22, no. 4), 389-424.

Khaldun, Ibn. 1967. *The Muqaddimah* (trans. Franz Rosenthal) (Princeton, NJ: Princeton University Press).

Kiernan, J.P. 1985. The Social Stuff of Revelation: Pattern and Purpose in Zionist Dreams and Visions. *Africa: Journal of the International African Institute* (vol. 55, no. 3), 304-317.

Kiev, Ari (ed.). 1964. *Magic, Faith, and Healing* (New York: The Free Press).

Kilborne, Benjamin. 1981a. Pattern, Structure, and Style in Anthropological Studies of Dreams. *Ethos* (vol. 9, no. 2), 165-185.

_____. 1981b. Moroccan Dream Interpretation and Culturally Constituted Defense Mechanisms. *Ethos* (vol. 9, no. 4), 294-312.

King, Arden. 1942. The Dream Biography of a Mountain Maidu. *Character and Personality* (vol. 11), 227-234.

King, Johanna. In press. Let's Stand Up, Regain Our Balance, and Look Around at the World. In Kelly Bulkeley (ed.), *Among All These Dreamers: Essays on Dreaming, Modern Society, and the Future of Dream Studies* (Albany, NY: State University of New York Press).

Konje, Prof. 1985. *The Lucky Star Dream Book* (West Hempstead, NY: G. Parris Co.).

Koulack, David. 1991. *To Catch a Dream* (Albany, NY: State University of New York Press).

Kracke, Waud. 1979. Dreaming in Kagwahiv: Dream Beliefs and their Psychic Uses in an Amazonian Indian Culture. *The Psychoanalytic Study of Society* (vol. 8), 119-171.

―――. 1981. Kagwahiv Mourning: Dreams of a Bereaved Father. *Ethos* (vol. 9, no. 4), 258-275.

―――. 1987. Myths in Dreams, Thought in Images: An Amazonian Contribution to the Psychoanalytic Theory of Primary Process. In Barbara Tedlock (ed.), *Dreaming: Anthropological and Psychological Interpretations* (New York, NY: Cambridge University Press).

Kramer, Heinrich and Sprenger, James. 1971. *The Malleus Maleficarum* (trans. Montague Summers) (New York, NY: Dover).

Kramer, Milton. 1982. The Psychology of the Dream: Art or Science? *The Psychiatric Journal of the University of Ottawa* (vol. 7, no. 2), 87-100.

Kroeber, A.L. 1957. Ad Hoc Reassurance Dreams. *Ethnographic Interpretations* (no. 2), 205-208.

LaBarre, Weston. 1970. *The Ghost Dance: Origins of Religion* (Prospect Heights, IL: Waveland Press).

LaBerge, Stephen. 1985. *Lucid Dreaming* (Los Angeles, CA: Jeremy Tarcher).

Lai, Whalen. 1982. Debendranath Tagore's Dream: The Soul and the Mother. *Anima* (vol. 9, no. 1), 29-32.

Lakoff, George. 1987. *Women, Fire, and Dangerous Things* (Chicago, IL: University of Chicago Press).

Landau, Rom. 1957. The Philosophy of Ibn Arabi. *The Muslim World* (vol. 47), 46-61.

Lanternari, Vittorio. 1975. Dreams as Charismatic Significants: Their Bearing on the Rise of New Religious Movements. In T.R. Williams (ed.), *Psychological Anthropology* (Paris: Mouton).

Laufer, Berthold. 1931. Inspirational Dreams in Eastern Asia. *Journal of American Folk-Lore* (vol. 44), 208-216.

Lefkowitz, Mary R. 1976. The Motivations for St. Perpetua's Martyrdom. *Journal of the American Academy of Religion* (vol. 44, no. 3), 417-421.

Levin, Ross. 1990. Psychoanalytic Theories on the Function of Dreaming: A Review of the Empirical Dream Research. In J. Masling (ed.), *Empirical Studies of Psychoanalytic Theories*, Vol. 3 (New York: Analytic Press).

Lewis, Jane White. In press. Dreams and Social Responsibility: Teaching a Dream Course in the Inner-City. In Kelly Bulkeley (ed.), *Among all These Dreamers: Essays on Dreaming, Modern Society, and the Future of Dream Studies* (Albany, NY: State University of New York Press).

Lhalungpa, Lobsang P. (trans.). 1985. *Life of Milarepa* (Boston, MA: Shambhala).

Lincoln, Bruce. 1981. *Emerging from the Chrysalis* (Cambridge, MA: Harvard University Press).

Lincoln, J.S. 1935. *The Dream in Primitive Cultures* (London: University of London Press).

Lorand, Sandor. 1957. Dream Interpretation in the Talmud (Babylonian and Graeco-Roman Period). *International Journal of Psychoanalysis* (vol. 38), 92-97.

Lucretius, Carus, Titus. 1977. *The Nature of Things* (trans. Frank O. Copley) (New York: W.W. Norton).

Luther, Martin. 1945. *Luther's Works* (ed. Jaroslav Pelikan) (St. Louis, MO: Concordia Publishing House).

Mack, John E. 1970. *Nightmares and Human Conflict* (New York, NY: Columbia University Press).

MacKenzie, Norman. 1965. *Dreams and Dreaming* (New York, NY: Vanguard).

Macrobius. 1952. *Commentary on the Dream of Scipio* (trans. William Harris Stahl) (New York, NY: Columbia University Press).

Malinowski, Bronislaw. 1987. *The Sexual Life of Savages* (Boston, MA: Beacon Press).

Maybruck, Patricia. 1989. *Pregnancy and Dreams* (Los Angeles, CA: Jeremy Tarcher).

Mayerson, Philip. 1984. Antiochus Monachus' Homily on Dreams: An Historical Note. *Journal of Jewish Studies* (vol. 35, no. 1), 51-56.

Mbiti, John S. 1976. God, Dreams, and African Militancy. In J.S. Pobee (ed.), *Religion in a Pluralistic Society* (Leiden: E.J. Brill).

Meggitt, M.J. 1962. Dream Interpretation among the Mae Enga of New Guinea. *Southwestern Journal of Anthropology* (vol. 18), 216-229.

Meier, C.A. 1967. *Ancient Incubation and Modern Psychotherapy* (trans. Monica Curtis) (Evanston, IL: Northwestern University Press).

Merrill, William. 1987. The Raramuri Stereotype of Dreams. In Barbara Tedlock (ed.), *Dreaming: Anthropological and Psychological Interpretations* (New York, NY: Cambridge University Press).

Miller, Patricia Cox. 1986. "A Dubious Twilight": Reflections on Dreams in Patristic Literature. *Church History* (vol. 55, no. 2), 153-164.

————. 1994. *Dreams in Late Antiquity: Studies in the Imagination of a Culture* (Princeton, NJ: Princeton University Press).

Milton, John. 1977. *Paradise Lost* (New York, NY: Viking Press).

Mindell, Arnold. 1982. *Dreambody: The Body's Role in Revealing the Self* (London: Routledge & Kegan Paul).

————. 1985. *Working with the Dream Body* (New York, NY: Mathuen Press).

Moffitt, Alan, Kramer, Milton and Hoffmann, Robert (eds.) 1993. *The Functions of Dreaming* (Albany, NY: State University of New York Press).

Morgan, William. 1931. Navaho Treatment of Sickness: Diagnosticians. *American Anthropologist* (vol. 33), 390-402.

————. 1932. Navaho Dreams. *American Anthropologist* (vol. 34), 390-405.

Morris, Ivan (trans.). 1971. *As I Crossed a Bridge of Dreams* (London: Penguin Books).

Mpier, Mubuy Mubay. 1992. Dreams among the Yansi. In M.C. Jedrej and Rosalind Shaw (eds.), *Dreaming, Religion and Society in Africa* (Leiden: E.J. Brill).

M'Timkulu, Donald. 1977. Some Aspects of Zulu Religion. In Newell S. Booth, Jr. (ed.), *African Religions: A Symposium* (New York, NY: NOK Publications).

Mundkur, Balaji. 1983. *The Cult of the Serpent* (Albany, NY: State University of New York Press).

Musurillo, Herbert. 1958. Dream Symbolism in Petronius Fragment 30. *Classical Philology* (vol. 53), 108-110.

Nashe, Thomas. 1965. *The Terrors of the Night, or, A Discourse of Apparitions.* In Stanley Wells (ed.), *Thomas Nashe: Selected Writings* (Cambridge, MA: Harvard University Press).

Ness, Robert C. 1978. The Old Hag Phenomenon as Sleep Paralysis: A Biocultural Interpretation. *Culture, Medicine, and Psychiatry* (vol. 2), 15-39.

Nielsen, Tore A. 1991. Reality Dreams and Their Effects on Spiritual Belief: A Revision of Animism Theory. In Jayne Gackenbach and A.A. Sheikh (eds.), *Dream Images: A Call to Mental Arms* (Amityville, NY: Baywood).

Nietzsche, Friedrich. 1967. *The Birth of Tragedy and The Case of Wagner* (trans. Walter Kaufmann) (New York, NY: Vintage Books).

Nock, Arthur Darby. 1934. A Vision of Mandulis Aion. *Harvard Theological Review* (vol. 27), 53-104.

Norbu, Namkhai. 1992. *Dream Yoga and the Practice of Natural Light* (Ithaca, NY: Snow Lions Publications).

Obeyesekere, Gananath. 1981. *Medusa's Hair: An Essay on Personal Symbols and Religious Experience* (Chicago, IL: University of Chicago Press).

Oepke, A. 1967. Onar/Dream. In G. Friedrich (ed.), *Theological Dictionary of the New Testament* (Grand Rapids, MI: William B. Eerdmans Publishing Co.).

O'Flaherty, Wendy Doniger (trans.). 1981. *The Rig Veda* (London: Penguin Books).

————. 1984. *Dreams, Illusion, and Other Realities* (Chicago, IL: University of Chicago Press).

————. 1988. *Other People's Myths* (New York, NY: Macmillan).

————. In press. Western Dreams about Eastern Dreams. In Kelly Bulkeley (ed.), *Among All These Dreamers: Essays on Dreaming, Modern Society, and the Future of Dream Studies* (Albany, NY: State University of New York Press).

Ong, Roberto K. 1985. *The Interpretation of Dreams in Ancient China* (Bochum: Studienverlag Brockmeyer).

Opler, Marvin K. 1959. Dream Analysis in Ute Indian Therapy. In Marvin K. Opler (ed.), *Culture and Mental Health* (New York, NY: Macmillan).

Oppenheim, A. Leo. 1956. The Interpretation of Dreams in the Ancient Near East. *Transactions of the American Philosophical Society* (vol. 46, no. 3), 179-353.

Osborne, Kenneth E. 1970. A Christian Graveyard Cult in the New Guinea Highlands. *Practical Anthropologist* (vol. 17), 10-15.

Otto, Rudolph. 1958. *The Idea of the Holy* (trans. John W. Harvey) (New York: Oxford University Press).

Padwick, C.E. 1939. Dream and Vision: Some Notes from a Diary. *The International Review of Missions* (vol. 28), 205-216.

Paolini, John. 1969. The Kabyle Handling of Grief. *The Muslim World* (vol. 59), 251-274.

Park, Willard Z. 1934. Paviotso Shamanism. *American Anthropologist* (vol. 34), 98-113.

Pauw, B.A. 1975. *Christianity and Xhosa Tradition* (London: Oxford University Press).

Peel, J.D.Y. 1968. *Aladura: A Religioius Movement Among the Yoruba* (London: Oxford University Press).

Philo. 1934. *The Collected Works of Philo* (trans. F.H. Colson and G.H. Whitaker) (Cambridge, MA: Harvard University Press).

Plato. 1956. *Crito* (trans. F.J. Church). In F.J. Church (ed.), *Plato: Euthyphro, Apology, Crito* (Indianapolis, IN: Bobbs-Merrill).

_____. 1957. *The Republic* (trans. A.D. Lindsay) (New York, NY: E.P. Dutton).

_____. 1961. *Phaedo* (trans. Hugh Tredennick). In Edith Hamilton and Huntington Cairns (eds.), *The Collected Dialogues of Plato* (Princeton: Princeton University Press).

Pobee, John S. 1986. I Will Lift Up My Eyes to Mozano. *International Review of Mission* (vol. 75), 123-127.

Pruett, Gordon E. 1985. Through a Glass Darkly: Knowledge of the Self in Dreams in Ibn Khaldun's Muqaddima. *The Muslim World* (vol. 75), 29-44.

Radin, Paul. 1936. Ojibwa and Ottawa Puberty Dreams. In *Essays in Anthropology Presented to A.L. Kroeber* (Freeport, NY: Books for Libraries Press).

Rambo, Lewis. 1993. *Understanding Religious Conversion* (New Haven, CT: Yale University Press).

Ray, Keith. 1992. Dreams of Grandeur: The Call to the Office in Northcentral Igbo Religious Leadership. In M.C. Jedrej and Rosalind Shaw (eds.), *Dreaming, Religion and Society in Africa* (Leiden: E.J. Brill).

Reay, Marie. 1962. The Sweet Witchcraft of Kuma Dream Experience. *Mankind* (vol. 5, no. 11), 459-463.

Reed, Henry. 1985. *Getting Help from Your Dreams* (Virginia Beach, VA: Inner Vision).

Reid, Howard. 1978. Dreams and their Interpretation among the Hupdu Maku Indians of Brazil. *Cambridge Anthropology* (vol. 4, no. 3), 2-29.

Reynolds, Pamela. 1992. Dreams and the Constitution of Self among the Zezuru. In M.C. Jedrej and Rosalind Shaw (eds.), *Dreaming, Religion and Society in Africa* (Leiden: E.J. Brill).

Roheim, Geza. 1952. *The Gates of the Dream* (New York: International Universities Press).

Rupprecht, Carol Schreier. 1990. Our Unacknowledged Ancestors:

Dream Theorists of Antiquity, the Middle Ages, and the Renaissance. *Psychiatric Journal of the University of Ottawa* (vol. 15, no. 2), 117-122.

Russell, James R. 1991. "Sleep" and "Dreaming" in Armenian. In J. Greppin (ed.), *Proceedings of the Fourth International Conference on Armenian Linguistics* (Delmar, NY: Caravan Books).

Saint-Denys, H. 1982. *Dreams and How to Guide Them* (London: Duckworth).

Schneider, David M. and Sharp, Lauriston. 1969. *The Dream Life of a Primitive People: The Dreams of the Yir Yoront of Australia* (Washington, D.C.: American Anthropological Association).

Seligson, Fred Jeremy. 1989. *Oriental Birth Dreams* (Elizabeth, NJ: Holym).

Severus, Sulpicius. 1949. *Writings* (trans. Bernard M. Peebles). In Roy Joseph Deferrari (ed.), *The Fathers of the Church* (New York, NY: Fathers of the Church).

Sharma, Jagdish P. and Siegel, Lee. 1980. *Dream Symbolism in the Sramanic Tradition: Two Psychoanalytical Studies in Jinist and Buddhist Dream Legends* (Calcutta: Firma KLM).

Shastri, Hari Prasad (trans.). 1985. *The Ramayana of Valmiki* (London: Shanti Sadan).

Shaw, Rosalind. 1992. Dreaming as Accomplishment: Power, the Individual, and Temne Divination. In M.C. Jedrej and Rosalind Shaw (eds.), *Dreaming, Religion and Society in Africa* (Leiden: E.J. Brill).

Shostak, Marjorie. 1981. *Nisa: The Life and Words of a !Kung Woman* (New York, NY: Vintage Books).

Siegel, Alan. 1990. *Dreams That Can Change Your Life* (Los Angeles, CA: Jeremy P. Tarcher).

Smith, Richard J. 1991. *Fortune-Tellers and Philosophers: Divination in Traditional Chineses Society* (Boulder, CO: Westview Press).

Spencer, H. 1882. *The Principles of Sociology* (London: Williams and Norgate).

Sperling, Harry and Simon, Maurice (trans.). 1949. *The Zohar* (London: Soncino Press).

Stephen, Michele. 1979. Dreams of Change: The Innovative Role of Altered States of Consciousness in Traditional Melanesian Religion. *Oceania* (vol. 50, no. 1), 3-22.

Stewart, Kilton. 1969. Dream Theory in Malaya. In Charles T. Tart (ed.), *Altered States of Consciousness* (New York, NY: John Wiley and Sons).

Strathern, Andrew. 1989. Melpa Dream Interpretation and the Concept of Hidden Truth. *Ethnology* (vol. 38, no. 4), 301-316.

Suri, Ellison. 1986. Religious Experience in Traditional Melanesian Cultures. *Melanesian Journal of Theology* (vol. 2, no. 1), 32-39.

Swedenborg, Emanuel. 1986. *Journal of Dreams* (trans. J.J.G. Wilkinson) (New York, NY: Swedenborg Foundation).

Tanabe, George J. 1992. *Myoe the Dreamkeeper: Fantasy and Knowledge in Early Kamakura Buddhism* (Cambridge, MA: Council on East Asian Studies).

Tanner, Morgan W. 1988. Dreams in the Hebrew Bible. *Epoche* (vol. 16), 33-62.

Taylor, Jeremy. 1983. *Dream Work* (New York: Paulist Press).

————. 1992. *Where People Fly and Water Runs Uphill* (New York: Warner Books).

Tedlock, Barbara (ed.). 1987a. *Dreaming: Anthropological and Psychological Interpretations* (New York, NY: Cambridge University Press).

————. 1987b. Zuni and Quiche Dream Sharing and Interpreting. In Barbara Tedlock (ed.), *Dreaming: Anthropological and Psychological Interpretations* (New York, NY: Cambridge University Press).

Tertullian. 1870. *The Writings of Tertullian, Vol. II* (ed. Alexander Roberts and James Donaldson). *In Ante-Nicene Christian Library* (Edinburgh: T. & T. Clark).

Toffelmier, Gertrude and Luomala, Katherine. 1936. Dreams and Dream Interpretation of the Diegueno Indians of Southern California. *The Psychoanalytic Quarterly* (vol. 5), 195-225.

Tonkinson, Robert. 1970. Aboriginal Dream-Spirit Beliefs in a Contact

Situation: Jigalong, Western Australia. In Ronald M. Berndt (ed.), *Australian Aboriginal Anthropology* (Sidney: University of Western Australia Press).

Topper, Martin D. 1987. The Traditional Navajo Medicine Man: Therapist, Counselor, and Community Leader. *Journal of Psychoanalytic Anthropology* (vol. 10, no. 3), 217-249.

Tracy, David. 1981. *The Analogical Imagination* (New York, NY: Crossroad).

Trafzer, Clifford E. and Beach, Margery A. 1985. Smohalla, the Washani, and Religion as a Factor in Northwestern Indian History. *American Indian Quarterly* (vol. 9, no. 3), 309-324.

Trimingham, Spencer. 1959. *Islam in West Africa* (Oxford: Clarendon Press).

Trompf, G.W. 1990. *Melanesian Religion* (Cambridge: Cambridge University Press).

Turner, Victor. 1969. *The Ritual Process: Structure and Anti-structure* (Ithaca, NY: Cornell University Press).

_____. 1986. Body, Brain, and Culture. *Cross Currents* (vol. 36, no. 2), 156-178.

Tuzin, Donald. 1975. The Breath of a Ghost: Dreams and the Fear of the Dead. *Ethos* (vol. 3, no. 4), 555-578.

Tylor, E. 1889. *Primitive Culture* (London: H. Holt).

Urban, Greg and Kent, Patricia. 1991. The Royal Road to the Collective Consciousness. Unpublished manuscript.

Van de Castle, Robert. 1994. *Our Dreaming Mind* (New York: Ballantine Books).

Van Gennep, Arnold. 1960. *The Rites of Passage* (trans. Monika B. Vizedom and Gabrielle L. Caffee) (Chicago, IL: University of Chicago Press).

Virgil. 1971. *The Aeneid* (trans. Allen Mandelbaum) (New York, NY: Bantam Books).

Von Grunebaum, G.E. 1966. Introduction: The Cultural Function of the Dream as Illustrated by Classical Islam. In G.E. von Grunebaum and Roger Callois (eds.), *The Dream and Human Societies* (Berkeley, CA: University of California Press).

Wallace, Anthony F.C. 1956. Revitalization Movements. *American Anthropologist* (vol. 58, no. 2), 264-281.

―――――. 1958. Dreams and Wishes of the Soul: A Type of Psychoanalytic Theory among the 17th Century Iroquois. *American Anthropologist* (vol. 60, no. 2), 234-248.

―――――. 1969. *The Death and Rebirth of the Seneca* (New York, NY: Vintage Books).

Wallace, W.J. 1947. The Dream in Mohave Life. *Journal of American Folklore* (vol. 60), 252-258.

Watson, Lawrence C. and Watson-Franke, Maria-Barbara. 1977. Spirits, Dreams, and the Resolution of Conflict among Urban Guajiro Women. *Ethos* (vol. 5, no. 4), 388-408.

Wayman, Alex. 1967. Significance of Dreams in India and Tibet. *History of Religions* (vol. 7, no. 1), 1-13.

Whitten, Norman E., Jr. 1978. Ecological Imagery and Cultural Adaptability: The Canelos Quiche of Eastern Ecuador. *American Anthropologist* (vol. 80), 836-859.

Williams, F.E. 1936. Papuan Dream Interpretations. *Mankind* (vol. 2, no. 2), 29-39.

Winget, Carolyn and Kapp, Frederic. 1972. The Relationship of the Manifest Content of Dreams to Duration of Childbirth in Primiparae. *Psychosomantic Medicine* (vol. 34, no. 4), 313-319.

Winnicott, D.W. 1971. *Playing and Reality* (New York, NY: Tavistock Publications).

Young, Michael W. 1983. *Magicians of Manumanua: Living Myth in Kalauna* (Berkeley, CA: University of California Press).

Zwemer, S.W. 1916. The Familiar Spirit or Qarina. *The Moslem World* (vol. 6), 360-374.

Index

Abram 39-41, 42, 217n, 229n
Achilleus 11, 13, 39
Achmet 25, 215n, 229n, 234n
Aeschylus 23, 39, 215n
Agabegijik 131-132, 138, 139
Agamemnon 23, 177-178
A'isha Qandisha 60, 63, 64
Akoboha I 135
Alkinoos 32
Allen, Woody 156, 233n
Almoli, Solomon 156-157, 174
Amory, Anne 180-181, 236n
Anggauwane 9, 14, 42
Apuleius 133-134, 230n
Arabi, Ibn 172-173, 176, 189-190
Aristides, Aelius 31, 36, 102-103, 105, 106, 124-125, 225n
Aristotle 117-119, 194-195, 198-200, 201, 227n, 228n, 238n
Artemidorus 25, 58, 69, 127, 170, 176, 215n, 219n, 221n, 229n, 235n
Augustine 61, 62, 64, 80-81, 111, 114, 219n, 222n, 226n

Baba 98, 103, 104-105
Baillet, Adrien 78-79
Barnes, Hannah 135
Barrett, Deirdre 222n
Basso, Ellen 237n
Beradt, Charlotte 159-160, 234n
Best, Elsdon 214n
Bharata 47, 49
Bilu, Yoram 220n
Blagrove, Mark 216n
Bland, Nathaniel 216n
Blau, Harold 95-96, 224n
Boaz, Franz 78
Bonnefoy, Yves 234n, 236n
Borges, Jorge Luis 4, 86
Bosnak, Robert 239n
Boss, Medard 237n
Boualem 20
Bourguignon, Erika 224n
Buddha 16, 30, 36, 110, 114
Brain, Robert 218n
Brennan, John 168-169, 235n
Briggs, John 228n
Brown, Michael 123, 229n

"C" 42-43, 48
Caraka 168, 175-176
Cardano, Girolamo 77, 82

264

Carlos 46, 48, 49-50, 52
Carroll, Lewis 160
Cartwright, Rosalind 37, 116, 216n, 227n, 228n
Cassian, John 220n
Casteneda, Carlos 79-80, 81, 83-84, 222n
Centlivres, Micheline 98-99, 225n
Charsley, Simon 224n
Chuang-Chou 69, 71, 72
Chuang-Tzu 69
Cicero 110, 144, 171, 226n
Clytemnestra 23, 24, 39
Cole, John 222n
Confucius 31, 36, 112, 114
Constantine 142
Corbin, Henri 133, 189-190, 221n, 230n, 237n
Cosmas 125
Coulianu, I.P. 238n
Covitz, Joel 124, 229n, 233n, 235n
Crapanzano, Victor 60, 214n, 218n, 219n
Crick, Francis 234n
Crito 113
Cuddy, Marion 220n
Curley, Richard 145-146, 232n

Damian 125
D'Andrade, Roy 224n
Daneel, M.L. 10, 102, 213n, 216n, 225n
Daniel 47-48, 170
Dasaratha 47
Davis, Winston 148, 232n
Dawood, N.J. 213n, 236n
Degarrod, Lydia 8, 46, 213n, 217n, 233n

Delaney, Gayle 218n, 228n
Demetrius 45
Dentan, Robert 216n
Descartes, René 78-79, 82, 195-196, 200-201, 238n
Devereux, George 92-93, 96, 214n, 233n
Dickens, Charles 117, 227n
Dilley, Roy 94, 224n
Dodds, E.R. 228n
Domhoff, G. William 223n
Driberg, J.H. 215n
Dronke, Peter 215n
Duerr, Hans Peter 73-74, 222n
Durkheim, Emile 237n

Edelstein, Emma 228n
Eggan, Dorothy 22, 93, 215n, 223n
Einstein, Albert 192-193
Electra 23
Eliade, Mircea 27, 36, 58, 63, 73-74, 136-137, 211, 215n, 216n, 217n, 219n, 220n, 222n, 226n, 231n
Elihu 43, 50
Enkidu 178
Erikson, Erik 206, 239n
Esau 40-41
Euripides 178, 236n
Eusebius, Pamphili 45-46, 217n
Evans-Pritchard, E.E. 108, 225n
Eve 26
Ewing, Katherine 137-138, 231n

Fabian, Johannes 167, 235n
Faraday, Ann 228n

Ferenczi, Sandor 206
Festugiere, Andre-Jean 216n
Feuer, Lewis S. 231n
Firth, Raymond 112, 226n
Fisher, Humphrey 147, 232n
Fitzgerald, Augustine 233n
Flannery, Regina 88, 223n
Foster, George 51, 215n, 218n
Foucault, Michel 220n
Fox, Robin 231-232n
Frank, Jerome 104, 225n
Freeman, Derek 56, 61, 214n,
    218n, 219n, 223n
Fremin, Father 188-189
French, Thomas 37, 116, 216n,
    227n
Freud, Sigmund 14-15, 27, 55,
    60-61, 62, 92-93, 96, 140,
    176, 198, 204, 206-207,
    208, 209, 210, 211-212,
    214n, 216n, 218n, 221n,
    223n, 236n, 238n, 239n

Gackenbach, Jayne 76, 222n,
    223n
Gardner, John 217n, 218n,
    236n
Garfield, Patricia 76, 218n,
    219n, 222n, 226n, 228n
Gasparutto, Paolo 187-188
Geijbels, M. 86-87, 223ı
Gendlin, Eugene 239n
Gennadius 80-81, 82
Gibbons, Francis 33, 216n
Gifford, Edward 236n
Gilgamesh 44, 48, 49, 50, 52,
    54, 178, 239n
Gillespie, George 76, 222n
Ginzburg, Carlo 68, 187-188,
    221n, 231n, 237n

Glaphyra 12, 14
Gnuse, Robert 226n
Graham, Laura 87-88, 93, 223n
Green, Celia 76, 222n
Gregor, Thomas 167-168, 182-
    183, 233n, 235n, 237n
Gregory of Nazianzen 136,
    138, 139
Gregory of Nyssa 112-113, 114,
    115-116
Grinell, G.B. 111
Guss, David 77, 190, 193,
    222n, 233n, 237n

Hall, Calvin 176, 216n, 218n,
    236n
Hallowell, Irving 70, 221n
Hallpike, C.R. 222n
Handsome Lake 149-150, 151,
    154
Handy, E.S. Craighill 101-102,
    166, 225n, 235n
Hanuman 178, 236n
Harold 18
Harrington, John 100-101,
    225n
Harris, Monford 90, 213n,
    223n, 235n
Hartmann, Ernest 50-51, 52,
    218n, 222n
Heraclitus 197
Herdt, Gilbert 132-133, 230n,
    233n
Herodotus 121, 228n
Herr, Barbara 59-60, 190-191,
    219n, 227n, 237n
Hitler, Adolph 159
Hiu, Kwan 87, 91
Hobbes, Thomas 164-165,
    235n

Hobson, J. Allan 83, 208, 210, 211, 215-216n, 223n, 236n
Holy, Ladislav 215n
Homans, Peter 235n
Homer 11, 32, 39, 113, 168, 177-178, 180, 213n, 235n, 236n
Homer, Joe 100-101
Hosain, M. Hidayet 215n
Houriya 20
Hsiang-shu, Wei 77-78, 81, 82
Hsieh, Liu 31, 36
Hufford, David J. 51, 218n
Hume, Robert Ernest 237n

Iphigenia 23
Isaac 40
Isaiah 152

Jacob 39-41, 170, 217n, 229n
Jayne, Walter 228n
Jedrej, M.C. 89-90, 218n, 219n, 223n
Jehu-Appiah, Jemiseham 135
Jeremiah 112, 115
Jerome 128, 144, 151, 152, 153-154
Jesus Christ 20, 21, 32, 35, 36, 44-46, 48, 49, 52, 69, 71, 110-111, 114, 129, 135, 142, 144, 146-147, 151, 163
Jiuxiao, Zhang 108
Job 43, 48-49, 50
Jones, Ernest 27, 214n
Joseph (New Testament) 110-111, 114
Joseph (Old Testament) 170

Josephus 12, 45, 213n, 217n, 220n
Juan, Don 79-80, 82, 84
Jung, C.G. 52-53, 97, 116, 140, 159, 212, 218n, 225n, 227n, 234n

Kakar, Sudhir 98, 225n
Kaplan, Bernard 73, 222n
Kapo 146-147, 151, 154
Kau-chu 58
Kelsey, Morton 136, 208, 209-210, 211-212, 220n, 226n, 229n, 230n, 232n
Kelzer, Ken 76, 222n
Kepelino 166
Khaldun, Ibn 156, 173-174, 176, 233n, 235n
Kiernan, J.P. 235n
Kiev, Ari 225n
Kilborne, Benjamin 214n
Kimaola 99-100, 103, 105
King, Arden 20-21, 215n
Konje, Prof. 107, 225n
Koulack, David 152, 233n
Kracke, Waud 109, 152, 214n, 218n, 226n, 233n, 239n
Kramer, Heinrich 220n
Kramer, Milton 37, 216n
Kroeber, A.L. 70, 221n
Kwinjinaambi 132-133, 138, 139

LaBarre, Weston 214n
LaBerge, Stephen 76, 222n, 223n
Lahiji, Shamsoddin 67, 71, 72, 74, 76, 189-190
Lai, Whalen 213n
Lakoff, George 213n

Lakshamana 47
Landau, Rom 172-173, 235n
Lanternari, Vittorio 146-147, 224n, 232n
Laufer, Berthold 87, 122-123, 223n, 228n
Lavie, Peretz 83, 223n
Levin, Ross 38, 216n
Lewis, Jane White 218n
Lhalungpa, Lobsang P. 222n
Lilith 56, 60
Lincoln, Bruce 230n
Lincoln, J.S. 208, 209, 210, 211, 213n, 214n, 222n, 224n, 226n, 232n
Liou 58, 60, 220n
Lorand, Sandor 56, 219n
Lucius 133-134, 138, 139
Lucretius 162, 165, 234n
Luther, Martin 164, 165, 234n

"M" 43
Macbeth 238n
Maccabeus 111-112, 114, 115
Mack, John E. 52-53, 218n
MacKenzie, Norman 208, 209, 211
Macrina 113, 114
Macrobius 171-172, 175, 235n
Mahwee, Dick 125-126, 138
Malinowski, Bronislaw 11, 213n
Martin of Tours 32
Martin, Robert 70, 71, 72
Mary 110-111
Matilde 8
Matthias 220n
Maya 110, 114
Maybruck, Patricia 226n
Mayerson, Philip 234n

Mead, Margaret 223n
Meggitt, M.J. 9, 184, 213n, 237n
Meier, C.A. 124-125, 228n, 229n
Merrill, William 187, 233n, 237n
Milarepa 78, 82
Miller, Patricia Cox 112-113, 226n
Mindell, Arnold 239n
Moffitt, Alan 216n
Monachus, Antiochus 163, 165
Monica 111, 114
Morgan, William 42, 217n
Morris, Ivan 216n
Moses (ben Jacob) of Coucy 90, 91
Mpier, Mubuy Mubay 74-75, 121, 222n, 233n
M'Timkulu, Donald 147, 232n
Muhammed 33, 36, 148, 177
Mundkur, Balaji 215n
Murray, Grace 121-122

Nabonidus 87, 91
Nabulusi, Abdalghani 174-175, 176
Nashe, Thomas 17, 164, 165-166, 214n, 234n
Natalius 45-46, 48-49, 50
Natholomoa, Akatitibi 135
Nausikaa 32, 39
Nebuchadnezzar 47-49, 50, 178
Nestor 177
Nielsen, Tore A. 239n
Nietzsche, Friedrich 50, 196-197, 201-202, 233-234n, 238n

Norbu, Namkhai 85, 100, 157,
223n, 225n, 233n

"O" 43, 49, 50
Oberhelman, Steven M. 125,
163
Obeyesekere, Gananath 152-
154, 233n
Odysseus 32
O'Flaherty, Wendy Doniger
169, 192, 213n, 219n,
223n, 226n, 235n, 236n,
237n
Ong, Roberto K. 77-78, 101,
112, 123, 214n, 221n,
222n, 225n, 226n, 228n,
234n
Onias 112, 115
Oppenheim, A. Leo 21, 34,
215n, 216n, 223n, 228n
Orestes 23-24, 178
Osborne, Kenneth E. 144-145,
154, 232n
Otto, Rudolph 2, 27-28, 63,
211, 213n, 215n, 220n

Pa Ahmadu 134-135
Padwick, C.E. 215n, 217n
Pam 118-119
Panzona, Maria 68, 71, 72, 76
Park, Willard Z. 19, 125-126,
214n, 229n, 231n
Patroklos 11, 13, 39
Patton, George 226n
Pauw, B.A. 213n
Peel, J.D.Y. 143, 232n
Penelope 168, 180-181
Pererius, Benedict 128
Perpetua, Vibia 21, 24, 42, 72
Phaedo 89

Philo 169-170, 176, 235n
Plato 61, 62, 64, 113, 165, 194,
220n, 223n, 226n, 238n
Plummer, Rosie 19, 24
Pobee, John S. 135, 230n
Pukutiwara 68, 71, 72
Pyanjuwa 144-145, 151, 154

Radin, Paul 12, 131-132, 159,
230n, 234n
Rama 47, 178
Rambo, Lewis 150-151, 232n,
233n
Ravana 178
Ray, Keith 231n
Reay, Marie 44, 58, 217n, 219n
Reed, Henry 228n
Reid, Howard 109-110, 226n,
233n
Reid, Thomas 83
Reynolds, Pamela 99, 225n,
231n
Roheim, Geza 68, 208, 209,
210, 211-212, 213n, 214n,
221n
Rupprecht, Carol Schreier
222n
Russell, James R. 34, 216n

Sachs, Wulf 7
Sahib, Ahmad 137-138
Sam (Chicago child) 28-29
Sam (Hopi man) 22, 24
Samuel 54, 229-230n
Sanchez, Pedro 221n
Sarashina, Lady 30-31, 36
Saul 54
Schneider, David M. 217n,
222n
Scrooge, Ebenezer 117

Sethos 121, 126
Severus, Sulpicus 216n
Shaikh Ahmadd Ahsa'i 133,
	138, 139
Shakespeare, William 238n
Sharma, Jagdish P. 226n
Sharp, Lauriston 45
Shastri, Hari Prasad 218n
Shaw, Rosalind 57, 134-135,
	152, 214n, 215n, 230n
Shaykh Ishaq 148, 151
Sheila 17-18
Shembe 147, 151, 154
Shipes, Henry 20-21, 24
Shiyuan, Chen 183
Shonin, Myoe 35, 36
Siegel, Alan 152, 226n, 228n,
	233n
Silvanus 65-66
Simonides 110-114
Sita 178-179, 181, 236n
Smith, Joseph F. 33, 36
Smith, Richard J. 108, 183,
	226n, 237n
Smohalla 149, 151, 154, 234n
Socrates 89, 91, 113, 114, 194,
	197-198, 201, 238n
Spencer, H. 222n, 236n
Spinoza, Benedict 231n
Stephen, Michele 90-91, 223n
Sternberg, Leo 59
Stewart, Kilton 80, 83-84, 222n
Strathern, Andrew 12, 69,
	214n, 221n, 233n
Sundar 98, 104-105
Swedenborg, Emanuel 34-35,
	36, 69, 71, 72, 76, 216n,
	221n
Synesius of Cyrene 157-158

Tagore, Debendranath 10, 13
T'ai-kong 58
Tanabe, George J. 216n
Tanutamon 21, 24
Taylor, Jeremy 219n, 228n
Tedlock, Barbara 152, 184,
	186, 235n, 237n, 239n
Tertullian 170-171, 235n
Theopompos 45, 48-49, 50
Thutmose IV 34, 36
Tianbao, Zhi 108
Tipu of Mysore 33, 36
Toffelmier, Gertrude 135-136,
	230n
Tonkinson, Robert 70, 93-94,
	221n, 222n, 224n
Tracy, David 217n
Trafzer, Clifford E. 149, 232n,
	234n
Trijata 236n
Trimingham, Spencer 122,
	228n
Trompf, G.W. 126, 229n
Trotter, Lilias 20, 44-45
Tuzin, Donald 214n
Tylor, E. 182, 222n, 235n,
	237n

Urban, Greg 93, 223n, 231n
Utnapishtim 54

Vadar, Darth 53
Van de Castle, Robert 19, 208,
	210-212, 213n, 214n,
	218n, 236n
Van Gennep, Arnold 131, 139,
	230n
Victoria 145-146, 151, 154
Virgil 235n
Von Grunebaum, G.E. 235n

Wallace, Anthony F.C. 149-150, 222n, 224n, 232n, 237n

Wallace, W.J. 158, 166, 233n, 234n, 235n

Wang Chiu-Lien 16

Wang Ch'ung 162, 165

Watson, Lawrence C. 214n

Wayman, Alex 172, 235n

Wesley, John 121-122, 126

Whitten, Norman E., Jr. 233n

Williams, F.E. 115, 227n

Winnicott, D.W. 224n

Ya Mabinti 134-135

Yakandali 9

Yoshikazu, Okada 148, 151, 154

Young, Michael 99-100, 225n

Zwemer, S.M. 57, 219n